Best wishes

Tony

[signature]

Tooting Common to the Stretford End

Tooting Common to the Stretford End

The Alex Stepney Story

ALEX STEPNEY WITH DAVID SAFFER

VERTICAL EDITIONS

www.verticaleditions.com

First published in the United Kingdom in 2010 by
Vertical Editions, Unit 4a, Snaygill Industrial Estate,
Skipton, North Yorkshire BD23 2QR

www.verticaleditions.com

ISBN 978-1-904091-43-1

A CIP catalogue record for this book is available from
the British Library

Cover design and typeset by HBA, York

Printed and bound by JF Print Limited, Somerset

CONTENTS

ACKNOWLEDGMENTS

Alex Stepney and David Saffer would like to thank the following people for their help in the research and publication of this book.

Firstly to Arthur Albiston, Martin Buchan, Pat Crerand, Alan Mullery, Tommy Smith and Nobby Stiles for providing 'player' memories.

We'd also like to thank statistician Gary Shepherd for producing Alex's career stats and Phil Goldstone for allowing us access to his vast range of football books. Among many sources of material used in the research process were the following books: *Millwall FC* (Breedon), *Chelsea FC* (Breedon), *Manchester United FC* (Breedon), *North American Soccer League* (Breedon), *Manchester United Book of Football 1-15* (Stanley Paul), *Manchester United in Europe* (Mainstream), *Football Champions* (Purnell), *Cup Final Extra!* by Martyn Tyler (Hamlyn), *Back Home* (Orion), *In Safe Keeping* by Alex Stepney (Pelham, 1969) and *Alex Stepney* (Arthur Barker, 1978). Other resources for information used were various *Jimmy Hill's Football Weekly*, *Shoot* and *Goal* magazines.

Finally, but by no means least, thanks to Karl Waddicor and Diane Evans at Vertical Editions for all their help.

FOREWORD

Alex impressed me straight away when he joined Manchester United. His first game was a derby clash against Manchester City at Old Trafford and he had an outstanding game. Derby games are always high-pressure encounters, we won 1–0 and Alex enjoyed a memorable debut in an intense atmosphere. Alex was a top class 'keeper and made all the difference to United in our bid to win the title in 1966–67. The day Matt Busby signed Alex from Chelsea was one of the best transfers he made for United.

When you train with fellows every day you get to know their qualities. Alex made everything look so easy and was never flash. He worked hard at his game, had a great pair of hands and possessed the qualities all top 'keepers need. Alex's angles were terrific; he was a great shot stopper, brave as anything and most importantly came off his line to catch a ball when danger threatened. Central defenders love a 'keeper that claims a cross confidently and Alex was accomplished at this aspect of his game. Alex gave everyone at the back total confidence and I used to love playing with him. Every time Alex picked up a ball, I looked for it to build an attack. Most managers in our era liked a 'keeper to hack the ball upfield but Matt preferred us to take the ball out from the back whenever possible. Alex played his part in this aspect of our game and you could class him as a good passer of the ball because he always passed intelligently.

I wasn't surprised at how quickly Alex settled at United. Footballers become an enclosed family even though they come from different parts of the country. Alex had a great personality and enjoyed the crack with all the lads in training sessions, during long journeys to opponents domestically and in Europe, and in the dressing room. Alex and I shared rooms and had great fun during United's travels. On a match day, Alex would always be up early making the tea, rattling his cup around while I was trying to sleep. It was always good-natured though; the crack was great and we shared many unforgettable experiences.

Over the years, Alex saved us in many games but his most important, as United fans love to recall, was his save from Eusebio with the score at 1–1 against Benfica in the 1968 European Cup final. We'd had the signal that only minutes remained before extra time and in that split second when Eusebio was about to shoot I said a little prayer because I thought the dream was over. Alex, of course, pulled off a fantastic stop and the rest is history. I shouldn't have worried though because Alex always made tough saves look easy. He did nothing flash—Alex was never spectacular—if a save needed to be made then he made it and that was it.

The thing that always amazed me about Alex was his lack of England caps. Gordon Banks was a terrific goalkeeper and but for his consistency Alex would have won many more caps. He did go to Mexico for the 1970 World Cup finals and should have played against West Germany instead of Peter Bonetti in the quarterfinals because Alex was one of those goalkeepers who had no nerves. The occasion would not have bothered him as he'd played in more big matches. I played with Alex over a long period and of course I was a bit biased towards my own 'keeper but he was a major reason why United won trophies. A successful team needs a top class goalkeeper and back four. Alex was one of best in the late sixties and early seventies, and a privilege to play alongside.

Paddy Crerand
(Manchester United 1962–63 to 1970–71)

1

FOOTBALL CRAZY

Wembley Stadium was the scene of my most vivid memories as a professional footballer. Winning the European Cup was a night to remember when Manchester United overcame the challenge of Benfica and I had my one-on-one moment of destiny with Eusebio. The match has gone down as an iconic day for United, and British football, as we were the first English club to win the trophy. It was also the day that Sir Matt Busby finally landed the biggest prize in Europe after more than a decade of trying. But it was not the highlight of my career. You see, as a kid growing up in the fifties, the big dream for me was winning the FA Cup and playing for England. That double was always my objective when I made my first tentative steps with Tooting and Mitcham. When I arrived at Old Trafford after experiencing relegation with Millwall prior to back-to-back promotions on top of a bizarre three-month spell at Chelsea, those aims were still the Holy Grail for me.

United's Division 1 title success in 1966–67 backed up by the European Cup triumph 12 months later were unforgettable experiences but I was desperate for my 'triple' medal, the FA Cup. And after missing out in 1976 against Southampton and walking off the Wembley pitch, I felt my dream had vanished. But I was wrong and 12 months later, I was back at the Twin Towers finally to pick up an FA Cup winners medal when we defeated Liverpool. Thereafter I enjoyed a brief sojourn in America playing in the North American Soccer League before rounding things off with my local club Altrincham.

I was privileged to play for Sir Alf Ramsey and Sir Matt whilst my relationship with Tommy Docherty had more downs than ups but he was the boss when United landed the FA Cup so at least things ended on a high. Playing with the likes of Bobby Charlton, Denis Law, George Best, Paddy Crerand, Nobby Stiles, Martin Buchan, Lou Macari, Steve Coppell and Stuart Pearson enabled me to experience the ups and downs that football offers a professional footballer. And tasting double relegation as a player, playing in front of a few hundred hardy souls in reserve team football, cup semi-final and final defeats all made me appreciate the domestic and European honours that came my way.

So where did it all start?

My parents, John (Jack to his mates) and Doris Stepney, had three children. Although the Second World War was in full swing both Eric (15) and Marjorie (13) were still living at home, unlike many kids who were evacuated, when mum gave birth to me on 18 September 1942 in the front room at 27 Percy Road, Beddington Corner, Mitcham Junction, Surrey. Dad was a labourer with Hackbridge Cables during the day and served with the Home Guard on Tooting Bec Common at nights. Too old to be called up, dad was proud as punch to 'Do his bit for King and country'. He never let on if any planes were shot down but dad did talk about the blitz when a bomb dropped near us. Not surprisingly, it made locals wary. Any unusual noise put everyone on edge. The horror of the war years would catch up with dad in years to come. All I vaguely remember about the hostilities was hearing the sirens go off following air raids. You could hear the drone of a doodlebug, which meant mum hid me under the kitchen table if time was short or grabbed me and ran to the air raid shelter at the bottom of our garden. I was only a tot so had no idea about the dangers but it must have been a scary time for those living in London. Despite the tough times our home, a typical terraced house in a suburban area, was a happy one. VE Day was a special occasion and I have vague recollections about a street party. It was a time when neighbours pulled together to create a community spirit that Winston Churchill would have been proud of.

Like everything in life, it's not what you know but whom you know. Having work was essential and dad was a grafter. Apart from his labouring job, on weekends he worked behind the bar at The Goat Inn Pub at Mitcham Junction so we enjoyed a few luxuries. Dad also had an allotment and he seemed to supply the whole street with vegetables during the summer. Mum used to go mad with him for not charging anything but that was dad, he liked helping people out wherever possible. Dad was a happy-go-lucky type of guy. Times were hard but he was really into looking after his family and never shy about putting in the hours. His generosity in difficult times made a lasting impression on me, as did his work ethic. I knew whatever profession I chose I'd have to graft. It was a great lesson and one I've always advocated. Mum looked after a disabled lady across the road who had a second home at Norman's Bay on the South Coast. She was always grateful for the help mum gave so I was able to spend time at her summer retreat fishing for cockles and generally pottering about on the beach like all lads of my age.

By the time I started school, Eric had joined the Merchant Navy and Marjorie was courting Fred Smith. Eventually Marjorie and Fred married and rented a couple of rooms in our street. I went to Hackbridge Junior School and soon after starting school was knocked down by a car walking to school. Apparently, I was with a mate and we were playing 'Chicken', a kid's game where you race across the road when you see a car coming close to you. My mate was okay but I was slow off the mark. I recall little about the incident other than not being quick enough to get across the road. By all accounts I was covered up with a blanket because witnesses at the scene thought I was dead. People ran to my mother and sister's home. They came running out and I was taken to hospital in Mitcham. Eventually, I came around. Like any six-year-old kid I didn't know what all the fuss was about and just got on with it. During my school days, kids were not dropped off at school, we walked. It was just the way it was in the post war years. I enjoyed school and it was during this time that I started playing football like most kids. I was also good at badminton and tennis but football was my favourite sport even at an early age.

At home, my Nan, Emma Stepney, lived with us but died when I was around 10. The only other grandparent I recall was mum's dad, Charles Wellman, who lived in Tooting. He was a real character who loved sports and lived to the grand old age of 90. Mum was a churchgoer and helped organise afternoon teas for the vicar. Church was part of my life and I was a keen member of Beddington Corner choir until I was 12.

Christmas was the highlight of my year and always a happy time in the Stepney house. Leading up to Christmas we'd make paper chains and put them up with the decorations and on the big day I knew mum or dad would come in with a few toys inside a pillowcase. My parents could not afford extravagant gifts but I never felt that I missed out at all. Parents in our area were the same with their kids. Families grew up together in similar houses. None of the kids got anything better than anyone else, it was one of the things that kept us united as a community. Our immediate family, mum and dad, my brother and sister with their families would always be together for Christmas Day lunch. It was a traditional time of the year and I loved it. Nowadays some of the magic of Christmas has gone with the materialism that has crept into society. It is sad but things move on.

In the early fifties we loved listening to the radio and eventually got a black and white television. The excitement in the Stepney household when our very own TV arrived was incredible. There were not many choices of TV set or channels but it was still terrific having a TV in our home. We kept the radio downstairs and I loved listening to the adventures of Dick Barton or science fiction. Comedy was also a favourite, especially Tommy Trinder and The Goons, which starred Spike Milligan, Peter Sellars, Harry Seacombe and Michael Bentine but when television arrived we'd watch it until the dot went off. Naturally, I was especially keen on anything sports related. Comics were also a favourite pastime for me. I read *Beano, Dandy* and later *The Eagle*. I even became a member of The Eagle Club, enjoyed taking part in the competitions and saved up so I could send off for a club member Eagle badge so I could wear it on my lapel at school. I earned around two bob a week on a local newspaper round, which was something all kids seemed to do. We didn't worry about safety as people do nowadays, we were just kids and got on with it. Football was never far away from my thoughts and I bought *Charles Buchan's Football Monthly* magazine so I could keep up to date with stars of the day.

When I was coming towards secondary education I discovered that I had a problem with my spine and had to go to a clinic in Wallington for what they called sunray treatment. My spine was bent but it did not affect me at all and I just carried on playing sports.

I didn't pass my 11-plus so went to Carshalton West Secondary School. It was not known in the area as being noteworthy for football or sporting prowess in general. In fact the games master, Mr Marley, was also a science teacher, but credit to him, he decided that as I played in goal during games lessons I should play in goal for the school and that was how my career as a goalkeeper started. I loved diving around and like all budding keepers, particularly enjoyed diving in the mud. Of course, the muddier it was outside the better, but my mother was not pleased at the extra washing it generated. That did not concern me though as I was flying though the air like top keepers of the day. Mr Marley certainly spotted something, picked me for the school team and I represented the U13, U14 and U15 sides.

It was bizarre that I ended up in goal because I played as a striker at Hackbridge Junior School and whenever I was with my mates kicking a ball about. It was so carefree in those days. We'd be on the streets or go down the Common, put down our coats and play for hours. Mr Marley changed my striking aspirations and it was not long before a couple of my mates' dads decided to set up a Sunday League team. Before I knew it, I kept goal for Achilles Boys Club. Life was great and it got better when I was selected to play for our local district team, Sutton and Carshalton. There were eight schools in the district and it certainly helped that Mr Marley was on the district selection committee for the team. Playing at this level meant I was advancing to a better standard.

Football was in my blood. I liked other sports, especially badminton and tennis, but there was only one for me and I loved nothing more than kicking a tennis ball around. We used to get the *Daily Herald* and I'd look for the football reports during the week and results in the paper on a Saturday night in the late sports edition. I'd also check out the Sunday morning papers for stories and results. Things just developed from an early age. Growing up in the fifties meant there was little football on television but there was football on Pathe News at the cinema, which was great.

Football was everything to me. I could not get enough of it morning, noon or night. My brother, Eric, played and I'd watch him represent Bedington Corner in a local Saturday league. There was a real community spirit watching them. Often there would be a couple of hundred people on the sidelines and the atmosphere was terrific. Eric played centre-forward and made it to amateur status with Leatherhead. At school the lads would wind each other up depending on how their favourite team had got on at the weekend. My team was Tottenham Hotspur. They were known as the Lilleywhites but that nickname has since been dropped. I hadn't seen them play but I'd read about them in the *Daily Herald* and Charles Buchan magazines. All the stars of the day were covered. Spurs had the famous 'push and run' team with Alf Ramsey, who of course went on to lead England to the World Cup, and then there was Bill Nicholson who would go on to manage Tottenham to glory, but such events were a million miles away in those carefree days.

In the early fifties the Division 1 title was not the big one to win, nor was the European Cup as it was still in its infancy and received little, if any, national coverage. The main two ambitions for aspiring players were to win an England cap and play in an FA Cup final at Wembley. I'd seen arguably the greatest final in 1953 when Blackpool, inspired by Stanley Matthews, came back from 3–1 down to defeat Bolton Wanderers 4–3 in the final minute. Stanley Mortensen scored a hat-trick and is still the last player to do so. I watched the game on TV and it was fantastic.

I hadn't been able to see Tottenham play because we lived too far away in South London. It was just one of those things that I accepted. The closest team that I could get to see was Chelsea. I was 13 at the time and went with Rodney Webb, a pal of mine who was a big Chelsea supporter. We played in the same school team and travelled to Stamford Bridge together. I did finally get to see Spurs play when they took on Chelsea. Roy Bentley was leading the Chelsea team and they subsequently went on to win the league under Roy's captaincy. We travelled by train from Mitcham Junction and then by tube from Tooting Broadway. I saw every home game in the title season. As kids we went down early each game to get at the front of the terracing opposite where the players came out onto the field. It was a great spot. Towards the end of the season Chelsea had a crunch game against Wolves, who, at the time, were the main challengers. Wolves had a cracking team and the crowd was packed earlier than normal. We got into the stand but were further back than we would normally be. Fortunately we did not need to worry as it was an era when it was common practice to pass kids down to the front of the stand for them to sit on the dog track that went around the ground. John Sillet scored a penalty for Chelsea to win the game and go a point clear of their archrivals in the battle for the title. A win over Sheffield Wednesday in the final home game clinched the 1954–55 Division 1 Championship. They were not my team but I'd followed them all season and it was a fantastic occasion. There were some fantastic games and I saw all the great stars play.

Roy Bentley was a goal scorer and star player in the Chelsea team. Naturally, as a goalkeeper, I observed the 'keepers in particular such as Jack Kelsey (Arsenal), Ted Ditchburn (Tottenham), Bert Williams (Wolves) and Bert Trautmann (Manchester City). I could not help but clock on to these guys to see how they commanded the penalty area and overcame aggressive centre-forwards because in those days there was no protection for keepers. All these guys were brilliant but, for me, Williams just edged it. Bert, at the time, was the England keeper so he was my main man as he wore that yellow England jersey I dreamed of wearing one day. It was rare to see footage of games but at the cinema there were always Pathe News snippets of England matches or FA Cup ties and it inspired me. Modern keepers do not realise how lucky they are, as keepers in the fifties took some stick. And they had to be brave to get the ball, diving full length into a ruck of players. It really was amazing to see those keepers in action. Of course, there were other great stars of the era such as Stanley Matthews (Blackpool), Tom Finney (Preston North End), Duncan Edwards (Manchester United), Nat Lofthouse (Bolton Wanderers) and Billy Wright (Wolves). In the summer, after watching a game, my mates and I would put our coats down on the local green for a kick around so we could emulate our heroes.

The following season I still went to Chelsea matches. During the season, as usual, we arrived early to bag a good spot. One particular week Chelsea were playing and when we got to our place on the terraces, I looked across the pitch and noticed a few kids standing behind the tunnel. I could not help but wonder what they were doing there when this old chap came out with a tracksuit and woollen jumper on, pointed at the kids and selected a few. And before I knew it, they were kitted out in tracksuits. They were all chosen as ball boys for the game. I thought to myself, 'I'll try that and I'll be closer to the action'. The next match was against Luton Town and I went to stand with the other kids at the tunnel. The guy came out and I couldn't believe it when he picked me. I remember Syd Owen was in the Luton side that day. It was a great experience.

I'd seen Newcastle United play at Chelsea and wanted to see them again because they were one of the most exciting teams around, so when they came to town, Fulham was the place to be, and I was not disappointed. The occasion was an FA Cup quarterfinal clash and it was the best game I ever witnessed. Newcastle had a superb forward line that included the great Jackie Milburn and had won the cup three times in the fifties. Newcastle were undoubtedly the cup kings of the era. They also had Jimmy Scoular, Bobby Mitchell and George Hannah in their line up. Ronnie Simpson, who later went on to star for Celtic, was in goal. I was behind the goal at the Cottage End that Newcastle attacked and they raced into a 3–0 lead through Casey, Milburn and Stokoe before Fulham grabbed a goal. At half time the Geordie fans were ecstatic but Fulham, who had the great Johnny Haynes in their lie up, had a lifeline and were urged on by a packed house. Chamberlain completed a hat-trick to take Fulham into a 4–3 lead. Six of the goals had been scored at the end I was standing. But the game was not over as Vic Keeble struck twice in the last 10 minutes to secure an astonishing 5–4 win. The match was the most exciting I'd seen and has rightly gone down in Newcastle cup folklore. Simpson was a great keeper but afterwards, I thought, 'Who'd be a keeper in a game like that?' It was an unbelievable match.

In my last year at school I played for the district team. The side was a good one and we reached the quarterfinals of the English School's Shield, which was incredible as we were pitted against the best sides around. We beat Swindon when a young Ernie Hunt starred for them on our way to the quarterfinals. Ernie went on to be play for Coventry City. Eventually we went out to the Isle of Wight. Our achievement was not without reward because the English School's FA made us, as a team, ball boys at Wembley for the England versus Scotland Home International match that season. The lads had a good day out.

Even though I'd impressed at school and district level with Sutton and Carshalton, I was always a reserve for London and

Surrey Boys. I was a promising keeper but ahead of me in the pecking order was Mike Kelly, who went on to play for Queens Park Rangers. Missing out was a blow because it reduced my chances of becoming an apprentice professional. There were times when I felt dejected and let down by the system but in some ways it kept my feet on the ground. Deep down there were initial feelings of rejection but it did not stop me hoping a chance may come my way. Scouts at clubs were always at games and able to take on around three apprentices every year so I hoped an opportunity would surface. Despite the disappointment, for me it was a case of playing football whenever possible and hoping to get spotted. And there were opportunities as I played for school on a Saturday, Achilles Boys Club on a Sunday and district team when selected.

Thoughts about following my brother into the Merchant Navy did not appeal to me so when I left school at 16 I got a job as a paint sprayer in a little firm near where we lived. And just as I'd hoped, out of the blue, Fulham contacted me to offer me a trial. I was delighted, excited and nervous. Bedford Jezzard was manager and gave me a 45-minute half. Afterwards he thanked me for attending but told me Fulham would not be taking it any further. At the time, it was devastating news but I was determined not to look upset. Of course it was a crushing blow because it was an opportunity I wanted to make the most of. Just like hundreds of other wannbee footballers I wanted to shine but, unfortunately, for the majority it doesn't work out. And it's even worse today because the conveyor belt of kids being given a chance from a ridiculously young age at soccer academies is mindboggling. But the modern era dictates that you have to spot talent early. The best run academies do make it clear what the chances are and make sure youngsters are well educated, but try telling that to the hopefuls wishing to make it.

Being let down like this is when your character becomes important. I had dreamt of making it in football and wanted to impress so much. I thought to myself, 'I'll show you'. Most kids buckle under the disappointment of bad news but others take it on the chin as they believe in their ability. I always had the philosophy that if you want something then you have to fight for it. I had to battle on.

2

STEPPING STONES

Two of my old footballing adversaries, Ian St John (Liverpool) and Jimmy Greaves (Tottenham Hotspur), used to joke that 'football is a funny old game'. Both were stars in their pomp and later found fame on TV when they hosted *On The Ball* and later *Saint & Greavsie* in the build up to matches on a Saturday. Their anecdotal quips were, of course, tongue in cheek but also spot on because you never knew what was around the corner as a footballer, whatever stage in your career. And that was certainly the case for me when I was looking for a break, because shortly after being rejected by Fulham I was invited to train at Isthmian League club Tooting and Mitcham United.

Tooting played at Sandy Lane and had a reputation for giving youngsters a chance. Training twice a week with the Colts (U18) I quickly discovered a step up in class but was not intimidated. The adrenaline rush was terrific and it was not long before I'd made the Colts side, which played on Figges Marsh. During the 1958–59 season we drew West Ham in the FA Youth Cup. Ron Greenwood was The Hammers manager and overseeing the youth set up was Malcolm Allison. Ronnie Boyce and Martin Peters starred as West Ham won 2–0. It was not an unexpected result but we battled throughout a hard fought encounter. West Ham were renowned for developing talented players. Peters was on the next rung of the ladder at the club, and of course would team up with Bobby Moore and Geoff Hurst for England in 1966. In more recent times the West Ham conveyor belt has provided Rio Ferdinand, Frank Lampard, Michael Carrick and Joe Cole, to name a few that have joined the ranks of world stars.

I found myself at Tooting at a historic time because cup fever gripped the club when the first team drew Division 1 outfit Nottingham Forest in the FA Cup third round after knocking out Bournemouth and Northampton Town. The Colts and reserve team players were allowed to watch the clash, which proved to be a classic as the 'Tooting Terrors' hit the national sporting headlines. Tooting, unlike Forest, had nothing to lose. And Forest were not pleased when they arrived at our quaint ground to discover a rock hard frozen pitch. The ground staff put down sand but the pitch was something of a leveller although Forest were still clear favourites with the bookies. Nobody outside Tooting gave us a prayer but our centre-forward Paddy Hasty harassed the Forest defence from the first kick. And incredibly Tooting led 2–0 at half time. A major cup shock looked on but Forest came back, although it took a freak goal to get them back into the match when Ted Murphy, who'd scored one of our goals along with Albert Grainger, played a back pass that took a wicked deflection off a piece of ice past our keeper. Forest then gained a fortuitous penalty when the ball bobbled and hit one of our defenders' hands. There was no intent, it was just a bad bounce and Forest equalised. The result drew great headlines in the sports pages over the next couple of days. There was a real spring in the step at the club but our joy was short lived in the replay as Forest ran out winners 3–0 before 40,000 fans. Forest went on to lift the Cup, so at least we could say we'd run the cup winners close. A regular at Forest at the time was left-winger Billy Gray who would become a mentor in the coming years as I made my way in the game.

My form in the Colts was solid and, unbeknown to me, I had a growing reputation. So the story goes, former chairman and influential committee member Bill Fell had heard about a budding keeper in the Colts side and when the first team were winning a game comfortably decided to drop in to a fixture at Figges Marsh. By all accounts he was not disappointed. I duly made my reserve bow in 1959–60 followed by 27 reserve games the next campaign but could not oust first team regular Wally Pearson. Despite this, my career was moving forward and, during the summer of 1961, my luck continued at the Epsom Derby. Going to the Derby was a ritual for my family. We'd find a spot near the middle of the course for a picnic before taking a punt on the horses. As a kid, you could run down to the start to watch the horses set off and get back for the finish. By now I was old enough to bet and took a punt on Psidium at 66–1. And it came first! Sadly, this would be the last time we'd go to the Derby as a family.

In recent years, dad's health had been a growing concern. He encouraged my football aspirations but was struggling with life generally but particularly with sleeping. We believed this was due to his experiences in the Second World War. After dad suffered a nervous breakdown he went into a sanatorium. Following treatment he returned home, which we were pleased about, but he was not the same person. The happy-go-lucky dad I knew as a kid was no longer there. Instead, dad was quiet and introverted. He did watch me play football but after one reserve match when we'd arranged to meet in the clubhouse for a drink, he didn't turn up. I assumed he'd gone home so I had a few drinks with the lads when I spotted him outside. He could not bring himself to join us, which was really upsetting. Dad was not well but I struggled to know what to think about his illness.

On 26 October 1961 I was on the verge of breaking into the Tooting first team when my life changed forever. Dad woke me as usual and gave me my morning cup of tea. Normally we had a quick chat but on this particular morning, we didn't. I thought nothing of it at the time; dad just seemed subdued.

Later, when I was at work, I received a call to go home immediately. My brother-in-law was a printer for the *Daily Express* and worked nights. He'd arranged to do some work in our garden with dad but on arriving, had discovered dad's body in the kitchen. When I returned home, my cousin was with a policeman outside our front door and I wasn't allowed to go in. Eventually I found out that dad had committed suicide and I was devastated. He was 58. Dad meant the world to me and I hoped that he'd proudly follow my football career but it was not to be. I've since accepted that dad needed to sleep. The worst thing was that because he'd committed suicide he could not be buried at the church where my mother had done so much voluntary work. In the end he was cremated in Streatham. I was furious when I first heard this and raced around to the Vicar's house to have it out with him. The Vicar gave an explanation but to me it was just an excuse. Since that day, I've never been a churchgoer.

During this difficult time, I was determined to make dad proud and it was in this period I progressed into Tooting's first team. There was a perk of picking up £5 per week boot money but for me it was far more important to pit my wits against the likes of Wimbledon, Leytonstone, Kingstonian, Wycombe Wanderers and Mainstone United in the Isthmian League. Among the first team regulars were Ken Holder,

Gordon Holden, Albert Grainger, Brian Bennett, Roy Agar and Len Farlam. I made 14 appearances during the 1961–62 season as Tooting finished fifth behind champions Wimbledon. Paul Bates led the goal scoring charts with 13 goals in eight games, which was some going. We went out of the FA Cup and FA Amateur Cup in the early stages but picked up silverware as we landed the Surrey Invitation Cup and Surrey Senior Shield. It was gratifying to see local papers, which had tracked my career to date and were noting my consistent performances. I was not a goalkeeper to make flying saves. Concentration and safety-first tactics were my game. On a historical basis, the season was notable for Tooting as they played in a Challenge Match against Arsenal to mark the switching on of new floodlights at Sandy Lane. Isthmian League chairman R. Donaldson had the honour of performing a ceremonial 'switch on' before kick off in front of a capacity 5,000 crowd, the biggest attendance I'd played in front of. I was determined to play well in such a landmark game.

Challenge Match, Sandy Lane
(29 March 1962)

Tooting & Mitcham: Stepney, Holder, Bambridge, Holden, Bennett, Wigham, Grainger, Agar, Hasty, Ward and Warnes.
Arsenal: McClelland, Wills, Magill, Ward, Snedden, Petts, Kinsella, Gould, Kane, Bloomfield, Whittaker.

Arsenal named seven first team players including a back line that featured Irish international keeper John McClelland and full-back Jimmy Magill. Of course, The Gunners were not going to play at full throttle but our 4–2 win was still a fantastic experience. Next day, the evening edition noted: '19-year-old Alex Stepney matches his agility with a super show in the home net, snatching balls from the air and diving at opponents' feet with the fearlessness of a veteran.' I was chuffed to bits. Hasty was the star though, rekindling his FA Cup escapades against Forest in 1959. Paddy scored one on top of making goals for Ward and Agar, who scored our final goal. Petts scored a penalty for Arsenal late on.

Having tasted first team action I could not wait for the new campaign and Tooting enjoyed some thrilling matches in the early months of the 1962/63 season. Tooting were challenging Wimbledon and Kingstonian for top spot. During a clash against Kingstonian I broke a wrist but there were no substitutes in those days so I played the remainder of the game on the wing! I was soon back in the side though and played in the FA Cup for the first time. As a non-league side we had to qualify for the first round proper and progressed past Ruislip Manor, Slough Town and Dulwich Hamlet before losing to Enfield, who also ended our FA Amateur Cup hopes but not before we trounced Welton Rovers.

FA Amateur Cup, Round 2, Sandy Lane (October 1962)

Tooting & Mitcham: Stepney, Holder, Applebee, Holden, Bennett, Pink, Grainger, Agar, Browning, Norcott, Warnes. *Welton Rovers*: Webber, MacLachlan, Millard, Margary, Collins, Edwards, Painter, Attwood, Skirton, Watkins, Canning.

On a day when everything went our way, Tooting thumped Welton 11–0. This would be the biggest win of my football career in any first class game but you'd never have predicted it as at half time we led 2–0. By the end, Warnes (4), Browning (3), Agar, Grainger, Holden (pen) and Applebee had written themselves into Tooting club folklore. One sports headline for me summed up the game: 'EUREKA! Tooting Find A Goal Mine.' As for my performance, there was not a lot to note. 'Alex Stepney became a solitary figure at one end while the other ten all leapt into attack.' The reporter concluded: 'The final whistle ended Welton's nightmare and their last Amateur Cup match. Next season Welton turn professional. I shouldn't imagine they have any regrets.' His comments were almost prophetic for me as a 3–2 defeat to Enfield would be my last in the competition!

Tooting's early season title challenge continued but after a 2–1 win at St Albans City in mid-December there would be no more games until mid-February due to the 'Big Freeze'. British weather in the early sixties was bad but the winter of '62 wiped out football. During this period I'd changed jobs. Dermatitis finished my days as a paint sprayer so I got a job in the publicity department of Philips Electricals in Croydon. To date I'd played around 50 games for Tooting but like all clubs we had a massive backlog of fixtures. There was no such thing as 'underground' heating so clubs had to improvise. Many put straw down to cover the pitch, more wealthy clubs hired hot-air blowers or sheeting but even those 'mod cons' failed. Things got so desperate that Wally Ardron, a wily old coach at Doncaster Rovers, thought polar bear hair from Belle Vue Zoo attached to his players' boots would grip the surface better. It didn't. It was freak weather and I always remember one picture of Blackpool stars Jimmy Armfield, today renowned as a match summariser on radio, and Tony Waiters clearing the snow on ice skates! Whilst we waited for the ice to thaw I received an unusual request from Millwall FC.

Every footballer needs a stroke of luck, whether it's getting a first team opportunity or chance to advance but in my wildest dreams I never thought bad weather would enhance my professional aspirations. As the worst of the winter weather disappeared, Millwall approached Tooting because they needed reinforcements to complete their reserve fixture list and my name cropped up, probably as I was being tipped for an amateur international cap. Ron Gray, a distinguished character, was manager and heard about my potential through scout Bill Collins. Gray asked if I fancied playing reserve games as an amateur. I jumped at the chance and received £8 expenses per game but my work-football schedule would make the modern day player cringe. Working at Philips Electricals from Monday to Friday full time, I then played for Tooting on a Saturday, Millwall (twice during the week) and Tooting again midweek. The only consolation was that training was not necessary!

Millwall reserves were made up mainly of young lads the club was trialling and a sprinkling of first teamers. The campaign went well as the reserves finished runners up in the Football Combination League. At Millwall, I enjoyed the professional outlook and banter in the dressing room. During the games I felt I'd made a mark and was delighted when, towards the end of the season, there was talk that Millwall along with Wolves and Blackburn Rovers were interested in signing me. It was great reading snippets in the sports pages but I knew nothing was concrete until a club contacted me.

After the last game Gray called me aside and proved that the rumours were true. Millwall wanted to sign me as a professional. Reg Davies had been first choice keeper for five seasons. Nicknamed 'The Cat' by Millwall fans due to his agility, Davies had a sound reputation but if I was to sign pro forms, I wanted assurances I'd start the season first choice. Gray listened and it was a bold move on my part but I felt I'd served my apprenticeship. Gray told me I'd impressed with my attitude and had the raw talent to make it as a pro. He also guaranteed I'd start the season in the first team. I signed for Millwall on 13 May 1963. Davies joined Leyton Orient not long afterwards.

Millwall's season was over but two games remained for Tooting and I was given permission to play in both against title rivals Wimbledon. In a three-horse race Kingstonian had finished their fixtures and led the way. It was now up to us but a 3–2 defeat at Wimbledon blew our chances of winning the league. In our last game I was captain but was at fault as we slipped behind to Wimbledon 2–0. The lads showed terrific character to draw 2–2 with a hotly disputed last minute penalty converted by Holden. Wimbledon went on to clinch the league following further games in hand. Finishing third behind Wimbledon and Kingstonian was an improvement on the previous season but desperately disappointing, as a Wimbledon 'double' would have seen Tooting crowned champions. Agar, Holden, Holder and Norcott were ever-presents. I played 27 of our 30 league games. Browning was top goal scorer with 23 goals.

I will always be grateful to Tooting for giving me my break, and they wished me well in becoming a professional, but at the time it resulted in a spat between the clubs. Tooting felt let down by Millwall as I'd helped out in a fixture crisis but it turned into what Tooting viewed as an 'extended' trial. And they had a point. Today this would not happen as there would be sell-on clauses, but although Tooting chairman John Dewar was quoted as saying I was worth £15,000 on the transfer market, he had to let me go for nothing. With no compensation agreed Tooting put a ban on professional scouts entering the board room and dressing rooms at Sandy Lane but they could not stop scouts attending games through the turnstiles. It was a shame that things had ended this way but Tooting still felt aggrieved from a previous transfer when Dave Bumpstead joined Millwall a few years earlier and a promised friendly had not taken place. Dewar pointed out that, as a gesture of goodwill, many league clubs made a donation to amateur clubs but that was not going to happen. In the end, good sense prevailed and Millwall agreed to play a friendly at Sandy Lane a few months later. Tooting kept the gate receipts.

My first contract meant I was earning £14 a week plus bonuses of £4 a win and £2 a draw during the season. In the close season I'd be on £12 a week. I was really chuffed as I'd almost doubled my salary at Phillips overnight. As a bonus, Gray handed me an envelope, which contained a £50 'signing on fee' and a 7s 6d FA Cup final standing ticket between Manchester United and Leicester City. Walking down Wembley Way, I thought to myself, 'I'm a professional footballer, something thousands of youngsters dream about and maybe one day I'll play at this stadium'. With £3 from my 'signing on fee' I decided to treat myself and upgraded my standing ticket with a tout outside the ground for a seat. United defeated Leicester 3–1. Watching Charlton, Law, Herd and Crerand display their skills I could see United were far better than the lowly position they finished that season in Division 1. Leicester came into the match favourites but were swept aside. Gordon Banks in the City goal was the far busier keeper. I watched Banks at close quarters and could see he was excellent. It was easy to see why he had just won his first England cap and was viewed as the long-term replacement to Ron Springett. Not having to report for training until early July, I decided to treat myself further during the summer, and with the remainder of my 'signing on fee' went to Tossa de Mar to soak up some sun on my first holiday abroad.

3

UP THE DOCKERS!

Millwall played at Cold Blow Lane and the Dockers fans were among the most fervent around. Looking ahead to the Division 3 campaign, Ron Gray was blooding younger players alongside a number of lads that had been at The Den since the start of the decade and that was reflected in the line up for my first team debut.

**Football League Division 3, The Den
(26 August 1963)**
Millwall: Stepney, Gilchrist, Cripps (captain), Harper, Wilson, Stocks, Jones, Broadfoot, Foster, McLaughlin, Haverty. *Reading*: Dixon, Neate, Meldrum, Evans, Spiers, Thornill, Wheeler, Shreeves, Morris, Kerr, Lofty.

Making debuts alongside me were Michael Foster and John McLaughlin. Before the Reading match, my so called best mates gave me plenty of stick. 'The Dockers are the worst fans going. They'll tear you apart if you make a mistake.' I gave them a wry smile as I'd already had the best advice going into the game from the boss and experienced pros.

'Give everything and you'll be fine,' was the message but above all was the advice, 'make a decision and be decisive'. Running out, of course, I had nerves but the crowd roar was amazing. Lining up in between the sticks I felt inspired.

Roars of 'Come on son!' and 'Good luck!' came from fans behind the goal. Millwall were among the pre-season favourites and got off to a great start with a 2–0 win. Haverty and McLaughlin scored. Back in the dressing room there were plenty of back slaps. A winning bonus and clean sheet on my pro debut was the perfect start.

But from the high of my debut, I fell back to earth with a bump as Millwall struggled for results and we had to endure the wrath of frustrated supporters. Eight defeats followed in 10 games including four-goal drubbings against Bournemouth and Wrexham. Walking off to a chorus of boos the Wrexham result ended in demonstrations outside the club offices. The back pages in the sport sections pulled no punches. 'Fans Storm Millwall Offices'; 'Lions Hit Rock-bottom' and 'Gray Must Go' were among the headlines on Sunday morning. I was experiencing a tough baptism but Gray kept encouraging me. At team talks Gray was always animated, revving up the lads to try their luck from distance. He was always convinced I'd make flying saves. It was his way of motivating us, though it was all a shade bizarre. Gray started to ring the changes, which included the return of injured striker Pat Terry, who had led the scoring charts the previous season. Terry was on target as we scraped a victory over Peterborough United but by the end of October we'd recorded just four league wins.

My debut season was turning into a relegation battle. Despite the situation, Millwall fans encouraged me, but the same could not be said about the older pros. A number gave me a torrid time when I made a mistake because it could cost us a win bonus. In those early days inside the inner sanctum of the dressing room, I didn't have the confidence to defend my corner. As rookie keeper I was an easy target but it was not just me making mistakes as defenders were missing tackles, midfielders were not creating openings and strikers, when they got an opportunity, blazed wide. I wondered what I'd taken on, especially after I made a hash of a goal kick in the last minute at home to Shrewsbury Town. With Millwall leading 2–1 a win was on the cards but the ball bobbled out to Shrewsbury's centre-forward who knocked in an equaliser. When you're a keeper there is no place to hide and I had to take the stick but the incident quickly hardened me as a pro.

Sadly, our misfortune continued as we departed from both domestic cup competitions inside 48 hours. The pressure was mounting when we took on non-league Kettering in a first round FA Cup replay at home. Losing 3–2 resulted in bedlam. Sitting in the dressing room we could hear Millwall supporters yelling abuse. They were also throwing stones against the windows and scuffles took place with police outside. It was really unnerving. Chants of 'Gray Out!' were deafening. It took time for the police to persuade fans to depart from the stadium as we licked our wounds and heard a few home truths from the manager. We'd let the club, fans and ourselves down. When Rotherham United thumped us 5–2 in the League Cup two days later Ron Gray's position was untenable.

Billy Gray was appointed player-manager. Billy had played for Leyton Orient, Chelsea, Burnley and Nottingham Forest. I'd seen him play for Forest when they defeated Tooting on the road to winning the FA Cup and our new boss had a lot to sort out. Players were arguing in the dressing room. In fact, he had to break up scuffles in an early practice match, but his arrival brought a brief change in our fortunes. The festive period is always a time when games come thick and fast. And Boxing Day brought a welcome win over Luton Town before another victory against Luton completed a 'double' 48 hours later. But the writing though was on the wall and changes of personnel were needed.

The New Year started with a defeat against Coventry City and I was at fault for both goals when we drew with Queens Park Rangers. Despite my errors, Gray backed me to the hilt and told me I'd stay first choice. The news hacks had, in general, been positive about my performances but after the Rangers game they slated my attempts to catch two crosses that allowed the goals. One journalist quipped, 'Stepney clutched the ball like a puppy does when a dog biscuit is tossed in the air'. I was miffed but the boss told me to get used to it. There was no middle ground with the press. You were a villain or hero.

With morale low, Gray tried to save our season. New arrivals included Len Julians and Jimmy Whitehouse. Both made immediate impacts. In his second game, Julians struck twice in a win over Walsall while Whitehouse notched key goals in victories against Port Vale and in the return fixture with Walsall. Brian Snowden came into defence while Hugh Curran, who later starred at Norwich City and Wolves, joined our survival bid but we were still inconsistent. On our day we clicked as Notts County discovered when we put them to the sword 6–1 but the win was one of two victories in our final nine games. Relegation was all but confirmed in our final home game against Bristol City. My error cost a penalty. One headline struck a chord, 'Penalty Pushes Lions To Brink'.

On paper we had a chance in the last match but we were clinging to a miracle at Mansfield Town, unbeaten at home all season. We needed Queens Park Rangers to thump Barnsley and at half time Rangers led 2–0. We were technically safe on goal average but Barnsley scored twice to send us down to Division 4. To complete a miserable day Mansfield thumped us 4–1. Relegation was a sickening feeling. I'd played in every game during the season and Gray told me I'd be first choice as he looked to build a squad capable of bouncing back at the first attempt. I knew the feeling of relegation, now I wanted to experience promotion.

Away from football, the summer was a busy time because I married Pamela Finch who I had known since our schooldays. After our honeymoon in Loch Lomand and settling into our bungalow in Meopham I returned for pre-season training expecting changes. I was right. Among players to depart were Broadfoot, Haverty and Jones who had been in the side on my first team debut. Broadfoot was a pacey outside-right who avoided no-nonsense defenders with neat flicks and deft touches. Joe was a crowd favourite on his day along with Haverty on the left flank. Jones had been among the goals for Millwall but struggled throughout the previous season and left league football. Gray was an advocate of the youth system. With a fresh outlook based around pros and talented youngsters, such as wingers Barry Rowan and Billy Neil, there was a winning feeling as we started the 1964–65 season.

With renewed optimism Millwall started the campaign with a 4–1 win at Stockport County and the opening 10 games brought just one defeat. Curran had been among the goals and his strike against Tranmere Rovers heralded four consecutive wins, the others versus Darlington and a Bradford City 'double'. City's neighbours, Bradford Park Avenue, jolted us with a 4–0 defeat but we bounced back in style with a Julians hat-trick in a 5–1 win against Halifax Town. At the halfway point of the season we completed the 'double' over Stockport and, with the festive period approaching, players and fans alike were in high spirits. Millwall fans did amuse me and I had a great rapport with them, but it was not the Dockers that had the loudest voices . . . the Dockers' wives shouted and screamed far louder! 'Get in there!', 'Scrap for every tackle!'

Comments such as these from behind the goal home, or away, never phased me. I could always rely on some comedian among the home faithful to raise a smile as we battled away.

The New Year began with a bang as Curran and Julians secured a win over Lincoln City. The triumph was welcome as a huge FA Cup tie loomed against Division 1 Fulham. We'd made the third round after gaining revenge over Kettering before thumping Port Vale. It was a plumb tie and fans packed Craven Cottage expecting a routine win for the hosts who boasted former England captain Johnny Haynes in the side. A superb playmaker in his heyday, Haynes was the first £100 a week footballer in British football. But, on a day when the underdog prevailed, we battled away to earn a draw. Cup fever gripped Millwall for a few days as fans flocked to buy tickets for the replay hoping to cheer us on to a famous upset. Over 30,000 fans crammed into the stadium while thousands more were locked out. These were the days before all ticket matches and segregation so it was a case of arriving early to secure a decent pitch. An upset was on the cards and we came through 2–0 with goals from Harper and Rowan to send home supporters wild. Of course, we were not going to win the Cup and went out to Shrewsbury—a big disappointment as we'd have faced Leeds United in the fifth round—but it felt good that winter's day to claim a big scalp.

A winning dressing room generates a fantastic atmosphere. Gray had belief in the team and gave the lads confidence. Billy was the type of manager who was always there for a player. Although outspoken, he backed his players and if we did something wrong he just had a quiet word. Training was also on a different level. Before his arrival, training sessions were monotonous. We'd arrive at Sidcup for a 10am start but there was no specific goalkeeper training. We worked out on a cinder track behind the stand. Modern day footballers would think they were on another planet in terms of our facilities. In my debut season it was a case of running, running and more running with the odd six-a-side game thrown in. Stamina was essential because of the poor surfaces and under the new manager there was still running as well as a lot more ball work, more six-a-side games of forwards versus defence and as a keeper, Gray organised specific sessions. Billy was an innovator, introducing his own methods to help us recuperate after a game. One day the squad was told a ballet dancer was coming to demonstrate new exercises and there were plenty of smirks among the lads but the boss was serious. Three days a week Doreen Hermitage taught us routines. When groin strains, pulled muscles and niggling leg injuries disappeared the smirks stopped!

Much credit for my eventual successes was down to Billy because he gave me good principles to follow. I improved enormously at Millwall. Gray was an imaginative coach and one of a generation coming into the game that looked at new ways to improve team performance. Billy would go on to develop a fantastic youth policy at Burnley that discovered the likes of Ralph Coates and Frank Casper but Millwall benefitted from his knowledge and I was delighted he kept me back after training. 'Pressure' sessions helped my agility, angles and footwork. Goalkeepers are different 'mentally' to other players at a football club and Billy recognised this. Pundits quip that only a goalkeeper is crazy enough to dive headfirst to make a save and there is probably some truth in that. There was certainly a kamikaze attitude to keeping but I loved it and Billy built my confidence in this area. He'd say, 'Son, you're brave, but remember when you go down at an opponent's feet you could break their leg if your timing is wrong so get it spot on'. A lot of work went into this area and I was never worried about making this type of save. Training was great and I could feel myself improving every session.

I was not a fan of goalkeeping gloves, but, of course, there was not much of a choice, unlike today. Ron Springett (Sheffield Wednesday) used a style that had pimples down the fingers and Peter Bonetti (Chelsea) favoured green, cotton gloves. The gloves made a difference when it was really wet but in milder conditions you had to spit or put mud on your hands to grip a ball. I tried both but went for Springett's because I discovered when the laundry ladies boiled them in bleach they shrank and the pimples went tacky, which gave me a good grip. Technology was new so we had to improvise!

In the mid-sixties football was beginning to change as television made its first moves to televise the game for a wider audience. *Match of the Day* began showing recorded highlights on BBC2 at the start of the season and it quickly took off. Shortly after our win over Fulham, Millwall featured in a BBC production presented by Danny Blanchflower, who had captained Tottenham Hotspur to the double in 1960–61, the FA Cup in 1962 and European Cup Winners Cup in 1963. After retiring, he joined the BBC and was tasked with looking at football in the lower leagues. I'm not sure how or why Millwall were selected but the BBC chose an away fixture at Barrow to get an insight into life at our level. Danny followed us in training and travelled with us to the game.

Barrow have long since gone from the league but in the mid-sixties it was a heck of a journey that took two days. We left St Pancras on the Friday morning, which allowed Danny to interview a few of the lads during the train journey before we changed at Crewe prior to arriving at Barrow in the late afternoon. Two-day trips were not usual as we normally returned after a game but Barrow was an exception because of logistics. We had tea at the hotel and went to the local pictures before bed. In the morning we had a stroll before a pre-match meal and a short coach journey to arrive at Barrow an hour before kick off. Barrow centre-forward George McLean had a reputation. An old-fashioned striker, McLean got stuck in and was a real character. One tale I heard was that in one game his manager was yelling at him to hold the ball up. Taking exception to the barracking McLean picked up the ball and yelled back, 'Like this boss?' I knew McLean would give me a rough ride and in the first half he duly caught me around the rib cage. There were no subs and the trainer came on, gave me the 'magic sponge', and I had to play on. At half time we were leading but I was passing blood, which shocked me. There was something wrong with my kidneys. Our trainer wasn't a qualified doctor. The home team had a doctor on hand and he came into our dressing room and said I'd be okay so I played the second half. We won 5–0 but I still felt rough on the overnight 'sleeper' train back to London. Arriving back at St Pancras on Sunday morning there was time for a quick hospital visit and I was back in the side next game at home to Hartlepool United! As for McLean, he'd left his mark!

A few years later George earned a place in Barrow folklore. This was when, in a Division 3 game against Plymouth Argyle, he scored a goal that ricocheted off a referee past a stranded keeper. To the best of my knowledge, this remains the only goal ever to be scored by a ref, in this case Ivan Robinson. Whilst I don't think it appears in any record books, it's definitely one for the statos!

Our good league form continued until we lost at Tranmere Rovers but it heralded an unbeaten 15-match run to the end of the season. Winning nine games, we shipped just seven goals. Our defence was the rock for our promotion charge. And in the final six games we won the last four, conceding one goal in the final game. Crucially we first disposed of promotion rivals Rochdale 2–0 in front of our biggest home gate of the season (15,359) before Gilchrist notched his only goal of the campaign to defeat Bradford Park Avenue. A Curran strike overcame Wrexham while Julians and Rowan provided the goals against Notts County. And the winning sequence was to prove essential as we finished four points clear of fifth placed Tranmere. Defeat against County would not have stopped us going up but it was a close call and showed how essential the Rochdale win was as it gave us a buffer. For the record, four teams gained promotion. Brighton won the league on 63 points, one ahead of Millwall and York with Oxford a point further back and Rochdale on 58 points. In a tight finish, five points separated the top six spots. Conceding 45 goals was Millwall's lowest since Coronation Year in 1953 and our seven defeats were the least since 1928. Leading scorers were Curran (18) and Julians (15).

Approaching the 1965–66 season I had two years' experience and the lads knew that defensively it was my call. Being relegated and then getting promotion gave me confidence about my game. If a ball got through our defence there was now a trust that I'd be ready and if I came for a ball but mistimed my jump one of the lads would be back on the goal line. Of course, that doesn't always pan out but the majority of the time it did. Relegation in some ways did us a favour as we needed to rebuild and for me it was an apprenticeship. It was tough settling into a losing side because supporters get on a 'keeper's back if goals are flying in but, though we were losing games, the manager backed me and it held me in good stead for the future. I had a lot to learn. Gray's key message was always, 'Don't give the ball away'. Billy hated me kicking the ball downfield and surrendering possession. Instead he encouraged me to use the full-backs and wingers. These were the days of outside-lefts and outside-rights so if the ball came from my right, I expected our left back and outside-left to get wide. They knew I'd get the ball and start a quick attack. The opposite scenario occurred if the ball came from my left. Communication was essential and, as rookie keeper, the experienced lads guided me. The lads in defence needed to feel they had a confident keeper that would back them up. They demanded clear direction so we could work as a competent unit.

There was a lot going on in South East London during the mid-sixties. It was an era when the infamous Cray twins ruled the roost and there were plenty of dodgy characters offering players drinks but after making small talk I'd politely keep my distance. Sportsmen were often in the local pubs and there were a number of well-known hostelries. The crack was great when snooker player Alex 'Hurricane' Higgins was about and heavyweight boxer Henry Cooper would be at the Thomas A Beckett pub on the Old Kent Road. Joe Lucy owned the Five Bells and his Lonsdale belt was always proudly on display behind the bar. There was never a problem at closing time! Nearer the ground you'd see the Dockers leaving pubs a little worse for wear on the way to a game. They'd shout encouragement such as, 'Give 'em hell Alex!' I was pleased to be running out for the home team! Chatting to footballers of the era from opposing teams I heard the same tale. They hated playing games at Cold Blow Lane because players and home supporters alike expected and gave no quarter. Crowd trouble has dogged Millwall down the years and it has damaged the club's reputation. But I've always maintained that, as with most clubs affected by hooliganism, it is caused by a hard core of fans rather than the majority of supporters.

Going into 1965–66 we felt a promotion challenge was on the cards and had a side with strength throughout. Among the key players in front of me was John Gilchrist, a tough tackling right back who also played centre-back when needed. John joined the attack at set pieces and took defenders away for our strikers to benefit. Cripps had broken into the side after the 'Big Freeze' of 1963 at left back when he replaced Gilchrist due to an injury. Making the position his own, Gilchrist moved to right back. 'Arry Boy' Cripps was a fearless tackler leading by example as skipper. Both Gilchrist and Cripps were hard as nails while at the heart of the back four was Tommy Wilson. Not only a stalwart in defence, he also played half back or right half in midfield. Tommy was a manger's dream in a crisis, stepping into the fold and always performing with great effect. Ken Jones was an unsung hero of the promotion team working tirelessly in every game. Well built, Ken played wing half or inside right with equal success. And in attack we had Julians. Having been a teammate of the boss at Nottingham Forest, Billy knew how Len would benefit the side. An experienced pro, Julians led the line and scored a stack of goals. In the dressing room and in tight games Len was a 'cool head' and especially important in the charge for promotion.

Feeling confident, Millwall got off to a flyer, continuing our good form from the previous season. George Jacks joined on a free transfer from Queens Park Rangers and immediately settled into the team as a man marker in midfield. Gray gelled the team superbly. He cleared out a number of players and brought balance to the side. No disrespect to Ron Gray, I appreciated my break at the club and he went on to serve Ipswich Town as chief scout but Billy put together a team with a winning mentality. From the opening win at home to Workington Town, a match notable for Jacks becoming the clubs' first substitute, Millwall were in the shake up for back-to-back promotions. Arguably, opponents may have underestimated us, which is possible with a newly promoted team but it can go both ways. Often promoted teams struggle, but we had belief and proved we could compete in a higher division. Nine wins from the opening 12 games was some going. Curran and Julians were on fire and the run included consecutive victories over Queens Park Rangers, Exeter City, Southend United and Swindon Town.

As a team we were clicking all over the park and I was gaining something of a reputation for saving penalties. I'd stopped six out of nine penalties awarded against us in the opening stages of the season, which was a terrific ratio. I loved the challenge of spot kicks and trying to psyche opponents out. My performances were getting sound reviews and we had reached the League Cup fourth round where we faced Peterborough United. Middlesbrough had been one of the sides that we'd defeated and it helped my growing reputation. But I was not able to play in the tie, which we lost 4–1, because I was selected to play for the England U23 team to face our France counterparts on the same night.

I'd played 104 consecutive league games for Millwall, and missed just one since joining from Tooting and Mitcham, when news of my international debut came shortly after I celebrated my 23rd birthday. It was the best belated present I could have had. To say it was a huge surprise was an understatement. I was the first Millwall player to receive international recognition for 27 years. It was not only big news locally but also made the headlines nationally. It was rare for a Division 2 player to represent England, and at the time Scotland, at any level. It was not such a surprise for Wales and Northern Ireland, but it was a sensation for a Division 3 player to represent England or Scotland. Gray was really chuffed for me and told me I deserved my chance. Billy was the first to inform me after training as we prepared for a clash at Shrewsbury Town. There were plenty of slaps on the back and I was on a high. But I was soon brought crashing back to reality when Shrewsbury claimed a 2–0 win with two spot kicks. The ace penalty saver wasn't so reliable after all!

Next day, the papers were still noting my call up against France and there was also speculation that a number of top-flight clubs were tracking my progress, which was always good for confidence. As a young pro I loved the gossip but I had to try to ignore the stories although it was not easy when my name was being linked with a potential move to Arsenal, Manchester United and West Ham. In fact, some pundits were convinced that that only Gordon Banks (Leicester City) and Tony Waiters (Blackpool) were ahead of me as an English keeper but I took that notion with a pinch of salt. It was nice to read that my valuation was around the £40,000 mark . . . not bad for a rookie keeper who not so long ago had been keeping goal in the Isthmian League.

The official line from Millwall was that I was not for sale and fans would not stand for it. Directors were no doubt mindful that when Charlie Hurley was transferred in 1957 it caused ructions as thousands of fans protested. The club wanted to avoid a repeat situation. Millwall chairman Micky Purser went public stating that the club wanted to build a strong squad but I knew his comments were the usual type of repost to transfer speculation. I was not stupid. If a sizeable offer was forthcoming, no player in the lower leagues would be held back. And of course, I was ambitious to take my career forward. Transfer gossip hasn't changed much over the years because at the end of the day, money talks. As things transpired in the months to come I moved to Chelsea at the same time that another player in the news, Barry Bridges, who had been dropped by England after gaining a handful of caps, attracted a £55,000 bid from Birmingham City. All that was for the future though as my big night loomed for the England U23s. I had no idea who had recommended me but was thankful. It was World Cup year and I'd been selected to play alongside some notable lads.

England U23 International, Carrow Road
(3 November 1965)

England U23: Stepney (Millwall), Lawler (Liverpool), Thomson (Wolves), Hollins (Chelsea), Mobley (Sheffield Wednesday), Smith (Liverpool), Thompson (Liverpool), Chivers (Southampton), Jones (Sheffield United), Ball (Blackpool) and O'Grady (Leeds United). *France U23*: Heinrich, Merelle, Brucato, Desremeaux, Polmy, Andrien, Dogllani, Blanchet, di Nallo, Gulnot, Roy.

Alf Ramsey and all the lads were fantastic. No one knew me as eight lads in the team came from Division 1 and two played in Division 2. Chris Lawler was also making his international debut. Receiving the official itinerary of arrangements was terrific and Alf told me just to play my normal game. Alan Ball and Mick Jones (2) scored our goals in a 3–0 win. There was some talent in the side. Of course, Ballie would go on to star for England in the World Cup finals and later won major honours with Everton, while I'd face Martin Chivers in his pomp for Tottenham Hotspur, Jones at both Sheffield and Leeds United, John Hollins, Mike O'Grady, Lawler and Tommy Smith for their respective teams. All would claim European and domestic medals. Playing with these lads you could see the extra class.

After getting my first cap, back at Millwall everyone was brilliant. The lads wished me luck in the future, which gave me a feeling that something was happening. I'm sure they realised, as I did, that it would not be long before I'd be moving on. Having had a taste of a higher level I naturally wanted more. Gray called me in for a chat to discuss my feelings and I was honest with him. If a club came in then I wanted to know. I was ambitious but Billy told me to bide my time and not do anything hasty. Billy informed me that Middlesbrough had made an offer but the clubs had failed to agree terms. Northampton Town had also made a bid but, with respect to both clubs, though they were at a higher level at the time, I declined. Overall, I was happy at Millwall. I'd signed as a professional and was grateful for my opportunity but inside three years I'd progressed to the England U23s. At Millwall, we were going well so we were earning win bonuses but playing at a higher level was my main priority. Having had a taste of mixing with top-flight professional footballers I wanted to do this on a regular basis. I trusted Billy because he'd been straight with me and knew my ambitions. I felt promotion to Division 2 was the furthest the Lions could go with me as part of the side. I was confident that more offers would come and until then I'd give my all for the club.

Millwall had given me my break, as for our supporters, I knew they'd feel let down if I moved on but I hoped they would understand. I had a good rapport with the home fans at games. Okay, when I made a rick I expected some choice words and fair enough because they were also the first to defend me but the banter was always good-natured. And they were always there when I needed them—in more ways than I could have imagined! After helping the England U23 team win, it was back to league action with a feisty derby at Brentford. We battled away and came up with a 2–1 victory but at full time there was some trouble between rival fans as we raced off the pitch. The odd missile was thrown and I was grateful to one diehard Docker when an opposing supporter had a go at me. Before I knew it the instigator was on the deck courtesy of a right hook that would have floored Muhammad Ali! Sometime later I bumped into the Docker who rescued me. He expressed his disappointment that things had got out of hand but parted with a wry smile! Shortly afterwards, I was retained in the England U23 line up to face Yugoslavia U23.

England U23 International, The Dell
(24 November 1965)
England U23: Stepney (Millwall), Lawler (Liverpool), Thomson (Wolves), Hollins (Chelsea), Mobley (Sheffield Wednesday), Smith (Liverpool), Armstrong (Arsenal), Hunt (Wolves), Chivers (Southampton), Jones (Sheffield United) and Rogers (Swindon). *Yugoslavia U23*: Pantellic, Fazlagic, Zemko, Sliskovic, Rasovic, Holcer, Blazevic, Nadoveza, Hosic, Skrbic, Djajic.

There were three changes to the side from the France game including wingers George Armstrong and Don Rogers. Armstrong was a tricky winger and would play in the Arsenal line up when Rogers starred for Division 3 Swindon in a shock League Cup final win in 1969 but George would also be a key member of Arsenal's double winning team of 1971. Jones and Chivers scored England's goals in a 2–1 win.

Back to domestic action and following a 2–0 win against Oxford United, I was brought back to earth when Millwall became another notch on non-league Hereford United's FA Cup giant-killing list. Hereford boss Bob Dennison commented that without me Millwall would not be promotion certainties, which was welcome but I was realistic enough to know it was not all down to me. Our defence was resolute and it was a team game. Back on the league trail our main title challengers were Hull City. Cliff Britain was Hull manager and he used available transfer funds to sign Chris Chiltern and Kenny Wagstaff in a push for promotion. The big spenders on Humberside did not faze us because our form was solid.

It always amazed me as a player how often teams competing at the top played each other over the Christmas,

New Year or Easter periods. Compiling a fixture list was random but come Christmas we faced Hull home and away in the space of 24 hours. Over 40,000 packed Boothbury Park to see Hull win by a solitary goal but we ended the year on a high with a 3–0 home victory to share the honours. Curran and Neil scored our goals. Julians had been prolific from the outset but Curran had picked up an injury so was in and out of the team. Curran would only play one more game during the season when we dispatched Southend United on New Years' Day in front of another bumper home crowd. Playing three games in five days took its toll on players but it was the same for all clubs. Nevertheless, when you lose a key player it is tough.

Throughout the winter our form stayed solid and during an unbeaten 11-match run I only let in eight goals and half of those came in a thrilling 4–4 draw at Scunthorpe United. Out of six wins Julians struck in five to continue his rich vein of form. Bizarrely though having kept clean sheets for fun we then got thumped 6–1 at Queens Park Rangers. The result was a real wake up call and we bounced back with four more wins in a five game unbeaten spell as we edged to our promotion target. Following a 2–0 victory over York City, I joined up with the England U23 side for my last game at this level.

England U23 International, Ewood Park
(20 April 1966)

England U23: Stepney (Millwall), Badger (Sheffield United), Thomson (Wolves), O'Neil (Burnley), Cross (Leicester City), Peters (West Ham), Summerbee (Manchester City), Hunt (Wolves), Jones (Sheffield United), Birchenall (Sheffield United) and Armstrong (Arsenal). *Turkey U23*: Artuner, Bugdaypinar, Ozkarsli, Becedek, Sen (Y), Uraz, Sen (M), Dogan, Sari Loglu, Lmastasoglu, Tunaoglu.

Of note was a trio of Sheffield United players and I'd soon

be pitting my wits against Mike Summerbee in a host of derby clashes while away from domestic matters Martin Peters made a similar impact to Ball earlier in the season. Both would make the World Cup squad. Two Armstrong goals brought a 2–0 victory. Playing for the U23s was terrific because I'd never got close to making the England schoolboy side. The only sad fact was that even though I had the honour of playing in all three games during the 1965–66 season no caps were awarded to players. The games are in the record books but no memento was provided as a keepsake. However, teams were tracking my progress and gaining selection for the U23s had improved my profile. Unlike my next league games when Millwall won, this time we went down to Oxford United followed by a draw with Mansfield Town but we were soon back on song with wins over Swansea and Walsall.

Prior to our penultimate game at home to Mansfield I played one further representative match when I lined up for Young England versus England in what was, at the time, a traditional eve of FA Cup final clash. For the record Everton defeated Sheffield Wednesday at Wembley. This challenge match is no longer on the calendar but was a regular feature in my era. The line up had real talent on display.

England Representative Match, Stamford Bridge (13 May 1966)

England: Bonetti (Chelsea), Armfield (Blackpool), Newton (Blackburn Rovers), Milne (Liverpool), Flowers (Wolves), Moore (West Ham), Callaghan (Liverpool), Hurst (West Ham), Byrne (West Ham), Greaves (Tottenham) and Eastham (Arsenal). *Young England*: Stepney (Millwall), Reaney (Leeds United), Knowles (Tottenham), Smith (Liverpool), Cross (Leicester City), Peters (West Ham), Ball (Blackpool), Chivers (Southampton), Saul (Tottenham), Venables (Tottenham) and

Thompson (Liverpool).

The representative match finished 1–1 with Byrne and Chivers scoring the goals. Looking back at these sides, there was a host of legendary players including Bobby Moore, Geoff Hurst, Peters and Ball who would all feature in the World Cup final. And that is not to forget Jimmy Greaves and former England skipper Jimmy Armfield. I may not have been in the frame for the World Cup squad like 10 of the players on the pitch that day but that representative game put me in the shop window. I'd soon be back at Stamford Bridge as a Chelsea player alongside my opposite number on the day, Bonetti, but only briefly!

From trying to keep Hurst and Greaves quiet, three days later I lined up against Mansfield in our final home game. And in front of a packed house we won 2–0 to clinch consecutive promotions. The celebrations were terrific but behind the scenes I knew that my days were numbered at the club.

For some time there had been rumours about clubs interested in signing me. It was hard not to take notice when I heard that Tottenham, Fulham, Wolves and Middlesbrough were watching my performances. Further snippets surfaced that West Ham and Hull City were looking to table a bid. I had to bide my time but trouble had been brewing between Billy Gray and the club directors over recruitment of new players should the club get promotion. Things came to a head and Billy departed. I could not believe the timing. In what should have been his finest moment, Billy, who was the inspiration behind the teams' double promotion success and my rise as a footballer, was no longer at the club. There was speculation that I'd leave and there was a 12-day gap before the last match at Grimsby Town. We could not win the league or miss promotion so it gave me time to take stock after 158 games for Millwall. And it did not take me long to decide. Gray departing was the final straw for me. Benny Fenton took over while Billy joined Brentford. Fenton would become the longest serving manager at the club since the 1930s but my time at Millwall was over. I made my feelings known and the club wanted to cash in on me joining a Division 1 club.

My transfer from Millwall had numerous twists. The saga started when I discovered Hull City had been refused permission to speak with me. I stormed out before the final match with Grimsby. Word came through to me that West Ham boss Ron Greenwood wanted to sign me. Ron was a diamond of a person and it was appealing to think I'd be playing with the likes of Moore, Hurst and Peters. A £45,000 fee was agreed, a world record for a goalkeeper. My salary would be £60 a week, a great salary in 1966. Having been on £14 a week plus bonuses for three years, I was delighted but West Ham made it clear that my request for a £3,000 signing on fee had to be part of any deal. Millwall would not budge so I refused to sign. Millwall were receiving a world record fee so I didn't think I was asking for anything out of the ordinary. In the end it seemed that Millwall had relented as I got a call to say I could collect my paperwork.

Everything was moving fast but more twists came on the day I was due to sign for West Ham. Firstly, I received a counter-offer from Chelsea boss Tommy Docherty. Chelsea were about to take on Barcelona in an Inter Cities Fairs Cup semi-final replay but Tommy was looking ahead and offered me better terms. To say I was stunned was an understatement. Tommy explained that Peter Bonetti was unsettled and wanted a move to another club. Mulling things over, the phone rang again. Hull City offered me a larger signing on fee. Hull had big plans but my priority was Division 1 football. I had to think about the bigger picture. I now had a straight choice of two London clubs: West Ham, FA Cup and European Cup

Winners Cup in recent seasons; or Chelsea, a 'bigger' club splashing the cash to compete. Before deciding, I had to collect my release papers from Millwall but was shocked to hear my signing on fee was not part of the West Ham deal. I went to see Ron Greenwood, who was a gentleman when I told him what had transpired. Ron wished me all the best but the deal was off.

In the meantime, Millwall and Chelsea had struck an acceptable deal. Tommy was terrific in our negotiations and a deal was tied up. We drove to Stamford Bridge where I signed a three-year contract that included a £1,000 bonus a year. The transfer fee was £50,000, a world record. At the time, my departure from Millwall was not ideal but my affection for the club has still not diminished after all these years.

As the summer of 1966 approached my career was on the up. Chelsea were a club on the move and Tommy was cementing his reputation as a wheeler-dealer. In the space of a few months The Doc showed his intent to challenge the big boys by investing over £200,000 on players. Incoming stars, apart from myself, included Charlie Cooke (£72,000—Dundee) Joe Kirkup (£35,000—West Ham) and Alan Harris (£45,000—Coventry City). Players also departed as Barry Bridges (£55,000—Birmingham City) moved on alongside Terry Venables (£80,000—Tottenham Hotspur). They were exciting times but I'd only be a 'Blue' for a matter of weeks!

Tommy Smith
Liverpool and England

Alex was a great keeper and I got to know him in his days at Millwall when we both played for the England U23s. We were good mates and would go for a bite before a game. Three of us shared a room before matches in those days and at our hotel before a match at The Dell, Southampton, apart from myself and Alex, there was another mate of mine from my days at Liverpool, Chris Lawler. While Chris and I were resting before one particular game there was someone fiddling at the door trying to get in. I thought maybe someone was trying to break in to steal something so got behind the door. When it opened I pushed the intruder aside and was about to have a go when I realised it was Alex. He'd forgotten his key. The look on his face was a picture but we soon laughed about it.

Alex was a top keeper in our era, there is no question about that and he deservedly went on to play for England. At club level there was always great rivalry between Liverpool and Manchester United. Building up to a game against United it was a case of 'they don't like us and we don't like them'. It's been going on nigh on 50 years but the players always respected each other and competed hard. People used to think, when we faced the likes of Everton and Manchester United, we'd be kicking the living daylights out of each other but it was not like that. We fought hard but the animosity stayed on the pitch. Liverpool fans always gave Alex stick in goal, it went with the territory but he could handle it. After all, Alex came from down South and was used to fans having a go after playing at Millwall!

4

MADCAP DAYS AT THE BLUES

After signing for Chelsea I flew with the team to Barcelona and stood in the stands as my new teammates got thumped 5–0. It was a harsh way to end the season but Pam and I were soon celebrating following the birth of our eldest son John. It was certainly a busy time at home and while I contemplated fatherhood, I was also excited about playing for my new club. Chelsea had a young squad that included terrific players such as Terry Venables, Ron Harris, Eddie McCreadie, Charlie Cooke, Peter Osgood and Bobby Tambling. Tommy was a players' manager. He knew the game and was great fun to be around. One moment Tommy would be explaining his tactical views in a serious manner and the next he would be joking with the lads. The crack was terrific because The Doc knew how to handle players, young and old alike.

Peter Bonetti, dubbed 'The Cat', gained his nickname due to his agility in pulling off flying saves. Peter seemed genuinely pleased I was joining. My move to Chelsea was massive news when the story broke but confusion erupted at 'The Bridge' when Chelsea and Football Association chairman, Joe Mears, died from a heart attack during England's pre-World Cup tour to Scandinavia. Joe's death had a profound effect at Chelsea as he was Tommy's main ally behind the scenes. Joe's successor at Chelsea made it clear that Bonetti was going nowhere. Suddenly, the new world record signing was an understudy although nothing would be resolved until after the World Cup finals.

As the tournament approached, all talk rightly focused on the World Cup and England's chances of winning under Alf Ramsey. Of course, England made it all the way to the final and while the tournament was in full flow, the players, bar Bonetti, reported for pre-season training. After meeting my new teammates and receiving our kits we made our way to the training pitches. Trainer Jimmy Andrews informed us that we had to run four laps. Like most keepers, running was not my strong point and lap running in particular was not on my radar. As we set off Jimmy barked out his instructions, anyone finishing behind him would do another circuit. Luckily I was not on my own but if I thought this session was tough it had nothing on the schedule to come. The Doc was known for wanting super-fit teams that played fast, high-tempo football. Stamina was essential and I soon had to get used to the schedule starting with a five-mile run. Finishing behind Andrews meant extra running and yours truly was among the runners crawling home after doing the 'extras'! Another session involved sprinting between two posts at timed intervals. Again, missing targets meant extra sprints and I copped for those too. I wasn't the only one but at least I felt the benefit because in practice games coming off my goal line I was razor sharp. The Doc may have been the joker with his one-liners but he knew how to get his players fit. I thought, 'Welcome to Division One!'

As the World Cup reached its latter stages we departed to Scotland, Switzerland and of all places West Germany during a pre-season tour. And as World Cup final fever gripped back home, we Chelsea players booked into our German hotel. We went to a designated room to watch the match live but the German guests had nabbed all seats at the front so the Chelsea lads stood at the back as England kicked off at Wembley. It was a surreal experience. English lads cheered on the boys but the Scots in the squad had split loyalties. On the after-dinner circuit, football supporters are always amazed when I recall this tale but I always jest that 'The Doc', being a proud Scot, didn't want to be in London when England won the World Cup!

Returning home, we finished off pre-season training but the goalkeeping issue would be on ice until Bonetti returned from the World Cup. It was clear though that Peter was staying put. Tommy was in a difficult position and he took me to one side to inform me Bonetti would start the season as number one. And Peter duly played in the opening four games. Chelsea were unbeaten, winning the opening two matches prior to two draws for a solid start. Bonetti however picked up an injury in the latter clash against Nottingham Forest so I got a call on the Friday to tell me I'd make my debut at Southampton. Arriving at the ground, there was a message waiting for me. 'All the best Alex, have a great game, Peter.' As things transpired, we won 3–0 and I played well. I let Tommy know afterwards that I deserved a run in the team.

I knew that Tommy had a major problem but things had to be sorted. It was all well and good Tommy saying to the press that he had the two best keepers in the league but the situation could not continue. On the Monday, Tommy called the two of us over during training to inform us he'd be playing us in alternate matches. The situation was getting farcical. If Bonetti was fit, he'd play in a midweek clash against Leicester City and I'd face Sunderland on the Saturday. I knew it was a non-starter and I was right because Bonetti played against Leicester and was named in the side after training on the

Friday for the visit of Sunderland the following day. Something had to give but before I could say anything, 'The Doc' pulled a masterstroke. Calling me to one side, he told me that if Peter's injury held up against Sunderland I could talk to Manchester United about a possible move. Matt Busby had made an inquiry about signing me and had agreed a fee, subject to Bonetti being fit. I was speechless and he told me not to tell anyone, not even my wife, Pam, who was house hunting in the Chelsea area.

Being sworn to secrecy over the coming days was torture as I waited to see if Bonetti had a reaction to his injury. Everything was fine so on the Tuesday I accompanied Tommy to a meeting at the White House Hotel near Euston Station with Matt Busby and Jimmy Murphy. Waiting in reception, I was both excited and nervous. Suddenly the swing doors opened. Matt walked in wearing his trademark trilby and puffing on his pipe. Jimmy was smoking a cigarette. 'The Doc' got up, exchanged pleasantries and I thought, 'Bloody hell!' Matt looked at me and said. 'Right son, we're going to sort this goalkeeping issue out but first Jimmy and I are checking in.' You could see Tommy was in awe of Matt as he went off to reception with Jimmy. Tommy didn't say a word and when Matt returned, he left with him while I went with Jimmy. Walking down the corridor my mind was buzzing. All I could think about was that Manchester United wanted to sign me. I was stunned.

Chatting to Jimmy, I could tell that he was a real character. I could barely believe he was trying to 'sell' Manchester United to me but for some 20 minutes Jimmy told me what great players Law, Charlton, Best, Crerand and Stiles were, and what a terrific set of fans United had. And then there was the city and people living in Manchester. Jimmy went on to say I'd love moving north and that I'd be looked after and reiterated that United had a great bunch of lads. It was crazy because there was nothing to sell. Jimmy said, 'Alex, you'll enjoy it son.'

All the time I was thinking to myself, 'Where do I sign?'

Then Matt walked in and Jimmy departed with Tommy. Matt said, 'Right son, we've done the deal. We'd like you to be our goalkeeper. I should have come for you before but I've seen you play and think the time is right now. Do you fancy coming to Manchester United?'

Before I could say anything Matt added, 'And before we go any further there are no back-handers or under the table payments. We'll pay you £100 a week plus £20 a point in our bonus structure. Right, son, do you fancy joining Manchester United?'

What a question. I knew United had Harry Gregg, Pat Dunne and David Gaskell on the books but Matt explained I was the future and would come in as number one. There was no decision to make. I asked, 'Where do I sign?' and we shook hands. Matt called Tommy and Jimmy back in to the room and there were handshakes all round. I signed for £55,000 in a second world record fee. In the space of three months I'd gone from being paid £14 to £60 and now £100 a week plus better bonuses. I could not believe my luck. My Chelsea career comprised 113 days where I played one first team game, one reserve fixture and a handful of pre-season games. Bizarrely I'd signed for Millwall on 13 May and Manchester United on 13 September. Tommy would resign from Chelsea just over a year later. Dave Sexton succeeded him and incredibly my career would cross both at United in years to come! But that was all in the future.

Having signed on the dotted line for United, Matt told me to meet him and Jimmy at Euston Station 30 minutes before the 10am train to Manchester the following morning where we'd sort out all the formalities. I would then watch the first team play in a League Cup clash at Blackpool. Tommy took me back to Stamford Bridge to collect my belongings and wished me well. I returned to my in-laws' home in Carshalton to break the news to Pam. It would be an understatement to say Pam was shocked, as we were about to buy a house in Surrey, but I explained what a great move signing for Manchester United would be. Within minutes the phone calls started as the news leaked out.

Next morning, five days before my 24th birthday, I was up early to catch the tube to Euston from Morden. I travelled up the Northern Line with commuters through Tooting Broadway, Stockwell, Balham and so on. The train was packed because it was the rush hour and my face was in all papers. I tried to keep my head down, which was not easy. I got quite a few stares and realised my life was not going to be the same again. Eventually I arrived at Euston and found Matt and Jimmy on the platform. They asked how I was and how my wife had taken the news. I said Pam was fine, but shocked. Matt reassured me that she'd be fine and the club would help us both settle into our new surroundings.

Matt told Jimmy to get the morning newspapers for the three-hour journey ahead of us. Sat in our first class carriage, my first thought was that it was a good idea because what were we going to talk about for all that time. Picking up a paper, I was reading an article when Matt suddenly passed a paper to me and in a stern voice said, 'Son, what's all this about?'

On the front page was a picture of Pam and a headline, 'I Don't Want To Live in Coronation Street.' I told Matt I didn't know anything about it. All I could think was a reporter had misquoted her.

Matt said, 'Don't worry son', and that was the end of the discussion. 'The Doc' was naturally quoted. In true Tommy

Doc style, he noted I was a keeper with potential but was happy to sell Busby the second best keeper in the country. I had to smile. 'The Doc' had all the answers!

The journey to Manchester flew by as Jimmy extolled the virtues of Charlton, Best, Law and all the playing staff at Old Trafford. Jimmy was a great character and I'd quickly discover his importance at United. Matt was the father figure but Jimmy was the players' friend. We could talk to him about anything. When I met Jimmy, I instantly knew and liked him. I'd never met Matt but knew all about him through the Busby Babes. In 1958, I had just finished school and had a grocery round at a corner shop where I first read about the Munich air disaster. I lived in London but was aware that the Babes were a great side. The whole country was affected by the tragedy and it touched all followers of football. United had great support but gained a new group of fans as Matt slowly strived to rebuild a team from the ashes of Munich. Following this disaster, Manchester United were on the way to becoming the world's biggest club and I was part of that building process, which was an amazing feeling.

When I signed for Chelsea there was a big reaction and plenty of reporters took up the story but it was nothing compared with the scale of joining United. When the train pulled in at Piccadilly Station, the press and fans were waiting. Walking through the station, with no disrespect to Millwall or Chelsea, I suddenly knew that I was in big time football. And in a few days I'd be making my debut. There could be no tougher baptism, as I'd be running out at Old Trafford to face newly promoted Manchester City.

5

THE REDS GO
MARCHING ON

The journey to Old Trafford from Piccadilly Station whizzed by and my head was spinning with all sorts of thoughts about the future. Behind the scenes everything had been taken care of to make my transfer straightforward. Chief scout, Johnny Aston senior was first to greet me as he'd organised digs while Pam stayed in London before we sorted out a house. Johnny had been a fine player in his day for United and his son, also called John, was following in his footsteps in the first team squad. I'd be living with the Wilds. Other United players at the digs were fringe players Jimmy Ryan and Terry Poole, who would go on to serve Huddersfield Town in goal. The Wilds were a lovely family and I enjoyed staying with them until Pam and I bought John Connelly's house in Sale, Cheshire when he moved to Blackburn Rovers. There were certainly no more Coronation Street headlines!

Aston senior took me on a tour of the stadium and it was impressive. Above the main entrance was a plaque commemorating the Munich air disaster. And in the car park I bumped into Noel Cantwell who led the team to an FA Cup win in 1963. A legend from his hometown of Cork, during a brief chat Noel offered a surprising tip when he advised me against rolling the ball out to Bobby Charlton in a defensive situation. I'd be better using Paddy Crerand as he was more assured in those situations. This did take me aback as Charlton was a world-renowned figure, but Noel was not telling me this to stir trouble, it was simply a tactic that suited the side better. As an attacking force, Charlton was exceptional but defensively he was prone to being caught out occasionally so I was advised to err on the side of caution. I thanked Noel for the advice, even though I must have looked a bit quizzical.

At the training ground I was not nervous about meeting my new teammates as Matt was convinced I'd settle in quickly. And who was I to doubt his judgement? The team were completing preparations to play Blackpool in a second round League Cup tie that evening. The League Cup was a new competition and it was an era when bigger clubs didn't always enter. This was the first season the final would take place at Wembley but United still rested key players. Matt was about to introduce me when I got my first taste of the competitive nature among United players in training. As we were walking along, Matt said, 'Alex, these are a great set of lads and there are never any problems'. Suddenly during a five-a-side match, Law crunched trainer Jack Crompton. Quick as a flash, Matt quipped, 'Five-a-sides are always competitive!' Meeting my new teammates, everyone was courteous but shaking hands with David Gaskell was awkward, as we both knew I'd be replacing him in the first team. Both of us knew the score though. Matt had to make tough decisions.

At Blackpool's ground, Bloomfield Road, Matt gave his final team talk in the dressing room before I went with Law to our stand seats. Law and Charlton were among the players being rested. There were plenty of back slaps from well-wishers as we settled down but it was instantly apparent that this legendary goal machine was the world's worst watcher of a football match. In years to come he'd become a terrific match summariser but whilst a player he could not sit still. Denis, desperate to be on the park, fidgeted away and barely spoke a word. It certainly did not help that United were being thumped. In the second half I was the only one watching as the Lawman was nowhere to be seen—he sloped off to sup cups of tea behind the main stand. United took a 5–1 battering with Blackpool centre-forward Ray Charnley plundering a hat-trick. There was no hiding place because the result was terrible especially with a 'derby' clash against Manchester City days away. But after some harsh words from the boss, I knew United would be at full strength for my first team debut.

After resting overnight I joined the first team squad on the Thursday morning for my first training session where we worked out with trainers Jack Crompton, Johnny Aston senior and Jimmy Murphy. Crompton and Aston both played in United's FA Cup winning team in 1948. There were some more tough words for the defence, which had been at full strength the previous night at Blackpool. Law was scoring for fun with eight goals to his name from seven league games but the goals against column had been an issue since the start of the season. United had opened the season with a thrilling 5–3 win over West Brom and followed up with a hard-fought win against Everton prior to a loss at Leeds United. Victories over Everton in the return fixture and Newcastle followed before defeats at Stoke City and Tottenham Hotspur. Attack-wise there was no problem but United had conceded 14 league goals, which was too many for Matt's liking and he reacted with my world record transfer. Praise indeed that he felt I'd be able to help build consistency, but I knew that I had to hit the ground running and there was no tougher task than making a debut in a derby against City. Joe Mercer was building a fine squad alongside flamboyant assistant Malcolm Allison and there would be fierce battles ahead in the coming years but my focus was on Saturday 17 September.

The atmosphere on the streets of Manchester was incredible. Everybody seemed to have a view. 'Make sure you beat City on Saturday, Alex' . . . '3–0 to the Reds!' . . . 'We'll murder them, no danger' were the encouraging messages from United fans while City supporters gave me plenty of gyp! The banter was great and good-natured. Travelling to the game, I was full of anticipation as well as nervous and excited. United came into the match favourites as the more established Division 1 side in recent seasons but I knew from Millwall's clashes with local rivals that form goes out the window with a derby. Even with my limited experience of derby games, United v City derbies, with respect to Brentford or Queens Park Rangers who I faced for Millwall, was on a different scale altogether. I'd never experienced such a high profile game and the feeling in the dressing room was that this was special. As United had a new keeper on show, the pressure was on. United v City was an awesome prospect and it was obvious what the game meant to both sets of players. Matt, as I'd quickly discovered, was a manager in control. There was no shouting or screaming, no ranting or raging; in a clear, measured voice his message was succinct. 'Come on lads, play your football and have a good game.' Matt shook my hand, 'Good luck son'.

Football League Division 1, Old Trafford
(17 September 1966)

Manchester United: Stepney, Brennan, Dunne, Crerand, Foulkes, Stiles, Best, Law, Sadler, Charlton, Aston. *Manchester City*: Dowd, Book, Kennedy, Horne, Heslop, Oakes, Connor, Bell, Summerbee, Pardoe, Young.

Running out in front of 63,000 spectators was incredible.

The roar from the capacity crowd was deafening. Any game at United generated a tremendous atmosphere but in a derby game you could sense the expectation from all corners of the ground. The only player I knew in the City line up was Mike Summerbee as we'd played in the England U23s together but there were plenty of other good players. The match may have been my debut, but for City players and diehard fans it was also massive. Not only was it the most high profile game but the first derby game since promotion in 1965/66 for the Blue half of Manchester. City supporters were on a high and wanted to see their team put in a top-notch performance. In my mind there was no doubt that we would win. The game fell the day before my birthday and clearly the local press had leaked the news because The Stretford End gave me a wonderful surprise with a rendition of 'Happy Birthday'.

I was desperate to get off to a good start and knew City would look to test me in the opening minutes. My feeling was 'bring it on'. And true to form Summerbee put in an early deep cross. Instantly, I called 'Keeper's ball!' and watching it all the way, caught it cleanly. It drew applause from United supporters and a huge weight lifted from my shoulders. The fans were behind me from the off and I felt great. Clutching the ball to my chest I'd signalled my intent to dominate the penalty area and build confidence in the lads. Credit to City, they gave everything but one of our classy players made the difference. In a frenetic game, Law scored the only goal with an opportunist overhead kick. I was delighted to win against the 'City Slickers' and also somewhat relieved as it had been a baptism of fire. My performance was viewed as being the best since Harry Gregg held down the number one spot on a regular basis. The comments were terrific but I was determined to play my own game. I felt privileged to play for the club and was determined to be part of a United squad that could achieve success.

Following a 4–1 win over Burnley, again at Old Trafford, one of the early front runners, Nottingham Forest, thumped us by the same score line at The City Ground. The result brought us back to earth but we responded in the best possible way by winning six games in an unbeaten eight-match run. This underlined our title aspirations as we defeated Arsenal, Chelsea, Sheffield Wednesday, Southampton, Sunderland and Leicester City during a scintillating spell of form. Defeating league leaders Chelsea 3–1 at Stamford Bridge was naturally special after the problems I'd experienced in my short spell. United were fourth in the table so it was an important clash. Aston (2) and Best (with a beauty) scored the goals that enabled us to leapfrog The Blues. Chelsea would have gone three points clear if they had triumphed but we played superbly on my return to The Bridge. It was also amusing to hear United supporters chanting, 'Ee aye addio, you sold the wrong one', the quip aimed at Chelsea boss Docherty. Credit to Tommy though, he made a point after the game to congratulate me in our dressing room. Making our way back to Manchester I felt lucky to be in the United side because I could sense we were going places. While Law, Charlton and Best hit the target with regularity during this period, Herd also took the plaudits for a four-goal haul against Sunderland in a 5–0 win. I was also delighted to concede just four in eight games. Matt had called for consistency in defence and we'd found a better return than earlier in the campaign.

I was still finding my feet but Matt offered advice to all the lads continually and had tremendous confidence in the players. He used to say that any player at Manchester United was welcomed with open arms. It's easy to make such a statement but Matt was absolutely on the mark. There were World Cup winners and international footballers on the team, but more importantly there were no prima donnas. All the lads got on. Dunne was a regular at full-back but Bobby Noble was just making his mark in the other full-back slot. Stiles partnered Foulkes in the centre of defence with Crerand in front of a back four. Sadler filled in at both centre-half and centre-forward but the forward line spoke for itself with Best, Charlton, Law and Herd together with Aston interlinking superbly. Best-Charlton-Law was a headline writer's dream but they never sought special treatment in the United camp. The trio knew that without the hard work of the other lads around them they could not deliver the goods on the park.

For me, playing in the First Division was easier than keeping goal in the Third and Fourth tier of English football. At the time I hadn't played in the Second Division, although my time would come! Of course, the stakes were higher in top-flight football but better players made fewer mistakes in terms of positional play, ball control and their all round game. If my new teammates got into a sticky situation, more often than not, they found a way to get out of it. Off the field, the thing that hit me most in the early days was that football in Manchester was 24–7. There was never any let up from locals whether I was in the street, dropping into my local, out for a meal or at a local store. And for Mancunians it was either United or City. No other team came into the conversation. When I lived in London, although I was recognised, it was not the same as there were plenty of fans following other teams locally whether it be the Division 1 clubs such as Arsenal, Tottenham, Chelsea, West Ham or Fulham, or lower league sides such as Crystal Palace, Queens Park Rangers, Millwall, Charlton Athletic or Leyton Orient. The banter also appeared to be less through midweek until match day. I was now truly plying my trade in a hotbed of football.

During training Matt rammed home that every game was

essential because winning the league meant we had another shot at winning the European Cup. We knew what the trophy meant to Matt and the club. He would not have many more opportunities at going for the big one so we wanted to deliver and we were in a good position to challenge. It was not like the modern era when four teams in England take part in the Champions League. There was only space for one club, the Champions, so it was imperative we kept our run going. There was a feeling that this could be our year but defeats to Aston Villa and then Sheffield United on Boxing Day knocked us back. The Villa defeat was particularly depressing. We lost 2–1 but it was one of those games when we could have scored a hatful. We dominated throughout but couldn't put Villa away and they snatched an unlikely victory with two strikes against the run of play. In between the losses, Herd had grabbed a hat-trick in a 4–3 win at West Brom and David struck again to seal a win over Sheffield United 24 hours after their win at Bramall Lane. The victory was welcome but none of us could have predicted it would be the start of an unbeaten run that would take us all the way to the Division 1 crown.

The coming weeks would see some titanic battles. Our main challengers were defending champions Liverpool, Nottingham Forest, Tottenham Hotspur and Leeds United. While Tottenham and Leeds were snapping away we could not shake off Liverpool and Forest. We'd drawn 2–2 with Liverpool at home prior to Christmas before facing the other three clubs at the turn of the year. A draw with Leeds was a reasonable result, though as with Liverpool, it felt like a point dropped as we were the home side but we made no mistake against Tottenham when Herd grabbed the all important goal at Old Trafford. But whenever we won, Forest also seemed to win. Managed by former United favourite Johnny Carey, among their team was Jim Baxter, Joe Baker, Ian Storey-Moore together with defenders Henry Newton, Terry Hennessey and John Winfield in a balanced team. When Forest came to town we were determined to avenge our defeat earlier in the season. And we showed our title intent when Law scored the only goal of a tight clash late on to keep us ahead of the pack.

We crashed out of the FA Cup at home to Norwich City a week later, which although a bitter disappointment at the time, was in reality a blessing in disguise as our mindset was focused solely on the league. And we bounced back against Blackpool, gained two creditable draws at Arsenal and Newcastle, before thumping Leicester City. But the latter victory saw Herd break a leg scoring our third goal past Banks. A clean striker of the ball, David was tough to shake off when in possession and had a terrific strike rate for the club. Tragically, his injury was the beginning of the end of his United career. By mid-March Liverpool were still alongside us at the summit so it was crucial that we did not slip up at Anfield at the start of the Easter fixtures. Liverpool had a crack outfit with skipper Ron Yeats marshalling a solid defence that included hard man Tommy Smith and Ian St John led the line with Roger Hunt. We had to be on our guard throughout and our resolve was total against Bill Shankly's team as both defences stood firm in a crucial 0–0 draw. We'd seen off Forest and now Liverpool lost heart. They knew we were not going to slip up and the unbeaten run continued. With Herd out, Charlton rediscovered his goal scoring touch with consecutive goals in wins over West Ham and Southampton and a brace at Hillsborough in a 2–2 draw with Sheffield Wednesday. A 0–0 draw at Sunderland and 3–1 victory over Aston Villa followed and the lads sensed the title was on although for me things were happening so fast I did not appreciate the enormity of what was occurring.

United had won the league two years earlier when they pipped Leeds United to the crown on goal average and many of the lads were part of that side. For me it was a new experience and I just concentrated on each game to avoid being wrapped up with the hullabaloo surrounding the club. We'd virtually won the title and victory at West Ham in the penultimate match would seal the Division 1 championship. We were in fine spirits but tragedy struck again when Noble had a terrible car crash on his way home after the game at Roker Park, Sunderland. Bobby had come into the side shortly after I'd arrived at Old Trafford. Blessed with a turn of pace, rock hard and possessing tremendous positional sense, Bobby was just 21 and lived for football. He was set for a glowing career not only with United but also as a future England player before the injury, which affected his co-ordination. Bobby battled to get back to fitness, but despite being blessed with natural ability he was unable to figure at the highest level again. Bobby received a £25,000 payout, a huge sum in those days, but he'd have given that back in a flash to pursue his football career. The incident was a stark reminder of how tenuous a footballer's career can be. One bad injury and in a split second your dreams can be over.

I hadn't missed a game since my arrival and we crowned a terrific campaign by putting on a virtuoso attacking performance at West Ham. The gates were closed an hour before kick off as the biggest post-war crowd was crammed into Upton Park that day. Some 38,424 supporters made for an electric atmosphere inside the ground with thousands more locked out. In the dressing room beforehand, Matt had named the same XI as my United debut and knew that a draw would clinch the title but implored us to go out and attack. Matt wanted us to nail the title with a game to spare.

**Football League Division 1, Upton Park
(13 May 1967)**

Manchester United: Stepney, Brennan, Dunne, Crerand, Foulkes, Stiles, Best, Law, Sadler, Charlton, Aston. *West Ham United*: Mackleworth, Burkett, Charles, Peters, Heffer, Moore, Rednapp, Boyce, Hartley, Hurst, Sissons.

Running out we were raring to go and got off to a flyer when Charlton capitalised on a mix up in the home defence to score on just two minutes. Bestie almost made it two moments later, but we were not to be denied when Crerand ghosted in to head home an Aston cross to double our advantage. The lads were on fire and when Big Bill Foulkes scored from a corner on the 9-minute mark the champagne was on ice. Bestie made it 4–0 from a Stiles cross on 25 minutes and the game was ours. West Ham scored a consolation goal when John Charles scored a 25-yard screamer that dipped late, giving me no chance. Charles became the villain when he bundled over Law for a penalty. Denis made no mistake and was on the spot again when Hammers' keeper Colin Mackleworth spilled a Bestie shot 10 minutes from time to complete the scoring with his 23rd strike of a memorable season. We may have been 6–1 ahead but you would not have realised that by looking at Bill, especially when Nobby told him he had his fourth championship medal. Only moments remained but Bill was still as focussed as when the score was 0–0 but that was the true professionalism of the man. Bill summed up what United was all about.

The opening 10 minutes did the damage and it was amazing to see how the lads were playing. I found out later that Matt had not got to his seat until the third went in but nobody informed him we were three up so he was tense for a while! There was a carnival atmosphere inside Upton Park but we had a job to see through and went on to play 'champagne' football. It was a brilliant way to clinch the title and my first major honour. These were the days when there was no segregation and trouble did occur on the terraces. Despite the match being played in a terrific spirit, records show that 12 people were treated in hospital and dozens had to receive treatment from first aid officials on duty. There were incidents before and during the game, and arrests took place. The trouble was lamentable but in no way spoilt the action on the pitch and the game is remembered for the lads pummelling the West Ham goal.

It was impossible not to notice United fans outnumbering the Hammers supporters in the stadium and hundreds of Reds invaded the pitch at the final whistle to celebrate the moment. It took me some time to get to our dressing room where the champagne was flowing. Towards the end of the game most of the lads were near the tunnel for a quick getaway so I was one of the last in and it was a wonderful sight with lots of backslapping. Champagne was flowing and I had a post-match celebratory cigarette along with a quiet thought for my dad who would have been really proud. In the bedlam of the dressing room as things settled down I was not the only player to spare a thought for Noble and Herd who had so cruelly missed out on an unforgettable occasion. This would be the only time I'd win a Division 1 medal and there is nothing like winning the title by your own efforts on the day.

Afterwards, we were due to travel back to Manchester by train. Everyone jokes that there are more United supporters in London than Manchester, well it may be true because our journey was blocked and we missed our connection but that did not bother us. We eventually caught a Liverpool train and changed at Crewe. The lads liked a beer but there was plenty of champagne all the way home. For Matt, it was his fifth title winning campaign as he completed 21 years at the helm. From the Busby Babes, Matt had created another side who had cracked the ultimate prize in club football. Apart from me, the team included just three big money signings. Law was the most expensive at £115,000 in addition to Crerand (£56,000) and Herd (£40,000). Matt knew a bargain as he had snapped up Dunne from Shelbourne for the princely sum of £3,000 while the other lads had come through the system including teenager Brian Kidd who was about to make an impact at the club.

Our title win meant Nottingham Forest and Tottenham Hotspur had to settle for second and third place respectively. Interestingly, when you look at our league record the key period came after our home win over Tottenham as it heralded eight straight league wins at home and eight draws in the corresponding away fixtures. Everyone says that is the ideal template for champions and I recall Matt telling the press that if we won at home on top of drawing away we'd be fine. It never normally works that way but it did during a key 16-match run. Of course, we then broke the sequence by thumping the Hammers and drawing at home in the last game against Stoke City with the title wrapped up!

The medals were handed out after we played Stoke to cap a memorable season. It was certainly a campaign to remember as over two million fans witnessed our 42 league games. Our average attendance had also shot up to over 50,000 every home game. United received plenty of plaudits for the title success arguably best summed up by the Football Champions Annual that year. Chronicling our title success, the overview noted: 'It is difficult to single out any player for special praise, because each one is an integral part of a footballing machine that runs smoothly and efficiently, a well drilled, well disciplined team, which thoroughly deserved to win the English League Championship.'

Manchester United's Division 1 title winning squad (appearances and substitutions are listed for the season) was Stepney 35, Brennan 16, Noble 29, Dunne 40, Crerand 39, Foulkes 33, Stiles 37, Best 42, Law 36, Sadler 35 (1), Charlton 42, Herd 28, Aston 26 (4), Connelly 6, Gaskell 5, Ryan 4 (1), Cantwell 4, Fitzpatrick 3, Gregg 2, Anderson (1). Our main scorers were Law 23, Herd 16, Charlton 12 and Best 10.

Matt was quoted as saying I'd made a major impact in the United team being able to win the title, which was great to hear but the victory was about the whole squad. Inside 12 months I'd gone from Division 3 to winning a Division 1 title, so I was pinching myself. Matt also described the title success as United's finest hour and told reporters that the side played like real champions. Well, no one could argue with that sentiment. After all, to claim the championship with a 6–1 away win is something special. Of course, he noted that his great ambition was to win the European Cup and we now had the opportunity after being crowned champions. The title win was United's seventh, equalling the record held by Liverpool and Arsenal. All these years later United and Liverpool are still locked together, on 18 titles, after both clubs enjoyed dominant periods in the intervening decades.

It was a great time to play football. Crowds were growing and there was a tremendous spirit up and down the country. Following our title success we embarked on a six-week post-season tour to America where we played Benfica in Los Angeles before moving on to Australia and New Zealand. We were still in celebratory mode when we faced Benfica. But Eusebio brought us back down to earth when he scored a hat-trick that included a penalty, which he smashed home in his trademark fashion during a 3–1 win. Eusebio was a class act but I was not impressed with his theatricals when challenged or when he ruffled my hair after his spot kick. Dundee also defeated us, this time at Kezar Stadium in California. There was no time for much 'r 'n' r', although Paddy found a bar to celebrate former club Celtic's European Cup win against Inter Milan!

We flew straight on to New Zealand where we thumped Auckland and Christchurch. The goal rush continued in Australia against Queensland before Charlton saved our blushes with a late strike to deny Victoria a famous win. As in our other games on tour, the stadium in Melbourne was packed, again demonstrating the worldwide United fan base. Our form returned to overcome Newcastle and New South Wales before we atoned for our near embarrassment in a return with Victoria by knocking in four goals. Our final games on the whistle stop tour saw comfortable wins over South Australia and Western Australia. Records show Bestie led the way with 13 goals among our total of 55 during the tour, which also saw Kiddo make his bow when Law picked up an injury. Brian, 18 at the time, took his chance by notching 10 goals to finish joint second scorer alongside Charlton. Denis's knee injury was a worry as he had been in a top form and it would take time to diagnose fully. With Herd's broken leg, the arrival of Kidd was a major boost to the squad. Rumours had circulated that Matt enquired about a number of players to bolster the team including Geoff Hurst, Tommy Baldwin and Jim McCalliog. Kiddo's arrival stopped all the gossip as we had discovered a future star.

Away from the scoring accolades, keeper Jimmy Rimmer got an opportunity as did full-backs Francis Burns and Paul Edwards. Former club skipper Cantwell was also on the trip but departed on our return to succeed Jimmy Hill at Coventry City. Hill, of course, began a long stint as a highly respected TV pundit. A true innovator in the game and former PFA chairman, Jimmy was also editor of a weekly football magazine. The popular *Jimmy Hill's Football Weekly* was forerunner to *Goal, Shoot, Scorcher* and *Striker* that were popular during different phases of my career. These magazines were just around the corner and formed essential reading for football supporters in the aftermath of the World Cup. It was always a thrill to be asked to contribute and over the years I was always happy to be interviewed.

Returning home, I had time to reflect on a memorable season. If anyone had predicted I'd start off at Stamford Bridge before winning a championship medal at Old Trafford I'd have thought they were crazy. But bizarre as it may have seemed, that is what had happened. In less than a season, I'd won the biggest domestic prize and was about to play in Europe's premier club competition. The league table reflects the best team over a season and United deserved the title. But in the aftermath of the title success the job was only just beginning. The European Cup was the big one. United had reached the semi-final stage three times, now it was time to go an extra step. I couldn't wait for my first full season at the club.

Nobby Stiles
Manchester United and England

Without doubt Alex was the best goalkeeper I played with at Manchester United. We had Dave Gaskell and Pat Dunne who were both good keepers but Alex made a big difference to United when he arrived. Alex was confident, never flash and we were always sure that when he had to make a save he'd make it. Alex just got on with it. There were many games when Alex saved us whether we were playing in a big league game, cup-tie or in Europe.

The match we all remember was against Benfica at Wembley when Eusebio went clean through. We had a corner when Benfica broke quickly. I was the one marking Eusebio and when I went for the ball he toe-poked it past me. I turned round silently praying, but fearing the worst. Eusebio was clean through. I thought, that's it and Eusebio didn't half smack the ball but the great thing about Alex was that he stood his ground and caught it! Eusebio came in to say well done but Alex wanted to get on with the game, which was typical. He never made a big fuss, just got on with things. That moment proved to be a massive turning point in the game.

It was a shame for Alex that Gordon Banks was playing for England at the time. Gordon was a great keeper and Alex was also tremendous. Off the pitch Alex was different class. He was a lovely chap, enjoyed a game of cards like all the players and was just one of the lads. I can't praise him highly enough during the time we played together at United. Alex had a great personality and was never cocky or big headed.

Alex was a confident 'keeper and that is what he gave to you when you were on the pitch. I played at the back alongside Bill Foulkes and always knew Alex was there. He had bags of confidence and only made the saves when he had to. Alex *would talk to the defenders about what he wanted and if I was lining up a wall, Alex stayed on top of things. He hasn't changed over the years—he's a great lad.*

6

CHAMPIONS OF EUROPE

The European Cup was, understandably, the main topic of conversation at United during pre-season and we were well aware of the challenge ahead. Winning the trophy had been Matt Busby's quest since the Munich air disaster. Only Bill Foulkes and Bobby Charlton were among the survivors still in the first team line up and had been in the side that reached the semi-finals in 1966 when they lost to Partizan Belgrade. This campaign was seen as Matt, Bobby and Bill's last tilt at the trophy. From my arrival at United I sensed the club was geared to mount a serious challenge for the top prize in club football but you can only take on each game as it comes. This is an old and well used cliché but as a professional footballer that is what you have to do. Resting key players before every European Cup tie was not an option because no team had such resources in the late sixties. All that, of course, has changed in the modern era where top clubs rotate star players for crucial Premier League and European fixtures. During my heyday however there was no such luxury, and in any case top players wanted to be a fixture in the side, it was the norm, so we played Saturday, Wednesday, Saturday on a regular basis.

Our training schedule was tough, as with most clubs, but Matt and Jimmy Murphy were always encouraging. They would walk around the touchline during training games continually offering constructive instructions without shouting or berating. 'Push on' . . . 'lay it off' . . . 'break away' . . . 'get close' . . . 'great touch son' and so on. By now I'd clicked with the back four. The lads asked me what I wanted and I made it clear where I expected the defence to be when I got the ball so we could break out quickly. Generally, I adopted a policy of throwing the ball out and not kicking upfield. And the best player for this tactic was Paddy Crerand. Paddy was renowned for hitting pinpoint passes from deep and would set up many a goal. Paddy never stopped. Whenever I got the ball, he was already running into space so I could find him and he'd hit his target. Both on and off the park we instantly hit it off. As well as being roommates for away trips we also enjoyed many memorable nights at Manchester restaurant Arturo's.

Paddy was a real character but his bad timekeeping caught him out on occasions. Once he was last to arrive at the train station before travelling to a game. As we waited on the train Bobby was down in the dumps because someone had stolen his golf clubs from his car while we were training. Paddy waltzed on board bragging that he'd just bought some golf clubs from a spiv. The lads cracked up. Bobby had his clubs back and Paddy was out of pocket! Paddy also got caught out when he was in cahoots with Denis Law but not before the two scallywags had fleeced the lads for a few forfeits. It was all innocent fun and came about when they were given two old pennies, one with two heads and the other with two tails. On away trips they'd clean up. I used to think . . . luck of the Scots. But one day in Blackpool before a game the coin landed on the floor and split down the middle. We all saw the funny side but not until the duo had shelled out for a few pints!

Much has been made of the 'drink' culture that existed during my era but it was no big deal. Players trained hard, played hard, relaxed with a few drinks and then ran it off on the Monday. If we played midweek we might have a drink after a game but we were always prepared for the Saturday. Lots of footballers also smoked but again it was the norm. When it came to diet, pre-match we'd have steak, chicken, poached eggs, basically anything we liked. Nowadays, of course, diet and drinking is strictly controlled while smoking has all but gone from football and I'm all for that. Fitness levels increase every year and standards move on, which is part of the game.

Everyone enjoyed the crack and team spirit that developed in training or travelling to matches. The banter was fantastic and there were plenty of pranksters in the side. On long coach trips we passed the time playing cards. Cribbage was the main game as the lads and backroom staff joined in the competition. And everyone was extremely competitive. Charlton and Stiles organised cribbage championships and made sure there were plenty of daft forfeits for losers. Carrying bags was top of the list until Nobby dropped Bobby's duty free and camera on one trip. Bobby was not best pleased! Cleaning shoes was another favourite forfeit.

We came into the new season as a unit ready for action as our opening match of the campaign was the Charity Shield, a traditional curtain raiser between the League Champions and FA Cup winners. United took on Tottenham Hotspur, who had defeated Tommy Doc's Chelsea side at Wembley. Both clubs looked to play football so fans were in for a treat and they weren't disappointed. The match was played at Old

Trafford and finished 3–3 but is best remembered for a freak 'wind assisted' goal scored by Spurs keeper Pat Jennings. And I am still reminded about my most embarrassing moment on a football field on a regular basis, much to the amusement of supporters up and down the country . . . and that includes United supporters! It's easy enough to laugh now but at the time I was not amused.

The match took place on a sunny but 'windy' day. When Pat punted the ball downfield towards the scoreboard end I doubt any goalkeeper could have anticipated what would transpire. I'd advanced to the edge of the penalty area as normal and saw the ball coming so shouted, 'Yours Bill!' I honestly thought Foulkes, who was marking Jimmy Greaves, would chest it down and pass back to me because in those days a keeper could collect a back pass. Whether or not Bill misheard me I don't know but he ducked and I'm not sure to this day how but the ball ballooned straight over me into the empty goal. I turned around in horror and disbelief as the ball hit the back of the net. I looked back and the bizarre thing was that for a split second the referee did not seem to know what to do. Was it a goal or not? Greavsie was yelling, 'Goal ref!' and of course the referee had to give it. Greavsie looked back at me, winked and laughed his cobblers off. I got plenty of good-natured stick at the time and continue to do so but it was just one of those things. The goal has gone down in history as a freak but I'm just relieved it did not happen in a major crunch game. Can you imagine the reaction if it had happened at Anfield, Maine Road or even Benfica at Wembley? I'd never have lived it down and the goal would be shown every season, you can be assured of that. As it happens, although it was my most embarrassing moment as a professional footballer, it's still a talking point 40 plus years on and whenever I see Pat we always have a laugh. The consolation is that it means we do get remembered and as I always point out to Pat that although he scored in open play I scored two goals later in my United career . . . but more of that later.

The Charity Shield gaffe was soon forgotten as we put the final touches to our preparations for the new season. I was ready for action. From my amateur days I had a set routine to prepare for a match. Every player gets nervous before a match but handles it in different ways. Back then there was nothing like the long drawn out stretching exercises of the modern era but all clubs had a certain pre-match routine. We had our pre-game meal three hours before kick off and I always arrived in the dressing room 40 minutes before a 3pm or 7.30pm start. First I'd glance through the match programme and then start to get changed. I'd be ready to head out of the changing room door when the bell sounded. There was no hanging about, that was it, I was mentally ready to play. The main team talk would have taken place after the final training session but while we got our strip on Matt would offer a few words of encouragement, tell us which players to watch out for, provide tactical information and so on. Finally, once I went down the tunnel I'd take a big deep breath and then run out on to the pitch. Superstitions are always a curious facet and again everyone is different. Some players got stripped in a certain order; others put boots on right or left first for some quirky reason while another popular favourite was to have a cap of whisky in the dressing room to warm the cockles before running out, particularly on a cold day. Once on the field, I always went directly to my goal and clicked both heels on each post. I also marked out a line on the six-yard box and put my cap in a certain spot at the back of the goal.

After winning the league, the championship flag flew

above the stadium. And coming into the opening league games we felt confident we'd go well. But the big excitement was whom we'd draw in the European Cup opening round. Celtic had become the first British team to lift the trophy so we were determined to become the first English side to win the trophy. This was my first season in European competition. Real Madrid had set the standard and Matt wanted to follow in their illustrious footsteps. There were plenty of great sides in the draw but you always have the chance of an easy first round clash and we got one when we pulled Hibernians—not the Edinburgh club but the champions from Malta. But before our onslaught on the trophy, the league campaign took precedent and we were far from our fluent best in the early encounters despite losing only one of our opening seven games.

Victories over Leeds United and West Ham were welcome but only one clean sheet was far from my expectations. It was early days though. Shanks's Liverpool had started well as had Tottenham and Nottingham Forest but overall the top of the league had an unfamiliar look as Sheffield Wednesday led the way with Sunderland, Wolves and Southampton also starting brightly. After the Leeds win, when Charlton scored the only goal, we were grateful to Foulkes for rescuing a draw against Leicester City after the visitors took the lead through winger Mike Stringfellow. Gordon Banks was no longer in goal for Leicester as he'd been surprisingly sold to Stoke City in favour of blooding a young 17-year-old keeper called Peter Shilton. Clearly, the Leicester management knew their goalkeepers because as we all know, Shilton would go on to star for Nottingham Forest and England in years to come. On the day, Peter pulled off a string of saves before being carried off late on. There were no goalkeeping reserves in those days but we still were unable to force a winner.

Senior players were getting us out of trouble and we were quickly indebted to Crerand for a last minute equaliser to deny Burnley after Andy Lochhead had scored twice. Our form was disappointing but Denis Law was on the comeback trail. I felt sure he'd add a spark on his return when we travelled to Hillsborough but his sharpness was still off the pace. Bestie scored our goal in another 1–1 draw but it was a better performance. Wednesday stayed in the top three behind Liverpool and Arsenal. Sitting in the away dressing room afterwards our focus soon switched because on Wednesday night our European Cup campaign would begin.

I was only 15 years old when Manchester United lost a generation of footballers in the Munich air disaster. Ten years on there was a will that this would be our year. United had been to the semi-final stage three times before only to miss out, and the defeat two years earlier to Partizan really rankled with the lads that played in those ties. Partizan lost to Real Madrid in the final but there was a feeling United should have been taking them on. United simply had not performed and it was a great opportunity missed. There was a feeling that this time it would be different as we started out against the part-timers from Malta. I had to confess I knew nothing about them and there was some confusion initially that we were facing Floriana, another side from Malta, but that was soon sorted out. The opening game against Hibernians, who were coached by a priest, Father Hilary Tagliaferro, took place at Old Trafford and we cruised to a 4–0 win with Sadler and Law scoring two apiece. It was so comfortable that my only save came in the closing minutes. The result was welcome but we were not going to take any chances for the return leg. Heat would be an issue so Matt got us some ultra-light tops for the game. The pitch at the Empire Stadium was also expected to be rock hard so we'd have to consider our studs.

The result settled us down and suddenly our season finally got going as we felt a bit of fluency coming back into our game. Next up was a humdinger of a clash with Tottenham. And what a game it turned out to be for the lads as we claimed a 3–1 triumph. Alan Gilzean poached a goal for Tottenham inside a few minutes although we soon had a golden opportunity to hit back but Jennings saved a Law penalty. Our disappointment turned to joy when Bestie struck a great goal. The match could have gone either way but we claimed the points when Law edged us ahead with his first goal of the season before Best sealed a great result. It was terrific to see Denis back to his brilliant best. Charlton had also enjoyed his best form and Stiles made sure Jimmy Greaves did not have a sniff on goal. Jimmy was some goal scorer and on his day there was no better goal poacher in the league. In fact, for me, during the mid to late sixties Law and Greaves were the best strikers around in the English game. The buzz was back in the dressing room.

Arriving at Luqa Airport, Malta, for our return clash with Hibernians I could not believe the reception. Thousands of United fans wearing red and white welcomed us. It seemed the whole of Malta followed United and we were treated like royalty. Local press described our reception as resembling 'Beatlemania'. A parade of around 100 cars, buses and motorbikes followed our coach. Horns were blaring all the way and United fans came out in huge numbers to line the streets as we made our way to the Phoenicia Hilton Hotel. It took time to get through all the well-wishers at the hotel reception. I knew the club was popular but this showed me the level of support Manchester United had around the globe. We attended a cocktail party held by the local United Supporters Club and the reaction was immense.

During our stay, wherever we went, local supporters followed our every move so preparation was hampered. There was no malice, it was all good-natured and I'd never experienced anything like it. It was just a shame that the match failed to live up to the hype. The pitch made sure that good football was impossible and we played a patient game. Dunne and Charlton both hit the woodwork but in the end we had to settle for a 0–0 draw. We planned to salute the crowd after the final whistle but a pitch invasion ended that idea as we raced for the sanctuary of the dressing room.

Returning to Ringway Airport there was no let up as our next clash was the short trip to Maine Road to face Manchester City. There is always a great expectancy for a derby game and this was the first of the season. City started well and scored early on through Colin Bell to put us on the back foot but we were not to be intimidated. When we needed something special we could always rely on Charlton and he delivered with a storming run before crashing the ball home for a great goal. A slip by Mick Doyle allowed Bobby to give us the lead, and despite having to soak up a lot of pressure we held out for a terrific win. The red half of Manchester had a good night out!

Liverpool and Arsenal were still leading the way but we were hot on their tails and The Gunners were next up at Old Trafford. And it turned into a tough encounter that we edged with an Aston header late on. Crerand put in the cross, which made up for an earlier slip that put me in trouble but I made a point blank save from Peter Simpson. Concentration is key throughout a game for a goalkeeper. On this occasion I stood tall and managed to block his effort. My motto is that a keeper must expect the unexpected at all times. The match though was remembered more for Law and Arsenal stopper Ian Ure being sent off. The two Scottish internationals were the highest priced British footballers at the time so predictably it generated back page headlines. Both got bans.

Every team had players with different temperaments. I rarely lost my rag. Likewise Dunne and Charlton seemed to be able to keep their heads under provocation. But Law, Bestie, Stiles and Crerand were quick to react to challenges. Everyone's personality is different and I'd describe all four as 'fiery' individuals but that is what made them tick and I would never want to change that. Without trying to make excuses for them, all four played in positions that arguably were under the severest pressure. Denis was an assassin in attack and opponents looked to take him out. Bestie was an exceptional talent who could win a game with a moment of magic, while Nobby was generally detailed to get stuck into our opponents' playmaker and Paddy was always in the thick of the action in the heart of midfield. Matt would implore time and again: 'Keep cool, don't lose your heads, let your football do the talking.' We knew opponents would come out determined to 'wind us up' but it was not always easy to hold back. As I said, all teams combined different personalities but one thing that also set us apart was that we were the team everyone liked to beat. And nothing has changed! And when a United player got sent off there appeared to be more headlines. This still remains the same, it goes with the territory of playing for United and certain players handle it better than others.

On a lighter note, shortly after the Arsenal clash we thumped Coventry City 4–0. Aston scored twice to grab the headlines but that particular game always reminds me of a chat I had with one of the lads just after I arrived at United.

The chat concerned my predecessor, David Gaskell who played in goal during the 1963 FA Cup final. The tale goes that Gaskell had an unusual superstition. Apparently when he was caught out of position to a long-range effort he'd yell out 'Bar!' or 'Post!' hoping the shot would hit the woodwork and incredibly it did on the odd occasion. I thought, 'Brilliant, I must try that'. Anyway, during the game, I was hopelessly caught out of position when Ernie Machin, who was a fine striker of the ball, had a dig. In that split second, I remembered the story and just had time to turn around and shouted 'Bar!' Amazingly, the ball hit the bar and bounced straight back into my grateful grasp. Ernie was not amused and back in the dressing room, the lads gave me plenty of ribbing, 'You jammy so and so!'

Following our inauspicious start, apart from the odd blip, we had played our way back into the title race, especially after a 2–1 win at Liverpool when Bestie grabbed both our goals. It was an important victory because Liverpool had started to become a real force under Shanks. In recent years they had won the league title twice and FA Cup. Playing at Anfield was always an occasion and the atmosphere was electric. Prior to the game at Anfield we lost at home to Leeds United who had gained a reputation that would stick with them for years. Dubbed 'Dirty Leeds' when they gained promotion in 1963–64, the likes of Billy Bremner, Johnny Giles, Jack Charlton and Norman Hunter were far better than the team's nickname suggested. And they had players blessed with skill such as winger Eddie Gray who could skin an opponent as only Bestie could. Managed by Don Revie, Leeds were on their way to becoming one of the most feared teams in the domestic game and picked up their first major honour during the season when they defeated Arsenal in a bad-tempered League Cup final. The tournament still failed to attract all the top sides including ourselves due to our European Cup commitments.

Our second round clash against FK Sarajevo was a tough draw. Sarajevo had lost a number of players that helped them win their domestic title to rival clubs but they were still a strong outfit. Defeating Liverpool was the perfect preparation for the first leg in Sarajevo. Our journey was arduous so United organised a charter flight to Dubrovnik. This was the first charter since Munich a decade earlier as United had travelled by train to European away fixtures but this time the journey was too difficult. There were a few nervous faces on board the BAC 111 but at no stage did I fear for my safety. After landing we then faced a 200-mile coach trip via Split through the mountains to Sarajevo. The trek was arduous, in fact it took so long we played two knock out crib tournaments, Paddy and Bestie coming out on top much to the dismay of one or two of the so-called 'elite' players. Eventually we made it to the remote town. There was a real sense of history about the place as we visited the site where Archduke Franz Ferdinand, heir to the Austro-Hungarian throne, was assassinated heralding the start of the First World War.

We had 48 hours to prepare so we also had time for some souvenir hunting in the local bazaar. Our hosts made us very welcome, which was more than could be said for our opponents. We trained at the Kosovo Stadium, which in itself was a strange experience as the changing rooms were up in the stand, so in some ways it was like being in a massive cricket pavilion.

Law was suspended for the game following his sending off against Arsenal and Stiles was out injured. Burns came in for Brennan and Fitzpatrick for Stiles. Matt warned us to be aware as Sarajevo were a physical side. His last message was to show composure, 'Lose your heads and you'll lose the match'. Although struggling domestically that season, his fears were correct because the Yugoslavs were fit, resilient, tough and the dirtiest team I'd played against. Sarajevo kicked us at every opportunity. They employed rough-house tactics throughout whether it was tripping, spitting or generally niggling at us in a bid to intimidate us into retaliating. By half time Fazlagic had been booked and Best, Kidd and Burns in particular had taken a huge amount of abuse from the Sarajevo team. Trainer Jack Crompton seemed to be on the pitch all the time, it was ridiculous.

A Musemic shot nearly caught me out but I got a slight touch to a shot and just recovered as the ball touched our goal line. There were frantic appeals but the referee and linesman were unsighted. Outside right Prodanovic hobbled off but Sarajevo continued to attack and attempted to batter us but we held firm with a solid defensive display for a 0–0 draw. Late on we actually looked the more likely to score and Kidd went close with a long range effort as 10-man Sarajevo tired. We were happy to draw but the referee was weak. Whether he was intimidated by Sarajevo I don't know but he was completely out of his depth. As we made our way to the dressing rooms Matt was livid. I'd never seen him so animated. Both teams had to pass through a glass door towards the changing rooms on opposite sides of a corridor. Matt was waiting in the middle when suddenly there was commotion as the Sarajevo players went into their dressing room. Matt yelled at them. I'd never seen him so irate. Back in our dressing room we were outraged but Matt congratulated us on our resilience under immense provocation. Calming down, our thoughts were on Sarajevo's return game at Old Trafford and we couldn't wait to face them on our own turf.

On our return home, Kidd was on target as we defeated Southampton and drew at Stamford Bridge. Chelsea were somewhat in disarray following the departure of Tommy Docherty but that was the last thing on my mind on the journey back to Manchester. The only conversation on the team coach was the return clash with Sarajevo—we felt confident but knew it would be a battle.

On the night, tackles flew in as expected but when Aston was on hand to slot home a goal after Mustic could only parry a Best header, any nerves were instantly gone. Bestie went close, as did Burns and Kidd before the break. Sarajevo needed to score but returned to their first leg tactics following an incident between Bestie and Mustic. Bestie took a swing but missed, otherwise he'd have been dismissed. Incensed, Prljaca scythed down George and received his marching orders. Playing against 10 men we took the initiative and Bestie grabbed a second goal midway through the half. I made a smart save from Antic before Delalic scored late on but there was no way we were going to let in another. At the final whistle, normally I'd have shaken hands with my opposite number but there was a lot of pent up frustration. A scuffle broke out in the tunnel and I've never seen Crerand move so fast as he clashed with Mustic. Henry Cooper would have been proud! But in the melee Matt clocked a punch as he tried to intervene. Eventually, after being ushered into our dressing room we simmered down. No further action resulted from the incident and it was a tie we were glad to get out of the way. Safely through to the quarterfinals in three months' time, our mindset returned to defending our league title, but news that we'd take on Polish champions Gornik Zabrze who had knocked out Celtic's conquerors Dymano Kiev was a sobering thought.

The build up to the festive fixtures is always an intense time but we were now battle hardened and it showed in our form. During a real purple patch we played some great football. Bestie was on fire against West Brom and he matched his two goals on Boxing Day when we thumped Wolves 4–0. Kidd was also on target and a few days later fired home the winner as we edged the return fixture 3–2 at Molineux. And our winning spree continued in the New Year at home to West Ham and Sheffield Wednesday but Tottenham brought us back down to earth when they held us at Old Trafford in a third round FA Cup tie. The game was the first of a trilogy of games as they won the midweek replay with the only goal of a match that went to extra time but we avenged the result by returning to White Hart Lane on the Saturday and winning 2–1, Charlton scoring the winner.

Exiting the FA Cup was a real kick in the teeth especially as the winner by Jimmy Robertson had controversy written all over it but we were still flying on two fronts. Big matches in Europe lay ahead and we needed a fully fit squad to compete. We'd adapted to life without Herd, who was finding it tough to get back in the side on a regular basis and Law's knee problem was becoming more of a concern and limiting his appearances. Another injury had kept Stiles out for a fair few games but Nobby was on the verge of getting back to full fitness and we needed him for the battles that lay ahead as Foulkes looked set to be out for a while. The title race now had Leeds and Liverpool as our main challengers.

With everything to play for, we suffered a blow when we lost at Burnley. Martin Dobson, a promising youngster, came off the bench to snatch the winning goal but we still led the league . . . just. We got back to winning ways against Arsenal but had to do so without Charlton who was playing for England against Scotland in a home international match that also served as a Nations Cup qualifier. This was an era when international games took place during the season on the same day as league games, a situation inconceivable nowadays. Can you imagine Wayne Rooney and Rio Ferdinand playing for England when United had a league game on the same day? As March approached we'd played 29 games and were three points ahead of Leeds and had five more than Liverpool. Manchester City were nowhere, but the picture would soon change although our initial commitments turned back to the European Cup.

Playing Gornik Zabrze was a tough challenge as they had a skilful side with a number of dangerous players including one of the top players in Europe, striker Wlodzimierz Lubanski. With Law out other players had to take up the goalscoring mantle. And we had them ready and willing, especially Bestie who had scored in the past five games during a spell when we won eight out of 11 league games. It was a tough match against the Polish side at Old Trafford but we came through 2–0 courtesy of an own goal by Florenski who was trying to keep out a strike by George and a last minute Kidd back-heel from a Ryan miss-hit shot. It was a fortuitous strike but Gornik were indebted to their keeper Kostka for a number of saves, otherwise we would have been out of sight. As things transpired, I played my part when Lubanski broke through late on. A goal could have put Gornik back in the game with a crucial 'away' goal for the return. Facing a player one-on-one I always tried to narrow the angle, forcing him to shoot across me (which was the most inviting option for a striker), chip me, take the ball around me or strike the ball firmly. My gamble worked as I cut out his cross shot to preserve our two-goal advantage. Throughout the game, Latocha had given Bestie no room to play and at the other end of the field we had to keep a keen

Held by my mum, Doris Stepney, at a street party to celebrate VE Day

Enjoying a day out as a ball boy for England v Scotland at Wembley

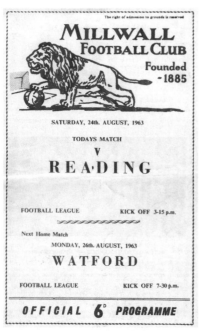

Millwall v Reading, making my professional debut

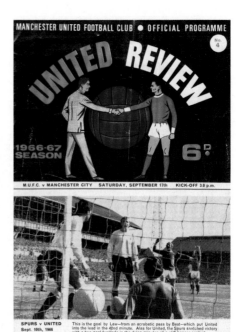

Manchester United v Manchester City, my United debut

Match programme for United's clash at West Ham when we clinched the title

Raising the Division 1 championship trophy

Sir Matt takes the applause from United's players and fans

Tipping over the bar watched by Sadler and Stiles. Manchester United versus Burnley at Turfmoor, February 1968

Part of the European Cup Champion team, Press Day, July 1968   © Howard Talbot Photography

European Cup Champion team, Press Day, July 1968   © Howard Talbot Photography

FOOTBALL ASSOCIATION
INTERNATIONAL MATCH

Wed.
22nd MAY
1968

England
v
Sweden

KICK-OFF 7.45 p.m.

WEMBLEY

EMPIRE STADIUM

Match programme from when I claimed my full England cap

Following England captain Bobby Moore out to face Sweden at Wembley

United defeat Real Madrid on aggregate to reach the European Cup final

Destiny awaits for United in the European Cup final at Wembley

Bobby Charlton raises the European Cup. I show my delight along with Bill Foulkes

eye on Szoltysik and Musialek. The match was played in a fantastic spirit, a far cry from the last round, and we applauded our opponents off at the end.

Back to league action and we went down at home to Chelsea 3–1. It was one of those days for me and I bemoaned my misfortune when I picked up an injury as Baldwin scored. The injury was a factor in the other two goals scored by Tambling and Osgood, but with no keeper sub I just had to get on with it. No excuses, Chelsea deserved the points. It was a crazy situation when you think back. The only positive I could take out of the game was that I had 10 days to recover for the Gornik return as we had a rare weekend off due to our opponents being in the FA Cup fifth round action.

Gornik moved the match from their home ground to the Slaski Stadium in Chorzow, halfway between Zabrze and a mining town called Katowice in Upper Silesia. It was one of the most uninviting, bleak places a footballer could play during the harsh blizzard winter months. Again we chartered the BAC 111 airplane for the journey. On top of the harsh weather, Crerand had played in Poland for Scotland three years earlier and warned us that the food was terrible. Although his warnings were welcome the backroom staff were experienced enough to travel prepared with our own food and especially water. Nowadays dietary requirements are second nature but in the sixties clubs were not so strict. We took no risks on a trip to a country such as Poland although the dining facilities had improved since Paddy had visited with Scotland so there were no major worries.

We knew that the match would be tight and 105,000 vocal fans would be present at the away leg. Incredibly, another 100,000 had applications turned down. There would be very few United supporters in the stadium. The Polish football season had just restarted and it had snowed solidly for two days prior to the game. We trained for an hour at the stadium, which was not ideal preparation. Unfortunately the ball would not roll normally given the conditions, it was a farce and we soon gave up. Trying to play football was a lottery. Our brand of flowing football was impossible on a snowbound pitch. Matt made it clear that he was not happy and there was a lot of debate over whether the match would go ahead. In fact, as we returned to our hotel the match was in doubt and remained so up to kick off. It was down to the managers and referee, Italy's finest at the time, Concetto Lo Bello, to agree for the game to go ahead, but he was on the overnight sleeper train from Vienna. A league match would have been postponed but there was enormous pressure to play the game. Gornik offered to flatten the snow so it would take a stud but the offer was rejected. In the end, a group of labourers put in a massive effort to clear the snow from the pitch. Although far from an ideal surface when we walked around the ground prior to the game it was a big improvement from 24 hours earlier and you had to compliment the effort made. The pitch was passed fit but it was obviously going to test us.

During the afternoon we had the opportunity, through our travel agent, to visit Auschwitz concentration camp. Most of the lads visited the notorious death camp where the Nazis killed millions of Jews during the war. On trips abroad there was little time to see historic places but we felt we had to see this terrible landmark. My own father had suffered after playing his part in the war against Nazi Germany. What happened during this period in history must never be forgotten.

Then after completing our pre-match preparations, we made our way to the stadium. Matt told us to play compact, as control would be tough. It would make it difficult to score so we had to keep it tight. Defensively, if in doubt, we had to take no chances and clear our lines. The temperature was well below freezing at kick off so we had to prepare as best we could and massaged oils into our bodies to try to keep out the cold. It was damp and dark in the tunnel as we waited to go onto the pitch and the noise from the capacity crowd was deafening as we ran out. Warming up I noticed the Gornik players wore polo-neck tops, gloves and tights. Clearly, they knew what to expect in the biting conditions while we had our normal tops on. The conditions were tough and with snow still falling the lines were painted red instead of the usual white.

Despite the weather, one thing Gornik could not anticipate was our desire to win. I knew the lads would battle away and true to form they took on board Matt's tactics from the start. Fitzpatrick had come into the midfield to bolster our defensive unit of Dunne, Sadler, Stiles and Burns. Dunne picked up an injury during the first half and was a passenger for most of the second half but to a man, the lads dug deep to keep our lead intact. Possession was the key and Charlton was superb, dictating play as we stayed firm until a bizarre refereeing decision 20 minutes from time. A goalkeeper in my era was allowed four steps before clearing a ball. With the score 0–0 I caught a corner cleanly but had to come between my six-yard box and penalty spot to catch the ball so couldn't stop because of the pitch. The referee pulled me up for an indirect free kick, which was ridiculous. The ball ricocheted to Lubanski who struck the ball off the crossbar into the back of the net. The last few minutes were tense but Stiles and Fitzpatrick were immense as we held on. All the lads were shattered afterwards but there were plenty of back slaps because it had been some effort. We had not scored an away goal throughout the run but more importantly we had only conceded once. Our tactics of tight controlled football had again worked and we were through to the semi-finals.

Back at the hotel we continued the celebrations. Matt was on top form and gave a memorable rendition of his party-piece song 'I Belonged to Glasgow'. We were now in the last four and what a choice of opponents . . . Juventus, Benfica or Real Madrid. Of all the ties, the crack Italian outfit Juventus looked like being the toughest as they were renowned for dour defending. Benfica had a fine reputation with Eusebio leading the line while Real Madrid were the glamour clash and the one the neutrals wanted us to avoid in the hope that we'd play them in the final. Looking at the options the lads wanted Benfica or Juventus but not Madrid as they were something of a bogey team for Matt at the semi-final stages. But all the speculation was soon over as news filtered through that we'd drawn Real. The days of legendary players such as Di Stefano, Puskas and Santamaria may have gone but Real, managed by another great from the all-conquering team, Miguel Munoz, were a crack outfit. Munoz knew all about the tournament having led the team on its first two of their six titles at the time. Granted, Real did not play the unorthodox, off the cuff attacking football of days gone by as a more modern approach of hard work was a big part of their game but they would be formidable opposition. At first there was a sense that the footballing Gods were against us but that was quickly replaced by the anticipation of playing in a classic tie. The dream of winning the European Cup at Wembley was very much alive.

Before the first leg encounter at Old Trafford with Madrid there were nine league games to play and we suffered a European hangover at Coventry City. We bounced back against Nottingham Forest before a midweek clash with Manchester City and our neighbours came out on top with a 3–1 win to blow the title race wide open. We got off to a flyer when Bestie scored inside a minute. But credit to the City Slickers, they equalised before half time and won the points with further goals from Heslop and a Lee penalty. The result was bitterly disappointing but it meant that Manchester as a city was buzzing with Mercer and Allison driving our local rivals on. Since gaining promotion in 1965–66 they had quickly settled into the top-flight playing an exciting brand of football. With Book, Bell, Summerbee and Young now household names, Mercer and Allison had also brought Bolton striker Lee to the club. And Frannie was making a significant impact alongside Oakes, Doyle and Heslop. City were challengers make no mistake and Allison was telling anyone that would listen that his team was ready to take our crown.

Again we reacted well by winning 4–2 at Stoke City but Liverpool came to Old Trafford and avenged our win at Anfield by the same score line, 2–1. Bestie gave us the lead but poor defending allowed Yeats to slide home an equaliser before Hunt slotted home the winning goal. In reality though we had been well beaten and with seven games remaining, recent results meant that having been title favourites our five-point lead had all but evaporated as City, Liverpool and Leeds battled against us in the tightest title race for years.

Prior to the arrival of Madrid we dropped just one point and it was great to have the Lawman back in the side. Denis's injury had limited his appearances but scoring again in wins over Fulham and Sheffield United was terrific because the first leg clash with Madrid was coming up. But the media had a field day, labelling us dour and sloppy against Sheffield. In fact, the Blades created by far the best chances and on another day a more clinical team would have won because Tom Fenoughty and Gil Reece both wasted chances from point blank range. Of course, it was my job to save the goals but would Madrid have been so wasteful if presented with gilt-edged opportunities? Only three games remained and we still led the way on 54 points with Leeds a point behind with a game in hand, City four points back with a game in hand and Liverpool six points adrift with two games in hand. The league would go to the wire but that was for the future as Matt pondered his line up against Madrid.

In the eyes of Real Madrid our key player was Bobby Charlton, dubbed 'El Monstruo del Futbol Ingles' (Monster of English Football) in the Spanish media. Bobby had bossed a recent European Nations Cup quarterfinal at Wembley, scoring the only goal, and Madrid feared him more than any other United player. On the arrival of the Madrid manager, Munoz, at Ringway Airport he believed his side would advance even if they lost by the odd goal. Munoz also noted that aside from Charlton, United had three other world class players in Best, Law and Crerand. With three of them fighting to be fit, Munoz would no doubt have been hopeful they would all be out but he had problems of his own because star striker Amancio was suspended from the opening leg after being sent off against Sparta Prague. Other players to watch out for would be right half Pirri, sweeper Zoco and experienced winger Gento. But Amancio was a big loss, having cost a Spanish record £60,000 plus four players from Coruna. Madrid were a class apart in Spain, having won six out of the last seven titles at home together with a European Cup in the same period after dominating the early stages of the tournament with five consecutive crowns.

During the build up the tension grew each day. I'd played

in some big games for United already but this was on a different scale. I was never one to get overly anxious before a big match but this game was playing on my mind and I struggled to relax when I woke up. Normally on the morning of a big night match I'd laze in bed but not this time. I could not wait for kick off and, excepting local rivalries, the whole country appeared to be behind us as a packed house crammed into Old Trafford. Matt was at the centre of the media hullabaloo with his quest for the big one, the European Cup, but in the dressing room there was no time for sentiment. We knew history beckoned but we had to concentrate on the match in hand. It would be an emotional night but we had to keep focused. There is always a special atmosphere at a home game, especially a big derby game against City or when one of the big guns comes to town, but even those games were no match for a European Cup match when the atmosphere cranked up a few notches. And as we ran out, the noise was tremendous and the Stretford End gave me a massive reception but you could still sense the tense atmosphere.

Both teams took time to settle in the opening 20 minutes. Crerand went close early on when he struck a post but that was the nearest either side came to a goal in the opening period. Bestie was clearly targeted by Madrid who detailed two players on him whenever he was in possession. We carried on probing and dominated possession but struggled to find an opening until finally, a slip by Gonzalez was pounced on John Aston on the left wing. Looking up, John played in a superb cross for Bestie to fire home a sweet half-volley from 15 yards giving Betancort no chance in the Madrid goal. Having a half time lead was terrific but we needed a second. As in the first half, we struggled to break down a strong Madrid rearguard. Real's attitude was damage limitation and they rarely threatened as an attacking force. Whilst Betancort was constantly in the thick of the action I had a quiet night. Dominating possession, time and again we probed but Madrid battled away to deny us a crucial second goal that would have put us in a dominant position. Twice last-ditch blocks halted our progress when Pirri and Zunzunegui got in the way of strikes by Crerand and Law. Madrid defended and defended with some purpose in front of keeper Betancort, satisfied with a 1–0 deficit. Back in the dressing room at full time there was a sense of frustration that we had not settled the tie but Matt told us to be optimistic. If we scored a goal Real had to get three and with our attacking options that was always a possibility. Also, we'd demonstrated against Sarajevo and Gornik that we were up for a challenge and Real would come out to play football as they would not be able to sit back in the second leg. By the time I left the ground, although we only had a slight advantage, I felt a sense that destiny was on our side.

Before taking on Real at the Bernabeu Stadium in the second leg though there was the title run in to complete but we lost our advantage when cup finalists West Brom won a cracker 6–3 at The Hawthorns. Credit to The Baggies, they were on fire that night and deserved the win. A 6–0 drubbing over Newcastle, when Bestie struck a hat-trick, kept us level but City led on goal average. The title was out of our hands and with both Leeds and Liverpool also faltering, City had the title in their grasp. Prior to taking on Sunderland in our final home game there was a chance to run the rule over a number of Madrid players at the Bernabeu with England playing Spain in the Nations Cup second leg match. Walking through the trophy room you got a clear understanding of the depth of feeling for the European Cup. I glimpsed the haul of six trophies on display in addition to domestic honours and it was an impressive sight to say the least. England won 2–1 and I saw for myself the cauldron that awaited us although it would be even more partisan. Sadly another defeat on the final day of the league season to Sunderland ended our campaign in depressing fashion. City duly clinched the title with a 4–3 win at Newcastle United. The home dressing room at Old Trafford was a despondent place to be sat. Yet it was during such adversity that strength comes through. Matt Busby, gracious as always, put on a brave face for a TV link up to congratulate Joe Mercer and his City team whilst we contemplated where we'd missed out. But it was not long before there was a steely determination to land the big one and our focus turned to the Madrid return.

Based at the Fenix Hotel in a mountain retreat away from the city centre the United squad relaxed. Now I'm not a religious person but before the game Paddy said he was going to morning Mass so I joined him and Nobby for the service. If divine inspiration was forthcoming then I was all for it so I tagged along. Changing in the magnificent dressing rooms at the Bernabeu we were focused on the job ahead. And walking out in front of a capacity 120,000, including 30,000 United fans, we knew that we had to keep things tight in the opening half to be in with a shout of building pressure on Madrid. It was no surprise that Law was out after failing a fitness test. In fact, Denis now knew his knee would require surgery so Kiddo retained his place in the side and Foulkes was also playing in defence despite not being fully fit. Bill had played in the last two league games and come through unscathed so Matt took the risk as he felt his experience was essential. Sadler would have a crucial defensive role to play but was also tasked with breaking forward at every opportunity when we had possession.

In the opening minutes Nobby, who was man-marking Amancio, made his presence felt in a challenge with Madrid's key player, and determined to get his own back, the two soon got into a scrap. When play resumed, chances came for both sides but Real were dictating play. Amancio scraped the bar and Crerand went close from a free kick. It was mainly one-way traffic though with the ball in our half as Madrid pressed for a goal. We held on to our aggregate lead for 30 minutes but our plans were knocked back when the Italian referee, Sbardella, awarded a goal kick then changed his mind after consulting his linesman to give Real a free kick when Aston tackled Grosso. We felt hard done by and momentarily switched off in defence as Pirri headed home Amancio's cross.

Real had their tails up and came at us with all guns blazing. We were under the cosh and the crowd was going crazy. Five minutes from half time, Gento picked up a clearance before evading Crerand and Brennan to score. We were on the rocks and desperate for a goal when out of the blue—maybe it was divine inspiration—we got a massive break. Kiddo had bags of enthusiasm so chased what appeared a lost cause when Aston knocked a ball into the Madrid penalty box. Kiddo's run put Zoco under pressure and the centre-half failed to note Betancort come off his line. Zoco must have been horrified as his sliced clearance sailed into an empty net. Incredibly, through an own goal, we were back in the match. But after Nobby joined Sadler in the referees' book for another foul on Amancio, Real's sharpshooter scored with a rasping shot just before the break for a 3–1 lead. Half time could not come quick enough.

Back in the dressing room, we sat down deflated and looking for inspiration. Amancio had dictated play and if things did not change quickly we'd be thumped. But true to form Matt's pep talk was a masterpiece. Matt's cool-headedness was astonishing that night. He didn't say anything to begin with during the break. Normally, Matt would go through tactical changes if necessary and Jimmy Murphy would emphasise them but not this time. Matt and Jimmy walked in and paced around the table in the middle of the dressing room. Matt then sat down on a stool shaking his head. Taking a puff on his pipe he tutted at us and then just as the bell rang, signalling the teams to go out he stood up and walked to the dressing room door. Matt turned around and looked at us all. He'd been thinking deeply about what to say, but I didn't know what to think. Matt knew what he was doing. Heads were down and there was an eerie silence, as we'd let down the boss, ourselves and United supporters. Needing inspiration, Matt looked at us all. 'What's going on? This is a European Cup semi-final. You should be enjoying yourselves because you're great players but you're not great players tonight. You're playing the worst football you've played all season. You haven't lost when you've attacked teams so go out and play your football. We are only 3–2 behind, not 3–1 behind. Get an early goal and they'll crack. They may score two but you'll score again. Even if we lose by a goal we'll get a play off in Lisbon. And if we are to go down then let's go down attacking. Come on, go out, play your football and enjoy yourselves.' I walked out of the door feeling 10 feet tall as did all the lads!

Jogging out, the referee had a stern word with Stiles and Amancio to stop the feuding. Also, looking at the Real players there was a sense that they felt the hard work was done and it was soon clear that they had given their best in the first half. The pace slowed down and gave us a chance to swap formation from 4–3–3 to 4–2–4. Committed to attack, we had a different mindset and got on top. Matt had told

Sadler to move into attack from his defensive position but it took a fortuitous goal to get us back into the game around 15 minutes from time. From a free kick, Bestie nodded down a Crerand chip, the Real players hesitated and Sadler, who had joined the attack nipped in to poach a goal. The score was now 3–2 on the night and it was game on. More importantly we were level on aggregate. Real players suddenly slumped, they knew we were in the ascendancy and could sense our victory. We'd also silenced the crowd who knew the balance of the tie had switched. They could suddenly see the Real players arguing with the referee and realised they were unsure whether to defend or attack. We only knew one way though and shortly after Sadler's goal came a sweet moment that will live long in the memory.

Bestie had been shackled all night but in a moment of magic found space after waltzing past Sanchis and headed for the byline with defenders in hot pursuit. In their haste to catch George they failed to spot an extra United attacker trundling up in support . . . Foulkes! With the United bench screaming for Bill to get back into defence our centre-back had other ideas. In training, Bill loved playing striker in five-a-sides but this was a European Cup semi-final. Ignoring pleas from the bench Foulkes continued to rumble forward as Bestie weaved his magic before eventually cutting back the ball into the danger area for Bill to calmly arrive in the penalty box unmarked and sidefoot home the equaliser past Betancort. We were now ahead on aggregate. Bill was United's longest serving player with eight goals in over 650 appearances and this goal was his last for the club but it could not have been better timed or more important. The goal signalled a massive celebration with the big man. Regrouping, there was no way we'd let Madrid back into this game though they did push forward at every opportunity.

We'd made it to the European Cup final and at the full time whistle there were all sorts of celebrations. I did a handstand, Paddy a somersault, Nobby his party jig while a number of lads sank to the ground exhausted. The relief was enormous. Bobby was pictured in the papers next day overcome with emotion. And back in the dressing room the scenes were euphoric. Matt Busby was elated and more emotional than I'd ever seen him. Years of striving for this moment were over as he hugged all the players. It was a magical occasion and nobody wanted to get changed. In fact, we were in the showers still wearing our kits. All we wanted to do was celebrate a truly memorable moment. Eventually, we got changed and making our way to the coach, a flying bottle from a group of Madrid supporters caught Nobby on the head, which needed stitching before he could resume celebrating. The incident joined a long list of mishaps to happen to the most accident-prone member of the side.

It was an era when we did not fly back after a game so I partied the night away with Paddy, Denis, George and our respective partners until the early hours. There was nowhere to hide from 30,000 United supporters who naturally were also celebrating. Decked out in red and white blazers, red and white top hats, scarves and rosettes, it was a wonderful sight along the Gran Via. The champagne corks were popping in all the local bars. There was no trouble, just unbridled joy and even the local police had grudging smiles. The game had coincided with a public holiday in Madrid, the Festival of San Isidro, the city's patron saint, but there were not many locals celebrating as for one night only Madrid belonged to Manchester United followers.

Back in Manchester, judging from what we were told later, the city centre was almost at a standstill as fans tuned in to wirelesses for the game before celebrating big time.

Next day we flew home to a fantastic reception back in Manchester while a number of the lads attended the FA Player of the Year dinner where Bestie picked up the Football Writer's Player of the Year trophy. All talk was naturally now on the final and it was something of a surprise when we heard that Benfica overcame Juventus. But we looked forward to the challenge of taking on a fine side and I could reacquaint myself with Eusebio, dubbed 'The Black Pearl'. As the build up started I felt more strongly that it would be our year. With Denis booked in for an operation on his knee, Bobby would lead the side at Wembley. The press naturally played on the 10 years since Munich and it would be an iconic moment if United managed to win for Matt Busby and his rebuilt team. There was mass media coverage as we did interviews for papers, press and TV. As a kid my dream was to play in an FA Cup final at Wembley but now I'd be playing in a European Cup final at the Twin Towers.

Before the big game Alf Ramsey selected me to play for England a week before the final in a friendly match against Sweden. It would prove to be my only full cap but when Alf informed me in his no-nonsense manner that I'd be playing it was one of the highlights of my career. Banks was being rested but Alf would not have selected me for England if I didn't deserve to play. Being selected also benefited United as I got a taste of preparing in the dressing rooms and playing on the famous Wembley pitch at the iconic stadium. Alf was not one to give caps away. They had to be earned. Sentiment was not part of his makeup but having the chance to keep goal for England was one of the proudest moments of my professional life as a footballer. And pulling on the England jersey was a wonderful feeling with the likes of Frank Swift and Banks that had kept goal before me.

England International, Wembley Stadium
(22 May 1968)

England: Stepney (Manchester United), Newton (Blackburn Rovers), Knowles (Tottenham Hotspur), Mullery (Tottenham Hotspur), Labone (Everton), Moore (West Ham United), Peters (West Ham United), Bell (Manchester City), Charlton (c) (Manchester United), Hunt (Liverpool), Hunter (Leeds United). Sub: Hurst (West Ham United). *Sweden*: Larsson (S), Carlsson, Kristensson, Nordquist, Grip, Eriksson, Larsson (B), Nordahl, Elderstedt, Lindman, Persson. Sub: Andersson.

There was a lot of hype about the game back in Manchester as Colin Bell at City was also making his debut. Standing in the Wembley tunnel behind Bobby Moore alongside so many greats of the era was everything I'd imagined as a kid hoping to make it in the game. On the night England won 3–1 with Peters, Charlton and Hunt scoring. The only dampener was letting a goal in from Andersson but I felt a great deal of satisfaction back in the dressing room. There was not too much time though to ponder on the moment because the next time I'd pull a goalkeeper shirt on at Wembley would be for the biggest club match a professional footballer could take part in.

We prepared for the final at Great Fosters Hotel, Egham—a luxury country hotel situated near Windsor that offered perfect surroundings. We had a side that encompassed the perfect combination of youth, experience and brilliance. Despite the loss of Law our line up had the balance required to succeed. In Charlton we had one of the world's greatest players, our defence was solid and Crerand would keep the ball flowing. I also knew that Eusebio would be in for a match as he'd be coming up against Stiles. In Bestie we had a mercurial match winner. On our day we needn't have feared any side. I was about to play at Wembley in the biggest game in club football with the world watching and could not wait. We knew we'd have to battle. Benfica had not come to Wembley to let us take the trophy back to Old Trafford. We'd have to earn the right. Our coaches had us in the right frame of mind and made sure our fitness levels were right. Any doubts over knocks were resolved and the banter was there between the lads. Pre and post-match arrangements were all organised, and during our stay at the hotel, the 11pm curfew was in no danger. Jack Crompton was usually tasked with checking on the lads but none of us needed telling that our rest was crucial. I shared a room with Paddy and there was an added degree of anticipation because we knew that this was the biggest day of our careers. Paddy was always less relaxed than me when it came to resting before a game. While I was able to drop off, I knew my roommate would be thinking through our opponents and going over the strengths and weaknesses we'd been detailed. I knew what was ahead and tried to keep my feelings low key until it was time to get my match head on.

There had been more publicity for this game than any other match I'd known but finally the big day arrived, and 29 May 1968 was a real sporting day as it was Derby Day as well which was ironic as it had been such an occasion for my family when I grew up. Over breakfast we caught up with the gossip in the newspapers before a stretching training session, just to get the muscles warmed up. It was a light work out and the banter was terrific. Only one place was up for grabs, which was in defence and the full-back slots. Matt had to choose between Francis Burns who had played up to the first leg semi-final against Real Madrid or Shay Brennan who had come back into the side. The options were whether to have Francis at left back and Dunne right back or revert to the side in Madrid with Dunne switching to the left and Brennan playing right. It was not an easy decision and would be tough on whoever missed out. But Matt would make that call. For Brennan it was elation and desperation for Burns. Shay experienced the heartache of missing United's 1963 FA Cup final but was elated to get his chance this time. We all felt for Francis but he had missed out in Madrid so it was not really a major surprise. Francis was a classy full-back who had a turn of pace and was fit as a fiddle but Matt decided on Shay's greater experience in the end.

United were led by a great man. Matt Busby made everyone at the club feel special from the laundry ladies to cleaners, groundsman, programme sellers, ticket office staff and ball boys. Our training was meticulously planned, travel schedules and player needs were always paramount in his thoughts, and if we needed a quiet word, Matt would be available. Over 40 years have gone by since Wembley 1968 but Matt is rightly held in the highest esteem. When I first met Matt I was in awe and it felt amazing that he wanted me to play a crucial role in his team. Matt made me feel so much at ease at the club. Day in and day out it was a privilege to work under him. In training he was always encouraging and come a big match if a change had to be made for the benefit of the team, no matter how difficult, he'd make it, but you'd understand why and push on. In the dressing room, he was a master of getting his point across succinctly. Matt loved his sides to entertain and encouraged us to play our football. During games he was also the best tactician I played under. Win, lose or draw he knew how to handle any situation. Matt created the aura that surrounds Manchester United and when great managers of all eras are recalled, for me, Matt is right there at the top.

Jimmy Murphy was Matt's right hand man. Jimmy had

been with Matt since Matt took over the manager's job at Old Trafford after the war and had worked closely with him to build the three legendary teams of the forties, fifties and sixties. And of course, Jimmy had taken the helm in the aftermath of the Munich air disaster until Matt recovered from his injuries. Jimmy also presided over the reserve and junior teams. An unbelievable talent spotter, he recommended who Matt should sign and with a track record that yielded Duncan Edwards, Bobby Charlton and George Best, Jimmy knew his stuff. A proud Welshman, Jimmy was a taskmaster in training and was not averse to demonstrating to the younger lads the gamesmanship issues they'd encounter. Whether it was kicking from behind, shirt-pulling or timewasting, Jimmy made sure we were prepared to deal with the unsavoury aspects of professional football. Jimmy was also an inspiration in the dressing room and available to have a quiet word when the need arose. He was respected by all the players and, like Matt, turned down opportunities to benefit financially elsewhere because of his loyalty to United.

Back at Old Trafford, United's backroom staff, apprentices, players' relatives and family members from the 1958 team gathered as the club had chartered a train to the match. For everyone it would be an emotional event but Matt made sure no one would miss the big occasion. And while they made their way to London with around 40,000 United supporters, another big sporting occasion was concluding as Lester Piggot won the Derby on Sir Ivor. Alongside the Grand National, the race was one of the big dates in the racing calendar for the country. And footballers didn't need much encouragement to get involved in a sweepstake, especially the biggest event in the flat race season.

After the race it was time for a pre-match nap for an hour before changing for the pre-match meal three hours before kick off. We then had our team talk where the boss officially named the side that would become the first English team to play in a European Cup final. We knew destiny awaited, although it was tragic Denis Law was not available due to injury and we'd miss his calming influence in the dressing room. 'Mr Cool' before a big clash, Denis was the only player I knew who could shut his eyes for 40 winks before a game. The Lawman was the hero for United fans and a real players' player. Razor sharp in attack, Denis was the master at pouncing on a loose ball to strike. Prolific in front of goal, Denis was blessed with a touch of magic that could conjure up the most amazing goals from seemingly impossible situations. Powerful in the air, tough and brave, Denis also had the ability to know instinctively where a ball would be in the box. His hot-headedness, at times, got him into a spot of bother but it also made him the world class striker that he became when the raised arm signalled another goal. Missing Denis was a major blow but that is part of professional football and I knew we had a team that could battle, play off the cuff and win.

European Cup final, Wembley Stadium (29 May 1968)

Manchester United: Stepney, Brennan, Dunne, Crerand, Foulkes, Stiles, Best, Kidd, Charlton (c), Sadler, Aston.
Benfica: Henrique, Adolfo, Humberto, Jacinto, Cruz, Graca, Coluna (c), Augusto, Eusebio, Torres, Simoes.

In defence I called the shots in the penalty area. If I called 'Keeper's ball!', then the lads knew I'd be there and like most teams we played on a swivel system. If the ball went down the left then the lads on the right would move a bit in and vice versa. As a goalkeeper I believed in angles and worked on them all the time in training. Wherever I was around the six-yard box, I knew where my goal was. I never believed in being flashy when saving a shot. If I could get a hand to the ball and tip it over the bar or flick it around the post then fine, it was a corner, regroup. Taking a chance to pull off a spectacular save when safety was the best option was never on my mind. I didn't catch a ball then drop on it to waste time. Keepers were hard men, worked hard, trained hard and that's how it was.

Shay Brennan won the nod at right back. An experienced player and Eire international, Shay converted to right back after starting out as a winger. In the dressing room, Shay was one of the jokers. An honest player, Shay organised the 'yellow jersey' presentation for the player making most mistakes in training. It was always a laugh but nobody wanted the dubious honour of wearing it the next day. Shay loved life, a drink, a bet and his golf. After a game he'd be the first to buy a round at the pub and he was great to be around. Shay was the first of the 1968 team to pass away when he died following a heart attack on a golf course in Ireland. It was tragic as he was only 63 but knowing Shay it's the way he'd have chosen to go when his time came. I'll always remember Shay for the person he was off the park and the player he was on it. Calm under pressure, Shay played the game simply, with no fuss and to the benefit of the team. During a game when the tension was at its height he'd make the right decision.

On the opposite flank was Tony Dunne, another Eire international, and a tremendous left back. A quiet man with a matching temperament on the park, Tony was coolness personified in the heat of a game and just got on with his job. Never seeking the headlines, Tony was a solid defender, terrific slide tackler, brave, anticipated danger and just did his job. As last man in defence, Tony's speed was a real asset as he cleared dangerous situations on many occasions. Tony rarely lost possession and like Shay, got the ball and gave it simply to Crerand or Charlton to build attacks. An invaluable member of our team, Tony was one of the first names on the team sheet.

Bill Foulkes was the heart of our defence, never spectacular but always solid. When the ball came into his area Bill would clear the danger. Hard as nails in the tackle, you didn't mess around with the big man even in training! Once in an indoor five-a-side game I was playing outfield, like all keepers did. I fancied myself as a striker and caught Bill late. He crashed into the wall and after a few seconds turned and glared at me. I realised I'd better get out of the gym sharp and was back in the dressing room away from retribution until Bill simmered down. We laughed about it afterwards but I'd had a close call and was delighted he was in front of me on match days as I would not want to be on the end of one of his bone-crunching tackles. Bill had a quiet nature and never moaned about anything. He was a colossus in defence and a stalwart of the side. Experienced, strong, dedicated and determined, Bill was not the quickest defender around but would put his boot and head anywhere to clear the line. Above all he loved facing old-style centre-forwards and they hated playing against him. The Munich air disaster was a taboo subject with Bill who showed incredible character in the coming years. His goal in the semi against Madrid was a magical moment that has gone down in United folklore.

In the heart of the action alongside Bill was Nobby Stiles. An experienced England player, Nobby was our 'hatchet' man, and took no prisoners. Off the field Nobby was a different character. Dubbed 'Cleuso' as he was accident prone, Nobby kept spirits up by getting into mischief but once he crossed that white line, Nobby put the fear of God into his opponents and had a reputation to match. Nobby wasn't the biggest or hardest player but his endeavour, courage and bravery were evident. He tackled at the right time and let opponents know he was around. When Nobby went in for a challenge, opponents felt it but he was not a dirty player although some of his challenges were rash! Nobby could put the boot in when necessary. It was part of his game but he could also read the game well and took the tackles in addition to dishing them out. Nobby man-marked Eusebio on the night like he did for England in the 1966 World Cup against Portugal and he certainly didn't baulk at the challenge. We played a back four but Nobby was the sniffer around Bill. Yet he was far more than just a destroyer on the pitch because Nobby read the game superbly to stop an attack, was tactically astute and nippy. Most of all though his presence enabled the likes of Charlton to move into the attack knowing there was cover in defence.

Paddy Crerand had made his name at Celtic when he joined United, which was a huge investment at the time. Paddy operated as a floater in midfield, more or less around the right hand side just in front of the defence. A Scottish international, he lacked true pace but never stopped running for 90 minutes and always found space. And Paddy was always my outlet. Whenever I got the ball, I never had to worry. Regardless of where Paddy was when I looked up, he'd be available to take the ball and move it. I always preferred to roll the ball out and Paddy's great strength was his passing. A perfectionist, if Paddy misplaced a pass he was livid with himself because he had such high standards. But a misplaced pass was rare. Possessing great vision and drive, when Paddy got the ball he'd hit 20, 30, 40 yard passes to feet or to the front men with precision to mount an attack.

David Sadler was our utility player and could slot in at either centre-half or centre-forward. Quiet, methodical and cool under pressure, David brought balance to the side wherever he played. With only one substitute available, having David was terrific because it gave Matt the opportunity to change our tactics in a flash without disrupting the side because we all knew his capabilities in different areas of the pitch. Assured on the ball, an intelligent player, solid tackler and cultured passer, with Law out of the final, David played behind Charlton and Kidd.

Kiddo was a precocious talent. A born striker, Brian was able to play across the front line whether as the target man or interchanging with both wingers, so if Bestie or Johnny Aston came infield, Brian would move out to the flanks. Kiddo came into the side and immediately demonstrated that he possessed a powerful shot, had fine heading ability and was not afraid to mix it with uncompromising defenders; Brian would take on opponents down the flanks or through the middle. Kiddo was at the start of his career and we had absolute faith in him to deliver the goods.

Bobby Charlton led the team by example and had thunder in his boots. When Bobby connected with the ball, I felt sorry for the opposing keeper because if Charlton was on target the keeper didn't have a prayer. With Bobby in the side United had that something extra because opponents knew they were playing against a true legend in the game. And as one of the Busby babes, we all knew what the final meant to him. A superb passer of the ball, above all Bobby instinctively knew where to be for an opportunity. By the time I arrived at United, Bobby was playing in a deep-lying role behind the strikers and it made him a dangerous player due to his shooting prowess. Bobby was a world class player and his status has only grown as one of the all time greats of the game. Wherever you go in the world everyone in football knows who Bobby Charlton is and there is no greater accolade.

John Aston offered balance down the left side but had to overcome stick from a section of fans at times, especially when we had an off day. Having his father, John senior, at the club must have been tough but he battled away. John had pace to burn and could destroy any defence when on his A-game. His moment would finally arrive on a night to remember and this could not have happened to a more deserving footballer who always prepared in the right way and acquitted himself to the benefit of the club.

Finally, we had Bestie in the starting line up. George took players on the outside but could also come inside and cause havoc for defences with a pinpoint pass or strike at goal. George's fitness was phenomenal along with his ball skills and bravery. If he was hacked down, he'd keep battling away with his opposing defender. George never fell over just to win a free kick, it was simply not in his nature. A perfect example was a famous film clip of Ron 'Chopper' Harris of Chelsea taking numerous hacks at him during a run. But that was George, he took the stick and kept going. And the ball was never more than six inches from his boot at all times. His defensive qualities as well were not always appreciated but George filtered back when necessary. George could score from anywhere but was guilty at times of over-elaborating because he loved taking players on or having a strike from distance but he scored more often than not and was idolised by supporters. Bestie had a terrific strike rate and was capable of scoring with his right foot, left foot and with headers as well. Bestie was 22 going into the final and at the peak of his powers—he had the footballing world at its feet.

During the main team talk Matt told us to go out and bring that cup back to Manchester. He explained there was nothing to fear and that Benfica would be more worried about us. We'd thumped them in the quarterfinals 8–3 on aggregate in 1966 and could win again. 'Go out, play like you can, attack them and you'll win the game', Matt said. After giving us individual instructions on set plays, man marking and opposition strengths and weaknesses, a police cordon escorted us to Wembley Stadium. My match day head was now on and this was the biggest night of our lives as Manchester United players. We'd all been at the club for different lengths of time but knew the importance of the occasion and what it meant to the club. Our philosophy was you are not the best until you have done something and we had the opportunity to capture the biggest club trophy in football.

Travelling to the game the nerves grew as we approached the stadium and going down Wembley Way was tremendous. There just seemed to be a sea of red everywhere I looked. Cars were decked out with red and white scarves and ribbons flapping in the breeze. Fans were dressed up with rosettes, while others carried rattles and replica European Cups. Back in the same dressing room that I'd been in a week earlier when playing for England, I'd changed under the same peg. And walking around the stadium and checking the pitch, United fans spontaneously sang happy birthday to Kiddo, who was celebrating his 19th birthday. There was a quick wave to the fans from our teenage striker but it was soon time to get changed and for me it was the usual routine. There was no warm up on the pitch back then as there is today. We had a few balls in the dressing room so I bounced the ball against the white tiles to get a feel but that was it apart from some stretching exercises. All the lads changed in their own way and some made a few nervous jokes to ease the tension but overall there was a real sense of occasion. While the likes of Charlton and Foulkes were men deep in thought, having seen it all before, Bestie was taking it all in his stride. Always last to change, George was ready to make a massive impact. Everyone was focused and raring to go. The sense of anticipation was greater than I'd ever known but we knew we had to keep a lid on it or we would not perform.

For the game we had a strip change to all blue, the same colour that United wore when they won the FA Cup in 1948 against Blackpool two decades earlier. Maybe it was an omen as John Aston's dad had played in the winning side. Matt had given his main talk but moved around having a quiet word with all the lads. Nobby had to stick to Eusebio, Bill had to be on his mettle to stay with Torres, the big Benfica striker, especially at crosses and Bestie had instructions to do his magic. Just before lining up in the tunnel, Matt again told us we were great players and Benfica were more worried about us than we were about them. Above all, he reiterated as always, 'Go out, play football and enjoy yourselves'. The pre-match routine had resembled any other game but now we faced the long wait in the tunnel that can either make or break a player. And I was pleased I'd experienced a big occasion for England. Lining up, Bobby and Coluna were at the head of the sides. The tension was unbelievable as all the players waited nervously, fidgeting on the spot. Standing behind Bobby, concentrating deeply, I looked for the official at the top of the tunnel to give the okay to start walking out. I wasn't looking at any of the Benfica players. I could hear the crowd and the noise was building. The majority were obviously United supporters. And then came the sign to go, and in the distance the light at the tunnel end grew bigger as we walked up. The roar as the two teams entered the stadium was incredible, and playing a night game brought its own extra atmosphere. There had been no problem getting tickets as we had the players' allocation but I was too busy concentrating to spot anyone in the crowd. After being introduced to dignitaries we ran away to our end of the pitch. A few words of encouragement to each other and it was game on.

My only slight concern was Italian referee Mr Concetto Lo Bello as he'd pulled me up for the four-step rule in Gornik when I had trouble with my footing but I put that to the back of my mind. The first half was a cagey affair. As in every game, I wanted to get an early touch and did from a free kick outside the box, which Eusebio took. The ball came through the wall and stuck in my hands, which was a real confidence booster. Benfica made their intentions clear from the outset because Cruz and Humberto gave Bestie incredible stick as they tried to put him out of the game. Humberto was soon booked and the Portuguese tactics had a surprising effect because it gave someone else a chance to shine. Someone needed to step up to the plate and we had such a player in Aston who would go on to enjoy the finest game of his career. Adolfo was playing square and Aston soon capitalized with surging runs but there were few chances in the first half. Eusebio was always a danger and on 11 minutes lost Stiles, then evaded Foulkes before thumping a shot from the edge of the penalty area against the crossbar. I never got near his effort as the ball dipped and fortunately bounced to safety. Lady luck was on our side but I screamed at the lads to close him down from distance. Eusebio had a short back lift so it only took a split second for him to get a strike in. Next time we might not be so lucky.

The game settled down but neither team could find any fluency. Stiles and Eusebio were having a few tussles. Nobby was harassing his opponent at every opportunity and a two-footed lunge, which missed player and ball, brought a sparky moment although Eusebio was not totally innocent as he used his experience to playact at times but it was all part of the game. I had to be on my guard at free kicks around our penalty area but there was no serious danger to our goal. Then just before half time, out of nothing Aston and Charlton created an opening. Kidd played a one-two with Sadler and David was clean through but he got caught in two minds whether to chip the advancing Henrique or go round him. In the end, Sadler scuffed his effort and the chance was gone. Walking off, I felt comfortable but it was a poor half overall, as nobody wanted to make a slip.

Matt's team talk was for us to keep playing our football but stressed that we had to tighten up in defence because at times we struggled to pick up Benfica's attackers. He also made one key tactical change, which was to push Bobby forward while Sadler should drop back a bit as cover. Soon it was game on again. We started at a faster pace and Aston, in particular, was posing problems, forcing a couple of saves from Henrique. Finally, we were exerting some concerted pressure and eight minutes into the second half got the breakthrough. Sadler playing that bit deeper found space out on the left after taking a pass from Bestie before cutting inside and floating over a cross for Bobby to glance a header past Henrique in the Benfica goal. Our supporters lifted the roof at Wembley. I was over the moon because things were now going our way.

The game opened up as Benfica had to come at us. We started to get nervy. Benfica boasted 10 internationals and were a mobile outfit. Eusebio worried us. Augusto and Tony Simoes moved onto the wings supporting while Coluna and Graca pushed forward. I was more concerned by Torres, their 6ft 5in centre-forward. Bill had a tremendous job holding him but handled the task very well. Pushing forward, Benfica were now short at the back and Bestie started to come into the game more. Taking on opponents, George went close with a couple of strikes but we could not find a killer second goal. With the minutes ticking by we started to get jittery as Benfica applied more pressure. Augusto, Torres and Graca combined before Augusto crossed, Torres got a flick on and Graca smashed the ball past me. I thought, 'We've been coasting and it's now 1–1. Have we missed our chance?' but Aston started creating havoc down the wing again and soon we had a great chance to move ahead when Bestie waltzed past his opponents before firing in a shot that Henrique could only parry. The ball fell to Sadler for a tap in but he scuffed his shot and the keeper saved the ball.

The match had come alive and two minutes from time came a crucial point of the game. I've been reminded about my save from Eusebio ever since by United supporters at functions I've attended since but never tire of recalling it. There was no clock letting players know how long remained so we had signals from the bench and I knew extra time was looming. Then from a United attack, Simoes launched a counter-attack after dispossessing Charlton. Pushing the ball forward, Eusebio got a touch past Stiles before charging through a gap made when Torres peeled away taking Foulkes with him. Foulkes and Dunne tried to get back but it was too late. Eusebio was running through in a flash. As I came off my line, I thought I had a chance of getting to the ball first, but in the split second I had, I realised the Wembley turf was lush so would slow the ball down. I was in no-man's land so backed off as Eusebio was bearing down on the ball. I could see panic in Dunne, Foulkes and Brennan as they tried to get back to the 18-yard box but they were a few yards short. I was in trouble. Sizing things up, I thought Eusebio would chip me. Then instinctively, I stood up to him and thought, 'He's going to go for glory and burst the back of the net'. Standing tall gave me leverage of half a yard when he smacked the Mitre ball with his left foot just to my left, chest high. The power of the shot knocked me back. Either side I'd have had no chance, and if I'd parried the ball he'd have knocked in the rebound. We'd had a let off. The power knocked me over but I managed to hang on to the ball. I joke now that the Mitre sign on the ball is imprinted on my chest! Next thing, Eusebio was standing over me, patting me on the back and applauding me. I was not sure if he was showing great sportsmanship or telling me I was lucky. At the time though I just wanted to get on with the game and spotted Dunne waiting for a counter attack. Much has been made of my save but all I did was keep us in the game. There was still a match to win. There was no time to think about the save, we had to go for a winner but neither side could find a way through before the regulation 90 minutes.

During the extra time break both teams had socks down resting. Matt, Jimmy Murphy, Jack Crompton and John Aston senior came out to massage aching muscles and offer words of encouragement. Crerand was great. He said, 'I'm knackered but look at them', referring to the Benfica players. Paddy was right, they looked drained and after a visual inspection of our team there was one guy who looked to be full of running and sent out a signal that he was going to do this—that was Bestie. As for Matt, he told us we were throwing the match away by poor marking and too many misplaced passes. We had to tighten up and get back to playing football. The message was loud and clear. Lining up again, Crerand and Stiles urged on the lads with clenched fists. Both were fired up. We needed to get at Benfica who seemed slow to get back into position. And three minutes into extra time we edged ahead for a second time. From a throw in Dunne and Brennan both passed it back to me as Benfica dropped back. I launched a ball down the pitch, Kiddo got a little touch and Bestie was on the move, touched the ball through Jacinto's legs and was now bearing down on goal. As Henrique came out Bestie produced a moment of magic. In full control of the situation, and casual as you like, George waltzed past him before passing the ball into the back of the net for a classy goal and a 2–1 lead. Bestie wheeled away, arm in the air in iconic style. This time there was no way back for Benfica and you could see their heads went down.

A minute later it was game over. Aston won another corner, which Charlton took and Kiddo, on his birthday, scored at the second attempt off the underside of the crossbar to make it 3–1. Our teenage striker was off to celebrate and no United player could catch him. Benfica were gone and we made certain before the extra time break when Kidd went down the right wing, clipped the ball over for Bobby to score with a half volley across the keeper. The noise inside Wembley was incredible. United fans were singing, 'We'll be running round Wembley with the cup' and I knew they were right but we had to concentrate until the end. Towards the end of the opening extra time period Eusebio forced me into a couple of stops but in the second period Bestie and Kidd went close to hitting number five before I made another stop from Eusebio. But the game was over. The outstanding player on the night was Aston. Johnny was a player no pundit thought would be the star of the show but that can happen in football. Benfica could not have imagined how well he'd play. From the back, I could see he was causing problems. While Benfica concentrated on countering George and Bobby, Johnny enjoyed a night to remember. Every time he got the ball, he'd knock it 20 yards and fly past Adolfo before getting the ball into the box. That was the Matt Busby way; get down the flanks and get the balls in, and apart from the second goal they all came from crosses.

Matt's dream had come true and at the final whistle all the lads ran to him. Normally when the whistle goes in a cup final you go to the nearest player but not on this occasion. Looking back, one can only imagine what Matt, Bobby and Bill must have been thinking having survived Munich. There was a lot of emotion and tears on the pitch as well as massive relief that it was over. Walking up to the Royal Box was special and it was fitting Bobby collected the giant trophy. I was behind Bobby with Bill following me and it was a magic moment. Jogging around for the lap of honour was fantastic. Nobby produced his party piece jig but it was chaotic with photographers looking for the best shot. It was an unforgettable experience running around Wembley with the European Cup and back in the dressing room, there was champagne everywhere and plenty of joyful tears. I have to confess the floodgates opened for me as the enormity of the occasion sank in. And suddenly, my brother Eric appeared from nowhere. He'd blagged his way in after jumping over the fencing and dog track onto the pitch. Matt wanted to know who he was so I introduced him. The two didn't meet again until the celebratory dinner after we won the FA Cup in 1977 but Matt never forgot a face and went over to ask how Eric was doing. That was Matt all over and Eric has never forgotten it.

After we changed, the lads and squad members went into the lounge at Wembley where we had a celebratory drink with the England lads. They had been watching the game prior to flying to Hanover the following morning for a friendly match on the Saturday en route to Italy to play in the Nations Cup finals. Back at the hotel there was time to change and attend the official banquet at the Russell Hotel. The Joe Loss Orchestra entertained and plenty of celebrities were present but the match had drained the lads. We all seemed to arrive at different times so Cliff Richard's hit song 'Congratulations' was played a number of times. In fact, Bobby didn't make the dinner and Paddy was late. Kiddo was presented with a birthday cake while Matt received the Manager of The Year award. Family members of the Munich players were not forgotten. All in all it was an emotional night as well as one of celebration. Matt even gave a solo performance to Louis Armstrong's hit 'Wonderful World', which summed up how we all felt. I knew at the time it could not get any better. Everyone was on a high and we carried on partying at Danny La Rue's club until the early hours. Well you have to celebrate, don't you?

I missed the celebrations at the homecoming in Manchester as I joined up with the England team for the Nations Cup finals. I didn't face West Germany in the friendly match or the Nations Cup matches because Banks was recalled in the team. Alan Mullery became the first England player to be sent off when we lost 1–0 against Yugoslavia to a late goal. We finished third by winning the third place play off against Russia 2–0. Italy won the final.

Being part of the England squad was a tremendous honour and at United there was banter between the English and Scots lads. When I first arrived there was ribbing about England being world champions, but of course Denis and Paddy were able to crow a year later when Scotland famously won 3–2 at Wembley to become the first side to defeat the World Cup winners. Denis scored and held the bragging rights that summer, backed up by Paddy at every opportunity, but normal business was soon resumed. I also never felt hard done by that Banks was in front of me. Gordon was a great keeper and if he'd played for a bigger team than Leicester or Stoke City he'd have won more honours. Apart from the League Cup he played in two FA Cup finals but never came close to winning a league title. Domestically, I was in the right place at the right time and with Alf I felt lucky to be involved with an elite squad of players. All the lads mucked in and became friends, which has lasted but there was no sense you had a divine right to be chosen. You knew that with Alf he would play those players that had done it for him. And one player always in the side was the late, great Bobby Moore. Everyone praises him and rightly so. Bobby was an ambassador for his country and club, West Ham. As captain, Bobby liaised with the manager on behalf of the players to make sure the lads were kept involved in the preparations for a game. Alf always listened to any suggestions so everyone was happy. And that is what it was all about, which developed a togetherness in the squad. There was no southern and northern split among the players. I roomed mainly with the keepers because Alf liked to keep players in similar positions together. I remained in the squad until the 1970 World Cup finals, which was a terrific experience.

During the close season I was able to look back on a memorable campaign. I heard that the civic reception was some occasion as 250,000 fans came out to welcome the lads home. The Lord Mayor of Manchester, Alderman Mrs Elizabeth Yarwood, hosted a civic reception at the Town Hall and by all accounts it was a grand occasion. Matt was already a CBE and became the first sportsman to receive the Freedom of Manchester. Shortly afterwards he received the ultimate accolade when he was knighted. Our European Cup victory was a team effort but it was terrific to see George, who was outstanding throughout the campaign, voted the Football Writers Footballer of the Year. And he doubled up when he also scooped the European Footballer of the Year honour, edging out Bobby Charlton and Dragan Dzajic. This is the only season that saw us receive the top two positions and his efforts made it a hat-trick for United as Charlton (1966) and Law (1964) were past winners. Since that time, United players would just fall short with David Beckham (1999) and Eric Cantona (1993) until Cristiano Ronaldo joined an illustrious list at Old Trafford in 2008. Other Football Writers past winners for United are Johnny Carey (1949) and Bobby Charlton (1966), Cantona (1996), Keane (2000), Sheringham (2001), Ronaldo (2007, 2008) and Giggs (2009).

Plenty of publications commemorated our triumph and they have since become collectors' items. I've lost count of the number of match programmes, Wembley tickets, rosettes and books I've signed down the years. All the Christmas football annuals covered our victory along with the official club seasonal book, *The Manchester United Football Book No.3* edited by *Manchester Evening News* football writer David Meek. I had a chapter in the book titled 'We're the Cream' where I told my story up to that point in my career. Down the years since that unforgettable night I've met up with Eusebio a number of times and he always says he doesn't know how I stopped his shot but he says it with a wry smile now! And the teams have also met, most recently when United drew Benfica in the Champions League a few years ago. We had a dinner at Old Trafford and Benfica reciprocated. Both events were memorable. The circumstances surrounding our triumph will live with me forever.

7

END OF THE BUSBY ERA

Sir Matt Busby had finally achieved the 'Holy Grail' with the European Cup taking pride of place at the club but the final XI at Wembley would not line up again for a professional game. We were determined to defend the trophy on top of challenging for the championship again having gone so close the previous season. Our aspirations were no different to any of the top sides and, of course, we'd also be playing for the World Club Championship against Argentinean side Estudiantes. There was plenty to look forward to on returning to pre-season training.

I was now starting my third season with United in top-flight football and had won the top two honours available but I was hungry for further success. I'd also faced all the big clubs and stars of English football. For the 1968–69 season, pundits predicted Leeds United would be the team to beat and they were proved to be right. Leeds possessed players that certainly knew how to mix it. Playing uncompromising 'method' football, if Don Revie's team got a goal ahead they would shut up shop rather than go for the jugular, which was the United way of playing football. Leeds adopted time-wasting European tactics like no team before and while it brought success it generated ill feeling among other clubs' supporters. Labelled 'Dirty Leeds' by the media for a number of seasons, it was a shame because Leeds had players with tremendous skill. But in a era when every team had a hard man Revie's Leeds possessed a fair few. Billy Bremner, Johnny Giles and Bobby's 'kid' brother Jack Charlton knew how to make their presence felt but of the side the one that got stuck in most was Norman Hunter. When Hunter tackled, opponents knew about it but he was not alone because Tottenham had Dave Mackay, Liverpool had Tommy Smith, Chelsea had Ron Harris and we had Nobby Stiles. For me the only side that didn't include a so-called hard nut was West Ham.

Games against Leeds were tough but there was also great respect and rivalry between the players. And it was the same with Liverpool. With their solid defence based around Ron Yeats and Tommy Smith not many teams prospered at Anfield but you had to have a go. My favourite games were always against Tottenham because both sides wanted to entertain. Fans looked forward to the games and were rarely disappointed. Before my time there had been two famous 5–1 matches featured on *Match of the Day* (in 1965–66) that have gone down in TV folklore with each side winning one of the clashes. As for my favourite ground there was nothing like playing at Highbury on a Wednesday night against Arsenal because it was such a compact stadium. Arsenal were a top team and when United were in town we knew the atmosphere would be electric. Opposition supporters always gave us gyp. City fans were the noisiest and gave me plenty of stick but I loved the banter and especially with the Liverpool Kop. They'd applaud as I jogged to goal but when my cap and gloves were in the back of the net the comments would start. Some smart alec usually made a wisecrack such as, 'Stepney, you so and so!', but it was never malicious so I became used to it and it never put me off.

Beginning the league campaign it was great to have Denis Law back in the side. We claimed a home win over Everton but our form soon proved to be inconsistent. Carlo Sartori had come through the United ranks, making his debut in October and Matt entered the transfer market after John Aston broke a leg in the third match at Manchester City. A 4–0 drubbing at home to Chelsea soon followed and the match coincided with the arrival of winger Willie Morgan from Burnley for £117,000. A talented winger, Willie was dubbed as possibly being another Bestie as he had the Beatle-style haircut and snazzy dress sense. That was ridiculous because he was not in the same league. Willie had great ball skills and was dangerous on the wing but was no George Best, although he was a shrewd signing and would make his mark when he moved into midfield.

After the Chelsea defeat, we bounced back against Tottenham at home before losing a nine-goal thriller at Sheffield Wednesday 5–4. With pressure building domestically United had opted out of the League Cup again as we embarked on our European Cup run against League of Ireland side Waterford. Such was the interest in the game, Waterford switched the opening leg to the home of Irish international rugby, Lansdowne Road. Waterford wanted to cash in on a capacity crowd and easily sold out. United had massive support in Ireland and Matt had benefited from his scouting system that included Billy Whelan, Johnny Giles and Tony Dunne. As a contest Waterford were no match. The Lawman missed a penalty but was on fire, hitting a hat-trick in a 3–1 win before scoring four more in the return leg to seal a comfortable 10–2 aggregate triumph. The loudest cheer though was reserved for Waterford's goal at Old Trafford and for Al Casey it was a moment to savour.

In between the two Waterford games we played the opening leg in the World Club Championship tie against Estudiantes. We were looking forward to the two-legged affair and hoped to go a step further than Celtic who lost a bitter clash against Argentinean side River Plate a year earlier. That match ended in controversy due to roughhouse tactics used by the Argentinean side. There was plenty of talk about whether we should play in the challenge match against Estudiantes. It was two years since the World Cup when Argentina captain Antonio Rattin was sent off in controversial fashion against England in a quarterfinal clash at Wembley. On that occasion, Alf Ramsey had described the Argentinean team as 'animals'. The aftermath left a bitter taste in Argentina and there was a concern the game would offer a chance of revenge, especially as Stiles and Charlton, who featured in the World Cup game, would be playing. The Argentinean media was no friend of English football and we should have known what to expect when Nobby was dubbed 'El Bandido', referring to his World Cup exploits. It was also clear he'd be targeted when our interpreter informed us the match programme described him as a 'brutal and a bad sportsman'. Now Nobby was many things especially a tough tackler but questioning his sportsmanship on the park was going too far.

Our Argentina trek began immediately after we defeated Newcastle United at home, Bestie (2) and Law scoring in a 3–1 win. We flew from Ringway Airport to Buenos Aires via London, Paris, Madrid and then faced a 10-hour onward flight to Rio de Janeiro. To say we were jet-lagged on arrival was an understatement. We stayed at a fabulous complex on the outskirts of the city called the Hindu Club comprising two golf courses, 24-lane bowling alley and tennis courts. Security was tight and we had a police escort everywhere we went. We trained at the Boca Juniors Stadium. Buenos Aires itself resembled Mexico City but whereas there was a mass of slums in Mexico, as I'd discover on England duty, here there were slums on one side of road with mansions on the other. The contrast was incredible. On the eve of the game both teams and media were scheduled to attend a cocktail party at Boca's ground after training. It was not our usual build up to a game but we felt obliged to attend even though we were suffering jet lag, as Estudiantes had arranged it. Then news came through that our opponents would not be attending. Matt made our apologies and we returned, somewhat miffed, to our hotel. We later heard that the Estudiantes players and directors had a row over bonus payments and refused to go. At the time though it seemed like an attempt to sabotage our build up.

The main stand in the stadium ran down the full length of pitch and was set as boxes. It resembled pigeonholes but with people in them. The rest of the ground had a moat around with fencing to keep fans off the pitch. Come the gameday, armed police with tear gas were out in force. You could sense a tense atmosphere in the crowd built up by the media. Walking around the pitch beforehand supporters glared at us; the hatred was palpable. I felt that things might erupt at any point. The atmosphere was intimidating but in the dressing room there was a real steely determination to win through. Matt made it clear we had to walk away from trouble. He told us to keep our heads and not get intimidated. We had to play our natural game, be strong and play the way we played best. We knew it would be tough. Making our way from the dressing room we waited in a tunnel under the ground. The entry on to the pitch was from behind the goal through a caged entrance and stood by entrance was Antonio Rattin with a coat over his shoulder snarling at us. Following Bobby onto the pitch, I'd never experienced a reception like it. The noise, red smoke bombs and firecrackers going off were incredible.

In an extraordinary atmosphere, from the first whistle, Estudiantes tore into us. I'd never played against a dirtier team. Targeting anyone in a red shirt the opposition players kicked, spat and went in late for every challenge. Estudiantes were not interested in playing football and there was no help from the referee who seemed incapable of controlling the game. Throughout an intimidating half, Bestie had to take evasive action from flying tackles, as did Charlton, Law and Stiles. At half time we trailed by a goal when I misread the flight of a Ramon Veron corner for Conigliaro to score. Matt told us to keep our heads to stay in the game for the return at Old Trafford. But it was tough, and especially so when we went down to 10 men after Nobby, totally frustrated with events on the pitch, was sent off after gesturing at a linesman after being ruled offside. The incident summed up the game for Nobby who had been battered with no support from a hapless referee who refused us a blatant penalty, although he was proved correct by TV replays to disallow a Sadler goal. No further goals were scored and the only positive outcome from the game was that we didn't suffer any serious injuries. There was no post-match reception so it was a case of bring on the return.

We had a long trek home but the Football Association had allowed us to postpone the Saturday fixture. By the return fixture we'd made the European Cup second round but our form was poor in the league, drawing against North London rivals Arsenal and Tottenham, and losing at Liverpool. Because of the antics employed by Estudiantes there was a lot of media coverage and we were fired up for the second leg. Estudiantes received the reception they deserved when they ran out at Old Trafford but silenced the crowd early on when poor defending enabled them to extend the aggregate lead from a breakaway goal by Veron. We equalised on the night through Morgan but could not force another goal. Estudiantes did play more football than in the home clash and were not as dirty but adopted every 'legal' way of wasting time through obstruction, shirt tugging and playing keep ball. Estudiantes came with a plan and carried it out to perfection. And late on Bestie was sent off after retaliating to an incident involving Hugo Medina. At the full time whistle, I was so frustrated I stepped out of line for the one and only time in my career. Running off from the Stretford End, I was incensed, especially at captain Bilardo who had been one of the dirtiest players in the two-legged affair. He had a massive grin on his face as if nothing had happened and as he tried to shake hands with the lads in the tunnel I caught him with a beauty. It was a split second of madness, and back in the dressing room I calmed down. Unfortunately a TV camera had recorded the incident. Matt didn't say a word but next morning after my picture was splashed across the sports pages I was summoned to his office. I was in hot water.

Arriving at Old Trafford the press was waiting but 'No comment' was my response. Entering Matt's office, I didn't sit down. Puffing on his pipe, Matt asked what I was thinking of and I tried to explain but he stopped me in my tracks.

'Son, how do you think Jimmy Murphy and I felt sitting on the sides watching the treatment being dished out to the lads, and how do you think the board of directors felt, the groundsman, laundry ladies, apprentices and thousands of United supporters? In football, whatever the provocation, control is essential. As I always say, lose your heads, you lose the match.'

I'd let the club down. My behaviour was unacceptable for a Manchester United player. I received a £50 fine and was told if I ever repeated such behaviour I'd never play for United again. I accepted my punishment and apologised. Matt escorted me to my car where hacks were waiting to hear the outcome of my disciplinary meeting. Matt said, 'Gentlemen, have you met my first team goalkeeper Alex Stepney?' From feeling three feet tall I instantly felt 10 feet tall as I drove off. The press boys looked downbeat as there was no story. I departed having learnt a valuable lesson. Whatever the intimidation, more was expected from me as a United player. And looking back, it was fantastic man-management. What could have dragged on was over in a flash. I was wrong and the way Matt dealt with the situation was superb, not just with the press but by putting me in my place and raising me up again with a few choice words.

Just seven league wins by the New Year put immense pressure on the club and it was clear that Matt was feeling the heat. He looked under pressure every time I saw him and the strain was clearly beginning to tell, especially with United being the biggest name in British football. The media seemed relentless in speculating who would be dropped or arriving at the club and of course, nothing has changed, but when you are a United player it becomes more difficult to perform as each poor performance or point dropped appears to be magnified.

The one piece of good news was that we'd made it into the European Cup quarterfinals after overcoming Belgium champions Anderlecht. But it had been a close call. Bestie was absent from the tie following his sending off against Estudiantes and Morgan was ineligible to play. With doubts over Denis's knee still in the background we had to be on our A-game elsewhere. In the opening leg at home I had to make a smart save early on to deny Devrindt before Kiddo opened the scoring. The Lawman sealed the match with two goals. Going into the return leg we had a number of injuries to contend with but felt we had a cushion to progress and when

Sartori gave us an early lead it seemed that his first senior goal had settled the tie. But the goal had a strange effect as Anderlecht suddenly relaxed and with nothing to play for but pride, tore into us. Mulder and Bergholz with a brace scored to put us on the back foot and we only just held on for 4–3 aggregate win. It had been mighty close and Carlo had come up trumps in what proved a tricky tie.

Just two league wins between December and February meant a lean time for us. Both wins were at home, against Liverpool when Denis struck the only goal, and versus Sunderland when a Law hat-trick did the damage. The poor form had seen us slip just above the relegation zone. With the league out of reach as Leeds powered to the title, breaking a host of records on the way, the double of FA Cup and European Cup was still on in terms of trophy success. Law was on song with another hat-trick as we thumped Birmingham City 6–2 in a FA Cup fifth round replay to set up a quarterfinal clash with Everton. And Rapide Vienna were also awaiting us in the European Cup last eight. Rapide were the surprise team from the previous round as they had knocked out Real Madrid. And on a special night at Old Trafford we took the lead just before half time through Best. Morgan had been involved in the build up for the first goal and got on the scoresheet with our second. Nobby Stiles set up Bestie to complete the win.

Before the second leg we faced Everton at home in the FA Cup but any chance of glory vanished in a moment of madness when I was to blame for a scrappy goal. Young centre-back Steve James, who had just come into the side as a possible future replacement for Foulkes, was also at fault but as the senior player I should have taken responsibility when a hopeful ball was pumped into the box. Steve and I were caught ball watching and in a split second of indecisiveness, Joe Royle snapped up a simple chance to put his side into the semi-finals. Back in the dressing room I felt particularly low due to my madcap moment. If we had gone through we'd have played City in the last four, which would have been some derby while West Brom took on relegation bound Leicester City. But there was no time to feel low as we departed for the Rapide return leg. On route I had a heart to heart with Matt as I felt my place was under scrutiny. Our form was scratchy but my schoolboy error against Everton had not helped. But Matt did what he was best at which was to fill a player with confidence. His words of wisdom helped me focus on preserving our lead against Rapide because we did not want a repeat of the Anderlecht comeback in the last round. And at the Prater Stadium, Bestie was on fire and while we failed to score we also did not concede so we were through comfortably on aggregate.

I was delighted to keep a clean sheet. Like strikers who feel pressure when goals dry up, so goalkeepers feels pressure when goals are flying in. Unlike strikers who can win a game, keepers have nowhere to hide when a goal goes in so in my opinion the feeling is more intense. You feel incredibly vulnerable but all you can do is play through and hope the ball begins to stick. I just had to knuckle down. We were through again to the European Cup semi-finals and drew Italian giants AC Milan with the first leg at the San Siro Stadium but first it was back to league action and a 1–0 defeat at home to City did put any thoughts of playing Milan on the back foot. A draw at Everton and defeat at Chelsea kept the pressure on but finally there was a major boost when we thumped Queens Park Rangers 8–1 at Old Trafford in a rearranged midweek clash. Morgan grabbed a hat-trick while Bestie notched two goals and the result set us on a mini-revival over the Easter period with three more victories including a double over Nottingham

Forest. But our injury jinx struck again when Dunne broke his jaw at West Ham. And with Francis Burns and Brennan also out injured, Stiles and Fitzpatrick played as emergency cover at full-back, which was not ideal. Our league status had improved but Matt decided my form was suffering so following a defeat at Coventry City dropped me for the first time since I'd joined the club. I'd miss a massive European night against Milan. Jimmy Rimmer was in. I was distraught but had to accept the decision. Matt also decided to bring Foulkes back for James, which surprised me because they were contradictory decisions. I had more experience than Jimmy but was dropped yet Bill had more experience than Steve James and was in. Whatever my feelings the decisions had been made but they backfired as little went right for United at the San Siro. Milan exposed Bill's mobility against Brazilian striker Angelo Sormani but he was not at fault when Sormani took the ball with his hand before firing home. We felt aggrieved but the lads continued to battle away. Unfortunately we fell further behind when Kurt Hamrin fired home a terrific goal just after the interval. With fire crackers going off the tension increased and suddenly exploded when Hamrin punched Fitzpatrick who retaliated. Both were sent off.

In the return at Old Trafford again I was a spectator. From the outset United bombarded Milan but we faced the masters of defence and could not penetrate an impregnable back line in the first half. Adept at breaking up the rhythm of a game, time wasting was their forte and Milan succeeded in frustrating us. Things reached a peak when keeper Cudicini signalled to the ref that a missile from the crowd had hit him. United fans were incensed and I agreed. Cudicini was playacting as he theatrically collapsed in a heap. Over the years I'd been hit by all sorts . . . penny coins, apples, pebbles and cans, but I never reacted as if heavyweight champion

Muhammad Ali had hit me! Cudicini, not surprisingly, continued after treatment but Milan continued to wind down the clock until Bestie jinked past an opponent to set up Charlton for one of his specials. The ball almost burst the back of the net. Another goal would force a play off in Brussels and a chance to play Dutch champions Ajax led by Johan Cruyff, who was beginning to make a name for himself on the European stage. And we looked to have bagged an equalising goal from a goal mouth scramble but French referee, Marcel Machin, ruled it out. Law was convinced his touch from Crerand's chip had crossed the line but the ref was having none of it. Morgan was closest and felt a defender cleared the ball when it was over the line into his grateful keeper's hands. Willie could have smashed the ball home but didn't. Television replays show we were robbed but there was no comeback as we exited 2–1 on aggregate. The European dream was over and the United dressing room was a despondent place. The result heralded big changes as the Busby era ended.

Early in the New Year, Matt made it known he wanted to 'ease up' and in reality, after winning the European Cup, we knew it would not be long before someone took over his legacy. During the close season early rumours suggested Celtic boss, Jock Stein, was in the frame and he certainly had standing in the game but nothing materialised. A special character was needed because Matt had been the central figure at Manchester United for so many years. United had to move forward and speculation continued. Everyone knew about the Liverpool 'Bootroom' where succession planning took place. And in years to come Bob Paisley would supersede the work of Shanks. The Liverpool philosophy possibly swayed the United board because after much speculation, reserve team trainer Wilf McGuinness was appointed our new manager.

McGuinness's appointment was surprising at the time as he was only 32 years of age. It did not make sense. He was simply too inexperienced for such an important job and I have not changed my viewpoint all these years later.

Manchester United were a massive club and needed a manager who could manage big name characters. Wilf was in his early 30s, had guided United's youth and reserve teams but did not have the right credentials. United did not need someone who had not yet cut his management teeth but if they were to go down that route then I belonged to the school of thought that considered former United skipper Noel Cantwell, who had served his managerial apprenticeship at Coventry City, to be a sound shout. Noel was on the books when I joined, had the players' respect and knew the United way of playing but it was not to be, as out of the blue the board appointed McGuinness. Openly there was no dissension. We'd give Wilf our support but my misgivings were soon evident. On the park, the season petered out and we finished 11th, a poor result after recent seasons. I knew, approaching the new decade, that it would be a period of transition as the European Cup winning side broke up.

Alan Mullery
Tottenham Hotspur and England

Alex was a great goalkeeper, good for a laugh before and after a game but always a serious 'keeper.

One match I always recall was at Old Trafford in 1967 when Spurs (FA Cup winners) played United (League Division 1 champions) in the Charity Shield. Pat Jennings scored a freak goal for us that I remember as if it was yesterday. The surface was wet but whatever the weather Pat could kick the ball for miles. Collecting the ball, Pat volleyed the ball from his hands and Alex was standing near the penalty spot. As the ball bounced in the penalty area 'D' the ball went straight over Alex's head into the back of the net. Of course it was a complete fluke but even though Alex is a great mate, every time I see him I have to remind him that he is one of the few goalkeepers that another goalkeeper has scored against! It always raises a laugh.

I played alongside Alex when he won his England cap against Sweden and the record books show that it's still the last time we beat them. Alex was unlucky as he played at a time when England had four top class goalkeepers. In fact, when we went to the World Cup in 1970 there was Gordon Banks, Peter Bonetti, Peter Shilton and Alex in the original 28-man squad. When you think of those keepers, blimey, they were all terrific. Banksy, because of the 1966 World Cup, held the number one spot but I've always said that if Alex had played instead of Peter against West Germany in the quarterfinals he would not have been as nervous when Peter got the call to play.

Playing for Spurs against Manchester United was always a huge game. Arsenal was the biggest game for Spurs but when we went to Old Trafford or United came to White Hart Lane they were fantastic matches. I remember beating United at our place 5–1 early on in the 1965–66 season when all our forwards scored. Two months later we went to Manchester and were beaten by the same score. They were great games to play in but when you think of the talent in the side during that era it's not surprising. Spurs and United had fantastic 'keepers in Pat and Alex, then when you looked around there were the likes of Mackay, Gilzean and Greaves for Spurs while United had Charlton, Best, Herd, Law and Nobby Stiles. It was always going to be entertaining.

As a 'keeper Alex was great at coming out to get balls quite easily and the only person who also did that over the years was Pat. Whenever I meet Alex there is good-natured stick. Recently at a golf day at The Belfry he told me that his handicap had gone up as he's only playing four days a week instead of six! That is Alex; we always have a laugh. On an England trip one time Spurs and United had reached the League Cup semi-finals. Alex asked me what our bonus was for winning the Cup it if we met in the final. I told him £750 a man. Alex looked at me shocked. 'Alan, you must me mad, go in and sort it out. We're on at least two grand a man!' Alex was always great at winding me up and the banter was terrific.

Joining up for England games we became good pals and when Spurs played United before a game many a time we'd chat in the car park. During the game of course, I did everything I could to win but after the game we'd have a beer together. And that's what it was all about in that era. There was great camaraderie.

8

TRIPLE CUP
HEARTACHE

With the World Cup around the corner pre-season training for the 1969–70 season started early to give Alf Ramsey's squad extra preparation time for the finals in Mexico. Naturally, I was hopeful of making the final squad as one of three keepers to make the trip but my first task was to get back into first team action before the summer footballing fiesta when Brazilian stars Pele, Rivelino, Gerson, Carlos Alberto and Jairzinho would be lining up for the pre-tournament favourites.

I was on the sidelines when the Division 1 campaign started in earnest. Wilf McGuinness selected Jimmy Rimmer and it was a real body blow. Except for the FA Cup, I'd won the biggest prizes club football had to offer. I only wanted to play for United but playing for the reserve team was not my idea of professional football. I had to bide my time. Probably I'd become a shade complacent, thinking my first team spot was automatic. Being dropped shook me out of any complacency. My return to the first team came quicker than I expected. Two defeats in the opening three games included a 4–1 loss at Southampton. Rimmer had been caught out with crosses and I was back in the first team. The Saints match however was a game of significance as it signalled time for our colossus in defence Bill Foulkes, who joined the backroom staff as reserve team assistant, while McGuinness also dropped Charlton and Law. The shockwaves resulted in Law being placed on the transfer list at £60,000 but Charlton was quickly back as skipper for our trip to Molineux that saw the debut of Ian Ure who had been signed from Arsenal. A rugged centre-back, Ure was an experienced pro but his best days were behind him. Ure was only ever going to be no more than a stop-gap. Draws with Wolves and Newcastle United meant six games without a league win and McGuinness's start as boss was proving to be a tough baptism.

The European Cup team was a distant memory with Brennan out of favour, Foulkes retired and Dunne, Stiles and Aston all injured. McGuinness was looking for balance but instead his appointment had coincided with our worst start for 16 seasons. Any honeymoon period he had was now gone as reporters noted when United had last made a similar start to a campaign it saw the emergence of a young Bill Foulkes! Ure had bolstered the defence as an initial successor to Foulkes alongside Sadler with Nobby sidelined. Paul Edwards had briefly appeared in defence but none stayed in the line up for any time longer than a short run of games. Our form needed a boost and after finally getting off the mark in the league when we defeated another North East team, Sunderland, we made it a double as my first club game in the League Cup for United ended in victory as we scraped past Middlesbrough. With confidence slowly returning we gained a great 2–2 draw at defending league champions Leeds United before overcoming Liverpool, courtesy of a Morgan strike, and Sheffield Wednesday. Another 2–2 draw, this time at Arsenal, was followed up by a 5–2 romp at home to West Ham. And by the New Year we'd made our way to mid-table security, which at the time was the best we could hope for but far from what United fans expected or deserved.

Our participation in the League Cup had seen us set attendance records in early rounds as we defeated Wrexham, Burnley and Derby County. And the semi-final draw pitched us against Manchester City, which was a shame as both clubs hoped there might be a Wembley showdown, an occasion that all Mancunians are still waiting to see as it would be some occasion. But this was the first all-Manchester semi-final. The atmosphere was cracking for the first leg at Maine Road and we ran out smarting as City had thumped us in a league clash 4–0 a couple of weeks earlier. We knew this would be a different ball game but suffered a setback early on when Colin Bell opened the scoring after a determined run by Francis Lee. We regrouped and equalised through Charlton in the second half. Bobby was bossing midfield with Nobby, getting back to his best after being out for six months, and we were unlucky not to edge the tie. But City won 2–1 with a disputed penalty by Lee. In the heat of the moment as we left the pitch, Bestie ended up in hot water for a spot of petulance when he kicked the ball out of the referee's hands. The incident resulted in a suspension for Bestie but not until after the return and we came into the game buoyed by a 4–1 win at Liverpool.

Old Trafford was buzzing, but in front of another massive League Cup crowd I was at fault when City opened the scoring. Failing to take a Lee shot cleanly; Ian Bowyer had a simple task of scoring. Bestie set up Law for a goal on a rare first team appearance and Edwards brought us level on aggregate but I had a rush of madness that cost us dearly when I failed to spot the ref signal an indirect free kick to City. Instead of letting Lee's shot go into the net I parried it and Mike Summerbee scored what proved to be the winner. Losing a cup semi is always tough but this was especially so as lady luck had been against us and me in particular during both games. When City were awarded the free kick outside the box, as usual I started lining up the wall but was concentrating so hard to get my angles right that I did not see a signal from the referee behind the wall. I received justifiable stick in the media but felt the ref should have made his signal clearer. For the incident to happen in such an important game was so disappointing. On the night we simply did not get the breaks. Bestie also had a goal ruled out for offside, which summed up our cup luck. The League Cup did not have the razzmatazz or standing of the FA Cup but playing at Wembley is always an occasion. Missing out on another trip to the Twin Towers was really tough. This was my first semi-final defeat and it was a dreadful feeling. I'm still jibed about the free kick by City fans but I guess that's part of the crack. City went on to defeat West Brom at Wembley as they continued their purple patch of trophy success having won the league and FA Cup in recent seasons. The rivalry with City during this period was fantastic although it pains me to say the blue half of Manchester would enjoy even more trophy success that season with the European Cup Winners Cup arriving at Maine Road. Their successes just spurred us on more.

Rivalries aside, City had a great team but they have not come close since that season while United have dominated proceedings for three decades. Back in the late sixties and early seventies, City were a top side and all the lads from both teams got on. We're still good pals. Book, Pardoe, Summerbee, Lee, Bell and Doyle . . . all the City lads were fantastic. And we went drinking with Malcom Allison! There was never any problem with the City boys. It was a golden era and we had some terrific battles. Having two strong teams in Manchester was good for the game. Bestie and Summerbee even ran a business together. While I always like to see United get the better of the derby each season, a strong City team is good for English football. In the modern era, games against Chelsea, Liverpool and Arsenal tend to be more important to the current generation of players while for supporters a derby will always be special. Loyalties have been passed through generations of families and as they say, once a Red or a Blue always a Red or a Blue. There was always great respect among the clubs and one tradition I always appreciated at Maine Road—after climbing off the coach to a chorus of boos—was Albert Alexander, City chairman, dropping in to the away dressing room to wish us good luck for the game. It was something Albert carried on until he retired and it was a fantastic gesture in the heat of a derby clash.

The League Cup loss to City made us all the more determined to have an FA Cup run and after accounting for Ipswich Town, we gained solace for our League Cup exit to City by knocking them out of the 'premier' cup competition. Bestie returned from suspension to grab the national headlines with a six-goal display as we hammered Northampton Town 8–2. 'Six of the Best' was the common theme on the Sunday. Middlesbrough failed to stop us in a quarterfinal replay at Old Trafford when Morgan grabbed the winner. And in the midst of our cup run there was a further celebration at home following the birth of our second son, Paul. In the semi-finals we drew Leeds United and proceeded to have three titanic clashes that are still recalled today by supporters. Leeds were going for an unprecedented treble at the time. Only Everton could halt them in the league and Celtic stood between them and a European Cup final.

With only the FA Cup to concentrate on we really fancied our chances and we should have won the Hillsborough semi. Leeds had the opening chance but I managed to thwart Mick Jones. After that scare though, we dominated midfield with Carlo Sartori stopping Leeds skipper Billy Bremner in his tracks. Charlton and Crerand pushed us forward at every opportunity and with more clinical finishing Sartori and Best could have put the game out of sight. In the second half Leeds tightened up and created the better openings. Allan Clarke went closest but I just got to his header in time. Clarke had joined Leeds from Leicester City. Nicknamed Sniffer for his ability to snap up chances, Clarke was fast becoming one of the most clinical strikers around.

Before the replay at Villa Park, Bestie caused a storm. Bless him, George was not the greatest when it came to resting before a big game but even he overstepped the mark when he spent the afternoon prior to the FA Cup clash with a lady friend at our pre-match base. A number of the lads knew what was happening because she was quickly sent packing but soon returned. McGuinness was weak—after a quick ticking off Bestie had a 'mare. George was a genius but there is a time and place for relaxation and Busby would not have allowed the situation to happen. The incident proved to me that McGuinness was out of his depth. Despite the incident the match was a better tie. Again we should have scored in the first half but Kiddo missed an open goal inside the first few minutes as the ball zipped off the wet surface and Bestie missed a great opportunity when clean through. Stiles, who had battled back to fitness, also went close with a shot cleared off the line by Jack Charlton but it was not one way traffic as Clarke had a goal chalked off for a push and I denied his strike partner Jones and also Eddie Gray. Extra time brought more thrills and Law almost stole the winner when he entered the fray as a sub late on but was just wide.

It was now a case of third time lucky but it was decidedly unlucky for us as Bremner fired home early on to score the only goal of the second replay at Burden Park. Leeds formed an iron defence after the goal and we just could not find a way through, so for the second time in the campaign I had to contemplate a semi-final defeat. They say you only appreciate a winning semi-final dressing room when you have experienced a losing one and I can vouch for that. Losing a semi-final is the worst feeling. This was my first FA Cup semi and it was heart breaking not to make it to Wembley. Winning the FA Cup was a childhood dream so I was devastated. I never thought for one moment we'd lose to Leeds and it really hurt. At the time you think you'll never get another chance and it would be years before the opportunity arose for me again.

Fortunately I'd experience the right result before the end of my career at United. Whenever I see the Leeds lads they remind me of the ties as we battled away in three unbelievable games. Supporters loved the blood and thunder that ensued but I'm glad to see that the days of playing till a winner comes through are long gone. Although supporters revel in the action, which is unrelenting, as a player it was tough both mentally and physically even though we loved being involved in such encounters. So a season that started out with high hopes ended in double cup semi heartache.

The remainder of the season had an anti-climatic feel about it, which was summed up by a crowd of well under 30,000 attending our penultimate home game of the season when we thumped West Brom 7–0. We eventually finished eighth so missed out on a Fairs Cup spot by one place but the campaign was remembered for losing out in two semi-finals. The fixture congestion top teams went through at times was ridiculous. We experienced it and so did Leeds that season because it ultimately cost them the treble as the condensed campaign, due to the impending World Cup, meant no reward for them at all.

Cup upsets aside, the atmosphere amongst the players at Old Trafford was not right under McGuinness. Succeeding Matt was nigh on impossible, even more so because Matt was still at the club in a General Manager capacity. Getting the balance right between promoting from within while Matt's influence was still present was no easy task. The manager had to have a strong personality and be able to make difficult decisions. Although tactically astute, Wilf struggled with the disciplinary side in particular and did not have a charismatic character.

I found his decision making weak and felt particularly aggrieved at the end of the season when he refused my request to travel down early to London the day before we were due to play a pointless encounter on the eve of the FA Cup final between Leeds and Chelsea. The game was between losing FA Cup semi-finalists and played against Watford at Highbury to determine third and fourth place. These matches only took place for a short period and have, thankfully, been scrapped since. I had valid reasons but McGuinness assumed I was attending an annual football writer's dinner when in fact I was taking my family to London where they'd be for the summer while I was at the World Cup. McGuinness never gave me a chance to explain. Totally frustrated, I went behind his back to Matt who I still called 'boss' as I knew he'd sort things out, which he did. Wilf grudgingly gave me permission but our relationship was strained. I wasn't happy about my actions but had no choice. For the record, United defeated Watford 2–0 but it meant nothing. Wilf, in my view, was out of his depth and I doubted he'd be around much longer.

My thoughts now focused on Mexico and making England's World Cup squad. Twelve months before the tournament we had been there on a post-season tour. An England B Team defeated a Mexico XI in Guadalajara before the full side beat Uruguay in Montevideo 2–1 and then lost by the same score in the toughest of games against Brazil at the Maracana Stadium. The trip was a success as we tasted challenging playing conditions. I was thrilled to be in the initial 40-strong squad for Mexico where we would face Brazil, Romania and Czechoslovakia in our group games. All the lads have tales about playing under Sir Alf Ramsey. A disciplinarian, when Alf said curfew was such a time then it was and if he told you to be at a team meeting, at training or a pre-match meal then you were. Alf did not stand on ceremony with the players or the media and we had the utmost respect for him. It was an era with very few agents or distractions from the media boys. The squad had an inner strength and belief that we could go all the way. It was fantastic to be a part of it. None of the lads spoke badly about Alf. He was a top manager and knew how to handle world class players. England were a top side feared by other nations.

Altitude was the great worry in our preparations as players could be caught short of breath playing at 5,212 feet at the Jalisco Stadium, Guadalajara. Those playing would lose around eight pounds in sweat during each game so dehydration was a big issue. The ball also tended to move around in the thin air. It was harder to judge what would occur when you struck the ball. For a keeper it was a potential problem so I had to watch the ball carefully.

Five keepers, Gordon Banks, Peter Bonetti, Peter Shilton and Jim Montgomery as well as myself, showed the strength in depth at Alf's disposal. You would not find five top class keepers of that quality today, let alone 40 players good enough to play for England. Pundits still cite the squad as the strongest assembled and first Alf had to trim the squad to 28, which included four keepers for a pre-World Cup tour in South America before the final cull to 22 for the World Cup tournament itself. We travelled out early to acclimatise and so that players could discover the final cut following games in Columbia (Bogota) and Ecuador (Quito). The 28-man squad comprised: Goalkeepers: Banks, Bonetti, Stepney and Shilton. Full-backs: Newton, Wright, McNab, Cooper and Hughes. Centre-backs: Moore, Labone, Jack Charlton, Hunter and Sadler. Midfield: Stiles, Ball, Bobby Charlton, Bell, Mullery and Peters. Forwards: Hurst, Lee, Astle, Osgood, Clarke, Kidd, Coates and Thompson.

When England won the World Cup in 1966, the 22-man squad shared £22,000 equally. In 1970, football agent Ken Stanley looked after the players' interests. Findus, Ford, Esso and BOAC all came on board. We also had a hit single, 'Back Home', by Bill Martin and Phil Coulter. The duo had written hit records including 'Puppet on a String' and 'Congratulations' so we were in lofty company. We recorded the track at Pye Studios in London and the record was a smash hit when released a couple of weeks before we flew out. 'Back Home' stayed in the charts for 16 weeks and reached the number one spot. All of a sudden we were pop stars and we appeared on *Top of the Pops* dressed in dinner suits. On coach journeys Jeff Astle would lead the singing. It was all innocent fun and we earned a bob or two along the way.

The party departed from Heathrow Airport on 4 May on board a BOAC Boeing 707 for a 14-hour flight to Mexico City 29 days before the first game with Romania. Brazil and

England were favourites to progress to the quarterfinals. Our World Cup base for the tournament would be in Guadalajara, Mexico's second largest city, 300 miles from Mexico City. After two weeks' acclimatisation we flew to Colombia and Ecuador for warm up matches. Playing at Bogota at 8,500 feet and then Quito at 9,500 feet would complete preparations for returning to Guadalajara at 5,212 feet. During the flight the lads mingled freely with the press, something unthinkable in the modern era. Journalists following our every step were Ken Jones (*Daily Mirror*), Desmond Hackett (*Daily Express*), Brain James (*Daily Mail*), Hugh McIlvanney (*The Observer*) and Geoffrey Green (*The Times*).

Alf made sure all the lads mixed to build team spirit from an early stage. Building work in the surrounding area meant the Mexican and Italian sides would be at the same hotel. Alf was not pleased but we just got on with our schedule. Everything was planned meticulously regarding flights, transport, meals, training facilities and so on. Nothing was left to chance. We even took our own supply of bottled water. Dr Neil Phillips was in charge of all things medical, making up the back up team with trainers Harold Shepherdson and Les Cocker. Heat and altitude were the key issues. The one thing Alf seemed obsessed about was the sun so he limited our time sunbathing. Our acclimatisation started at La Marquesas. Olympic marathon runners trained at the site and the air was thin. Team building consisted of cricket, darts, dominoes, cribbage and the odd round of golf at the Reforma Club. The British Embassy also took us to a rodeo, which was an experience. Training sessions took place after a short rest period. Some sessions were for the benefit of the media but the main ones were behind closed doors as we planned tactics. Training was a real eye opener when we saw that locals washed their clothes in a stream and lived in squalid conditions. This made our facilities seem palatial in comparison.

After two weeks we travelled to our warm up games. Our travel instructions made it clear not to carry much money or jewellery as pickpockets were rife. The rules were for our own good but it left a flat atmosphere as we were a crowd of young lads on an overseas trip and we wanted to enjoy ourselves. Of course it was in Bogota that Bobby Moore visited a jewellery store that would shortly have repercussions.

The effects of training at altitude were amazing. Shuttle runs are normally easy but at that height the impact was incredible. It took it out of us but we knew it would prove beneficial for the finals.

Now the squad was cut to 22 players and a meeting was arranged on a Sunday where Alf would announce who would be leaving. The likes of Banks, Moore, Charlton, Peters, Ball and Hurst knew they'd be in the squad but I was a fringe player although confident of making it along with Bonetti as we both had more experience than Peter Shilton at the time. Before the meeting though chaos ensued as my United teammate David Sadler demanded a meeting with Alf after his wife, Christine, had told him he was not in the squad. The media had mugged Alf, who under pressure from the press to get the details in the Sunday morning editions had released the final squad not taking into account the time difference. Unscrupulous reporters had rung families to get a reaction. Alf was apologetic but livid and I realised why he had such a mistrust of the press. He'd been badly let down and was upset about his error but it was too late. The damage was done. For Alf that was the final story with the media. The players to miss out in addition to David were Peter

Thompson, Ralph Coates, Bob McNab, Brian Kidd and Peter Shilton. All had the option to stay but most decided to return home.

The full England squad was officially named as follows: 1 Gordon Banks, 2 Keith Newton, 3 Terry Cooper, 4 Alan Mullery, 5 Brian Labone, 6 Bobby Moore, 7 Francis Lee, 8 Alan Ball, 9 Bobby Charlton, 10 Geoff Hurst, 11 Martin Peters, 12 Peter Bonetti, 13 Alex Stepney, 14 Tommy Wright, 15 Emlyn Hughes, 16 Nobby Stiles, 17 Jack Charlton, 18 Norman Hunter, 19 Colin Bell, 20 Peter Osgood, 21 Allan Clarke, 22 Jeff Astle. The 22-man squad journeyed to the Hilton Hotel, Guadalajara but our plans were rocked. In Quito there was no direct flight to Mexico so we had to go via Bogota and had a five-hour wait at the airport. For the intervening period Alf arranged to return to our original hotel and watch a Jimmy Stewart western. But at the hotel the police arrived and escorted Bobby Moore away for questioning over an alleged theft from a jewellery story in Bogota. While diplomats sorted out Bobby's predicament we travelled to Guadalajara. Bobby joined us later amidst rumours of a 'put up' job. All charges were dropped. However annoyed Bobby felt about the incident he showed incredible strength of character and turned out to be one of the players of the tournament.

Whilst we completed preparations, back in England the country was tuning in every day to various World Cup programmes. There had never been so much coverage of a World Cup with breakfast, lunchtime and evening updates. Nowadays it's 24–7 but in 1970 it was a novelty and football fans lapped it up. All the matches were televised and from what I was told later it was fantastic coverage with 'expert' panels giving opinions. Pundits included Jimmy Hill, Brian Clough, Derek Dougan and Malcolm Allison. A special edition of A *Question of Sport* was pre-recorded with Bobby Moore, Geoff Hurst and Alan Mullery taking on former England greats Johnny Haynes, Tom Finney and Stan Mortensen. *The Radio Times* produced a special publication and there were plenty of World Cup 1970 brochures. Of course, we were oblivious to it all at our base.

There were no surprises when Alf announced the team to face Romania at the Jalisco Stadium, the venue where we'd play all our games. Selecting the first 11 players on the official squad list, Bonetti got the nod as substitute keeper, which I expected so took my place in the stands for what proved to be a cagey affair. It was essential we didn't slip up and we sneaked a 1–0 win when Hurst scored. It was a case of job done. Alf gave the squad a night off but there was a strict 11pm curfew. We knew the ramifications as earlier in the trip, a few of the lads went over the curfew and Alf made it clear at the team meeting that if it happened again there would be no second chances. A return flight home would be the outcome.

The whole squad were soon back at the stadium to watch Brazil take on Czechoslovakia and they were impressive in a 4–1 win. Pele particularly was on song and the world's greatest player even had the audacity to chip the keeper from the halfway line. He only just missed! Next up for England were Brazil for a midday clash and a match the media had been waiting for since the draw was made. Training went well and Alf announced that the England XI would be the team that finished against Romania. That meant Wright was in for Newton who had failed to overcome an injury. It also seemed that Osgood would start instead of Lee but Alf had made an error and let Peter know at the end of training. He was visibly upset and Moore had to have a quiet word with Alf.

A capacity crowd of 72,000 made their way expectantly to

the stadium where, unlike our opening game, the atmosphere would be electric for a match between the last two winners of the competition. In the dressing room the lads not selected carried out the run-around duties of getting tie ups and cigarettes for the lads that needed a last minute drag. The good news for us was that Gerson was out injured. Gerson was a danger and Paulo Cesar would deputise but he was some deputy! Before kick off Alf gave his last minute instructions and they were simple, 'Don't lose possession, play keep-ball because in the heat it will prove crucial as the game wears on. Patience is the key and then take your chances when they come'. When the lads walked out the temperature was 98 degrees. By the end of the match it would be over 100 degrees.

The events of the match have been well documented with the first half memorable for Banks's amazing save from Pele's header. It was incredible because it looked a goal all the way before Gordon somehow scooped the ball over the bar. I could only marvel at Banks's agility. At half time we had more than been in the game but Brazil got the vital breakthrough on the hour when a slick move saw Jairzinho strike. Banks had no chance. Bell came on for Charlton and Astle for Lee as we searched for an equaliser. In the stands all I could think of was 'Just give us one clear chance', that's all you ask for against a side like Brazil. And that chance came when Cooper played a ball into the box that the Brazilian defence made a hash of but Astle with an open goal wasted the chance. With that our opportunity of a result disappeared. We had a couple of strikes at goal but Astle had the opening that mattered. At the end Pele and Moore exchanged shirts in what has become an iconic moment of the game. There was despondency in the dressing room although in defeat we received more praise than when we had won against

Romania but the lads had no points to show for their efforts. It was now down to the last game against Czechoslovakia, who were all but out as they had lost to Romania 2–1. A win over the Czech team, who had nothing but pride to play for, meant we would be in the quarterfinals.

With Brazil defeating Romania 3–2, England had to avoid defeat against Czechoslovakia. And prior to the game we watched West Germany defeat Peru on the TV. Avoiding a loss in our final game would mean a quarterfinal clash against West Germany in Leon. Alf, as expected, rested a few players after the exertions against Brazil. Newton returned to the side at full-back, Jack Charlton came in for Labone at centre-back but surprisingly Bobby Charlton was not rested. His appearance took him level with Billy Wright for all time England appearances. Ball was rested and Bell came in, whilst in attack Clarke and Astle replaced Hurst and Lee. At a half full Jaliso Stadium the first half was a disjointed affair that brought no goals but we were in control. And early in the second half Clarke scored from the penalty spot to relieve any tension that was building. Ball and Osgood replaced Bobby Charlton and Astle. There were few chances but we were through to the quarterfinals thanks to Clarke's goal.

England versus West Germany was the pick of the quarterfinal matches on the coming Sunday. The winner would face Italy or Mexico in the semi-finals. On the other side of the draw Brazil faced Peru while Russia faced Uruguay with the winners meeting for a final place. After a light training session a couple of days before the West Germany clash the squad went to a TV studio to watch the Germans in action to complete our preparations. As no hotel was available until the following afternoon (Saturday) we were allowed to chill out at the Guadalajara Country Club.

Lots of managers and players from the First Division were at the finals relaxing. Also present were the wives of Moore, Hurst, Peters and Bonetti courtesy of sponsors. The 'wives' situation since our arrival in Mexico had resulted in some resentment from a number of the players but Alf could do nothing about it as his own wife was at the finals. At times there was plenty of mickey-taking by some lads especially when they made phone calls to 'check in' with their wives. Visits were limited but joking apart it caused unease as many lads saw it as a 'perk'. It's been documented Bonetti was agitated at times and for me, Peter was not mentally prepared for a game but it was not for me to say. Alf was manager and he was in constant contact with all the players. After the finals Alf noted the wives issue was his biggest mistake. Nowadays of course 'Team England' would handle this situation with appropriate accommodation. Back in 1970 though we were trailblazers.

Throughout the tournament, one or two of the lads had suffered with the 'runs' but it just seemed like a 24-hour bug. The backroom staff had been meticulous over our diet and from what we heard, the England squad fared better than most teams. In the build up to the West Germany game roommates Newton and Bobby Charlton had complained about feeling off. And 24 hours later their other roommate Banks had come down with a bug but by the Saturday morning at breakfast appeared to be on the mend. We then faced a 150-mile journey to Leon where we were scheduled to train at the Guanajuato Stadium that afternoon. During the journey though Gordon was not well again. Dr Phillips gave him some medication and asked me to stay with him. Arriving at the The Motel Estancia across the road from the Guanajuato Stadium the Doc and I had to escort Gordon to the chalet we'd be sharing. There was real concern and local journalists soon cottoned on but an official press release just said Banks was feeling unwell.

The Bulgarian side had previously stayed at the motel but it was not a patch on The Hilton. Looking back it was crazy the FA had not taken into account that we might have finished runners-up in our group behind Brazil and consequently had not pre-booked a hotel, unlike the German FA who had been nicely settled for the weekend. While they relaxed all day before the game we were trekking across a desert. The German wives and girlfriends were also staying at our hotel. The planning was shambolic. Even the press was caught out because a number ended up at a local monastery. Whether it went against us in the final analysis is difficult to tell but there was no question over which side was more rested on the day of the match . . . and it was not England.

While Gordon rested, the remainder of the squad trained at the stadium but we were delighted to see Banksie feeling better in the evening. There was plenty of speculation in the media what the side would be but the general consensus was that Alf would revert to the Brazil line up. The only debate was whether Clarke may retain his place or if Osgood would come in for Lee who seemed to be struggling in the heat. After a reasonable night, Gordon seemed fine as we went to breakfast and was named in the side at the pre-match meeting. Alf selected what he considered his strongest XI. Bonetti was again on the bench. I went to the chalet for my camera before going to the stadium with the other squad players not involved but quickly realised Gordon was in a bad way. I called Doc Philips. Alf came quickly as well with Harold Shepherdson. Alf took one look at Gordon and said, 'Alex you're on the bench, grab your boots.' I was thrilled to be involved but sad for Banks as I made my way to the coach.

All the lads were on the coach when Alf told Bonetti he'd be playing less than two hours before kick off. Peter looked shell-shocked. For me he had not been mentally ready to play for some time but it was Alf's decision. Forty years on nobody knows for sure what happened to Gordon. Rumours at the time suggested his food had been spiked. Whether that was the case or if he had just picked up a bug will never be proved but his absence was disastrous.

As for the match, Mullery got us off to the perfect start in the first half with his first goal for England and Peters made it 2–0 in the second half. We were off the bench in excitement thinking we're in the semi-finals. But just over 20 minutes from time with England in control Alf told Bell to get ready. As he was waiting to come on Bonetti let a long-range effort squirm under his body. Bell duly replaced Charlton and the match was suddenly on again but we still felt confident the lads could see it through. Hurst then grazed the woodwork with an effort and this was followed by Muller and Bell going close. Ten minutes from time, Alf sent Hunter on for Peters to help us close the game out. Both substitutions seemed logical with fresh legs in the centre of the park but it proved to be the wrong call as within two minutes Schnellinger hoofed a ball into the box, the defence was caught flat-footed and Seeler back headed the ball which looped over Bonetti into the net. Suddenly from nowhere the score was 2–2 and after a couple of half chances for each team it was extra time just as in 1966. With Charlton off, Beckenbauer was suddenly able to play his normal game instead of man-marking Bobby. Before this, neither had made a big impact on the game but that suited us, as Beckenbauer was Germany's most influential player. Now he was dictating play against our re-shuffled midfield. And in the second period Muller scored the winning goal. Hurst had a goal chalked off and Bell looked to be scythed down by Beckenbauer but our appeals were waved away. At the final whistle our dream of retaining the World Cup was over.

In the dressing room there was deathly silence and some of the lads were in tears while others seemed shell-shocked. Everything appeared surreal and nobody could quite believe what had happened. From having total control of the match we were suddenly out of the World Cup. I'd never experienced such a desperate dressing room in my career and never would again in the future. Alf told us that we had made him proud and we should be pleased with our performance but we could not take it in. Alf thanked us for our efforts and shook everyone's hand but we were gutted because we should never have lost the match.

As all the matches were being shown simultaneously, Gordon had no idea England had been knocked out. Local TV had shown Mexico-Italy and Brazil-Peru live with the others following on so when I got back to the room, Banksie was watching a delayed transmission of the game and England were 2–0 ahead. He took one look at me and could not believe we'd lost. Gordon refused to believe me but the Doc confirmed the news when he arrived after me. Whilst the inquests in the media started, we drank away our sorrows. There was no hatchet job on Bonetti within the squad and we all felt the substitutions were right at the time. Being out, we just wanted to get away from Mexico and two days later we made the long journey home. Bizarrely, we all received medals for participating but at the time they meant nothing.

By the start of the new season a number of the lads from the World Cup squad no longer featured in the England set up; most notably Bobby Charlton after setting a new appearances record in the West Germany match. I was soon out of the frame but very proud to have been involved. I'd played in the U23s as a Millwall player in Division 3 and progressed to win a full cap and been part of the 1970 World Cup squad, which was Boys Own stuff. I am still asked if I wish I'd won more caps but I had the greatest keeper ever in front of me. I sat on the bench many times and knew that Alf Ramsey would not have put me there if he did not think I was capable. My one cap has always meant the world to me.

9

GLORY DAYS TO RELEGATION WOES

Returning to Old Trafford after the World Cup, there was an uncertain atmosphere with Wilf McGuinness at the helm. United got back into action in a new-style tournament called The Watney Cup, which included off beat rules that rewarded attacking football. Playing semi-seriously was a good way to warm up and we reached the final before losing to Division 1 newcomers Derby County. Managed by Brian Clough, Derby would soon make a mark like its outspoken boss. Cloughie, as he was affectionately called, gave new meaning to the term 'opinionated' with his views on the game.

Wilf told me I was first choice keeper but there were issues developing especially with man-managing senior players in the squad. My initial feeling that his inexperience may be a problem was growing but I had to put it to the back of my mind as the season kicked off. Following a defeat to Leeds and draw against Chelsea at Old Trafford, we got thumped 4–0 at Arsenal. But the score was skewed because I dislocated my right shoulder following a collision with George Armstrong. David Sadler went in goal but he could not be blamed for the defeat. After four weeks I was fit to return but Wilf told me I was no longer first team choice. I had confidence in my ability so was stunned and frustrated. After mulling things over, I asked for a transfer but the board, fortunately as it turned out, refused my request. Every player goes through highs and lows. I had to wait for a chance but watching the lads struggle month after month was tough.

McGuinness was unclear how to change the club's fortunes. Wilf tinkered with the side that now included promising youngsters and recent signings together with some of the old guard but results remained poor with just six wins prior to Christmas. On the upside, we were crowned national champions of the *Daily Express* five-a-side tournament at Wembley when Bestie was the star of the show. We defeated Tottenham in the final but the TV tournament, first played for in 1968, was just a bit of fun. December 1970 proved to be the downfall month for McGuinness. Manchester City and Arsenal both won at Old Trafford, and then Aston Villa, at the time in Division 3, knocked us out of the League Cup at the semi-final stage. Bestie had not missed a game but after the Villa defeat went AWOL on Christmas Day as we prepared for a Boxing Day clash at the Baseball Ground. It was not unusual to train on Christmas Day but his absence started a chain of events that culminated in the manager's departure.

Behind the scenes the lads openly talked about their concerns over George who should have been approaching his peak years but Bestie seemed more like a pop star than football star having adopted a rock 'n' roll lifestyle. Something had to give. George was axed from the team to face Derby and fined but by kick off he had been reinstated after Matt intervened. And true to form, Bestie was among the goal scorers in a 4–4 thriller! Despite the result the writing was on the wall for McGuinness. The board decided that enough was enough and following the game Matt ended his successor's tenure. Wilf had been at the club for many years, so as a gesture of goodwill, reverted to his previous role as reserve coach but only stayed two months before quitting. After a short break he took a managerial post at Greek side Aris Salonika.

Hindsight is easy but looking back, McGuinness was on a hiding to nothing when he became United manager. It was no secret we clashed but in my view Wilf handled certain situations badly, especially with senior players who he needed to steady the United ship. Axing Charlton and Law early in the 1969–70 season was done as a statement of intent to show who was boss but the decision backfired. A manager has to make tough decisions but there are ways of handling senior players especially. Taking over from Matt was arguably an impossible task for anyone, let alone a 'rookie' boss. In football the buck stops with the manager and I was not surprised when the United board called it a day.

Despite our struggles United were still the biggest club in the country and it takes a special person to handle everything that entails especially when it comes to big stars and fans' expectations. Wilf tried his best but I've always felt he was too inexperienced at the time to do the job. During his brief tenure, United reached three domestic cup semi-finals and he led us to an eighth place finish. For most clubs that would be a decent return but it was not enough for Manchester United. With the players available at the club, even though it was a transitional time, we should have performed better. Matt may have been the toughest act to follow but the biggest problem was internal discipline and especially Besties' off the field antics. George had gone off the rails and Wilf could not cope. The board decided to go for the one person that could pull the squad back from the brink on a short-term basis . . . Matt Busby.

I was not in the side when Middlesbrough knocked us out of the FA Cup at the first hurdle. Rimmer had made errors and it brought about my return between the sticks at Chelsea. I was determined to make the most of my opportunity. For the first time since I'd joined United there was nothing to play for but pride. Matt rang the changes due to a mix of injuries and loss of form with Edwards, Aston and Stiles returning to the first team at Stamford Bridge along with striker Alan Gowling. Walking into the dressing room there was an instant change of atmosphere. Gowling and Morgan scored in our 2–1 win. The buzz was back. Wilf's departure proved a turning point in my career. Not that my return made a big difference, but I was in the fold on a run that yielded seven wins in 10 games.

Morgan was Matt's last signing and back from injury. He made an instant impact with the winning goal against Chelsea and then third placed Tottenham to claim our first home win in three months, much to everyone's relief. Bestie also scored against Spurs in a 2–1 win and with Crerand back in the line up Matt played familiar faces he knew would not let him down. Gowling had struggled to make an impact since his debut in 1967–68 but hit top form with four goals to down Southampton. I was also particularly pleased to see Law back among the goals with strikes against Huddersfield, Nottingham Forest and a hat-trick at Crystal Palace. Bestie also struck twice at Selhurst Park in a 5–3 win as he returned to what he did best. George was back on track and there was a familiar look in the final games as Charlton, Best and Kidd earned a win over Ipswich Town in our last home game before Law gained a draw at Blackpool. In our last match of the season we defeated City 4–3 with Best (2), Charlton and

Law scoring.

Kiddo had struggled for consistency yet ended the season with 18 goals, and despite being in and out of the side Law struck 15 goals. Denis worked hard in training to get back to full fitness. His sharpness was never going to be the same as in his heyday but Denis knew where the goal was and could still be a dangerous striker. We ended the campaign eighth but there was frustration among the United faithful who expected success. The season marked Matt's 25th year in charge and he received a silver tea service to mark the occasion. Matt's appointment was only ever going to be temporary as he returned to his General Manager role upstairs. The key now was to get the right manager to take us forward but whoever took the helm would have many challenges and not least our mercurial number 11. Things had started to slide for George when Matt retired but people are quick to forget that the adulation Bestie received was unprecedented. George had to take responsibility and that would be a major issue for the new boss when it was announced.

Times were moving fast at United. By the start of the new campaign Crerand had joined the back room staff and Stiles, following two seasons of frustrating injuries, had moved on to Middlesbrough. All media attention however was focused on United's new manager. The board was against internal promotion this time around so an experienced boss was sought. There was speculation that Don Revie (Leeds United) and Jock Stein (Celtic) were being sounded out and either made sense to develop the squad. The papers were full of stories and many big names in the game were touted. When the official announcement came though I was taken aback that the board had appointed Frank O'Farrell. Don't get me wrong, O'Farrell had a reputation for being a decent chap but this was the biggest job in British football and I was not sure if Frank had the charisma required. O'Farrell's track record showed he had guided Torquay United to promotion prior to taking Leicester City to an FA Cup final after replacing Matt Gillies during a season when he was unable to stop the team avoiding relegation. Leicester bounced back in style by returning to the First Division as champions. On his arrival at Old Trafford, Frank made it clear he was respectful to the club's history and there would be no rash changes.

For me the jury was out on O'Farrell's appointment. I had to give credit to the new management team that included Malcolm Musgrove, a sergeant major type number 2, because the positive banter that players thrive on suddenly returned to training at The Cliff. And the change of personnel brought instant dividends on the field at the start of the 1971–72 season. Keeping faith with the squad Matt had left behind, O'Farrell watched dutifully during the pre-season games and made two tactical changes by pulling Gowling and Morgan back into midfield with Kidd and Law as twin strikers. The midfield switch gave Charlton freedom and he revelled in the role because it gave us goal threats all over the park. Central defence was still an issue as Sadler partnered James while O'Neil and Dunne slotted in at full-back.

Initially the changes worked as we got off to a flyer in the league. Early results were terrific. Following a creditable draw at Derby we defeated Chelsea, Arsenal and West Brom. The latter two victories were particularly welcome as Old Trafford was shut for two games due to crowd disturbances the previous season so we took on the Gunners at Anfield (Liverpool) and the Baggies at the Victoria Ground (Stoke City).

Our league campaign quickly gathered pace. Defeats against Everton and Leeds were our only losses before Christmas, as we led the way by five points. A competitive side needs a balance of youngsters with experienced pros to show the way and credit where it's due, O'Farrell had an effect although we were still worryingly shipping goals. During a run of 11 wins in 14 games Bestie was back on song with hat-tricks against West Ham (4–2) and Southampton (5–2). He also struck the only goal in hard fought encounters with Derby and Newcastle. St James' Park was always one of my favourite grounds to play at because the atmosphere was electric. The Geordies know their football but we silenced the crowd when George got the only goal. Also hitting the target against Saints was Kiddo and a 17-year-old making his name, Sammy McIlroy. I was really delighted for Brian because he'd been frustrated at the back end of the previous season so it was great to have him firing again. And his partnership with Denis brought the best out of the Lawman. You can never keep a top goal scorer down for long and sharpness in the penalty box never deserts a striker. Tottenham, Leicester City and Nottingham Forest all had reason to curse Law as he cracked home goals galore during a purple patch.

The only disappointment was exiting the League Cup in a fourth round tie that went to two replays against Stoke City. John Ritchie was a strong, mobile striker and notched the winner but the forward that gave us most trouble was Jimmy Greenhoff. An intelligent player, Jimmy would become a hero at United in the years to come. Stoke went on to lift their only major honour at Wembley later in the season against Chelsea. One avenue to trophy success was gone and although we may have been league leaders pundits and rival managers such as Revie (Leeds), Clough (Derby) and Allison

(Manchester City) predicted our defence would prove to be our 'Achilles heel' based on recent results. November 1971 summed up our form as we slammed in 17 goals but shipped 10. Sadly, the so-called experts would be proved right because from the build up to Christmas right until mid-March we failed to win a league game. Aside from our poor form, O'Farrell was struggling to communicate with the players behind the scenes. When we needed direction and motivation it was lacking.

In a terrible run of form we lost seven games on the bounce, the heaviest a 5–1 thumping at Leeds as our season came off the rails, although there was some respite in the FA Cup. After overcoming Southampton and Preston, we defeated Middlesbrough in a fifth round replay when Stiles made an emotional return to Old Trafford before taking on Stoke at the quarterfinal stage. 'Lady luck' though was not on our side with two bizarre decisions against us. Greenhoff scored for Stoke but TV replays showed we should have had a goal kick before Jimmy slotted home from a corner. Then we had just equalised through Bestie, and looked like stealing a win, when Charlton smashed home the winner but the referee chalked it off. In the replay at The Victoria Ground we had opportunities before Terry Conroy, a tricky winger, gave me no chance in extra time.

Scoring was not a problem but we had still not replaced Bill Foulkes adequately. United managers had delayed going into the transfer market but we were not developing a suitable replacement from our youth ranks. Steve James was not up to the task although he tried his best. Whether clubs were holding prospective defenders to ransom who knows but we needed someone. O'Farrell pontificated too long to give us a chance of getting back into the title race but eventually he looked to the future by signing Martin Buchan from Aberdeen for £130,000. Buchan was seen as a long term replacement especially with our utility player, Sadler, struggling with a knee injury. O'Farrell also moved for Ian Storey-Moore of Nottingham Forest in a club record deal of £200,000 and the winger made a scoring start to his all too brief United career as we finally returned to winning ways against Huddersfield. Storey-Moore followed up with further strikes as we thumped Crystal Palace 4–0 and defeated Coventry City 3–2. By the next match though I was considering my future again following a 3–0 home defeat to Liverpool.

Being dropped is one thing but finding out when the team sheet is pinned up on the players' notice board is out of order. The incident summed up how communication had slumped off the field. As a professional footballer I never had an issue if a manager decided to have a quiet word about my form or take the decision to drop me if I had a bad spell. Whether you are a senior player or 'rookie', if a player is to be dropped then a manager should pull that person aside at training or find a suitable moment to explain why instead of allowing them to discover out of the blue. The spirit was sinking fast in the dressing room. I did come back into the side after three games but the incident left a bitter taste.

The remainder of the season, which saw the departure of Ure, Burns, Aston, Gowling and Sartori, petered out. Finishing eighth was simply not good enough after the start we'd made. Derby claimed the title after Manchester City, Leeds and Liverpool blew opportunities.

It had been a season of highs and lows for the club as well as for George Best because he finished top scorer with 18 goals yet also quit briefly after a bust up on international duty with Northern Ireland. He did revert what was a rash decision after a heart to heart with O'Farrell, who was desperate to keep George at United. Bestie was only 26 but his career was becoming a saga of wondering whether he'd quit or not. Clubs nowadays don't embark on summer tours but at United it was common practice. However a clash in Tel Aviv brought the wrong headlines when Bestie went AWOL. We all knew that although George was undoubtedly a genius, sadly his unpredictable behaviour meant his best days were behind him.

Approaching the 1972–73 campaign it was difficult to anticipate what to expect as a tough period of transition continued. Nobody could have predicted the turmoil ahead for United. The league season started disastrously and we ultimately only just kept our top-flight status. An opening day defeat at home to Ipswich Town saw the last goal by Law for the club and we failed to win our opening nine fixtures. United were rock bottom and O'Farrell wielded the axe by dropping Kidd and Law. In a bid to resurrect the club's fortunes O'Farrell moved into the transfer market. Welsh striker Wyn Davies was signed for £60,000 from Newcastle United and joining Davies in attack was Ted MacDougall for £200,000 from Bournemouth.

MacDougall had scored for fun in the lower leagues and this was his big break. Most famously he hit the headlines when scoring nine goals against Margate in an FA Cup tie but the step up to United was massive. Wyn at least knew the demands of topflight football and expectations of fervent supporters. I'd faced Wyn for United and he could be a handful but I would not class either signing among the best around at the time. Credit to the duo though, Davies scored the opening goal in a 3–0 win on his debut against defending champions Derby County as we finally claimed a win and MacDougall struck the only goal on his home debut to scrape a win against Birmingham City. And the new strike force teamed up with a goal apiece as we defeated Liverpool and Southampton. MacDougall was again on target as we defeated Norwich City to record three wins in four but the Davies-MacDougall partnership was no long-term solution. Five wins in 20 games meant we were third from bottom two points clear of Leicester and Crystal Palace having played a game more. Over half the season remained but United were in deep trouble.

Behind the scenes the biggest problem was that O'Farrell had become distant from the squad. The atmosphere was not conducive to success and the relationship with senior players in particular was not good. Charlton loved the club through and through, and still does. He's United's greatest ambassador but during the early months of the campaign it was obvious Bobby was frustrated. Law had signed a new short-term contract after his renaissance the previous season but he barely featured after a handful of appearances. He was no longer the Jack In The Box character of years gone by and his days at United were clearly numbered. Bestie still generated the most column inches as he continued to go off the rails. It's been well documented George went AWOL at times and threatened to quit but he was super fit and did give his all in training when he turned up, but he struggled with being George Best. I enjoyed hearing his latest escapades in the dressing room, all players have a tale to tell, but the bravado was hiding inner torment that would surface in coming years. My relationship with Bobby, Denis and George was never strained and we continued to be friends after our careers. But it was sad to see how things were changing at United as the board found it impossible to move on from Matt. The fun had gone, morale had sunk and it was clear, like it had been with McGuinness before him, that O'Farrell was out of his depth.

Prior to the Liverpool win, rumblings had started in earnest following a 4–1 defeat at home to Tottenham when Martin Peters struck all four goals for Spurs. At half time we came off to a chorus of boos as we were three goals adrift. And the boos and catcalls were louder at the final whistle. A derby defeat at City didn't help O'Farrell's cause and, despite a three year contract, his position became untenable approaching Christmas after a 2–0 home defeat to relegation rivals Stoke and rock bottom Crystal Palace. Credit to Palace they deserved the 5–0 win at Selhurst Park but with respect to the South London club, something was seriously wrong at Old Trafford with a result like that. Among the headlines the following day was 'Frank O'Failure'. It did not take a genius to work out that O'Farrell's days at United were up. When we were flying at the start of his tenure everything was fine but the team's inability to halt defensive frailties brought his ultimate demise.

O'Farrell departed after compensation had been agreed, so for the third time in a short period United were looking for a new manager. The board also decided a clean slate was needed so sacked Musgrove and John Aston senior. Severing links with John was particularly tough as he'd been associated with United for years but hard decisions are often made at a club and again a package was sorted out. As for Bestie, the board finally lost patience and placed him on the transfer list. Bestie was out of control. Without Matt towing him in, George was a liability. Off the field he was clubbing, living the fast life and had various business interests which were funding his glitzy lifestyle. Football was no longer the main thing in his life. He had the fast cars, glamorous girlfriends and a state of the art house but the press hounded his every move. Majorca was the in-place so Bestie was travelling backwards and forwards. His showbiz lifestyle had destroyed his football career. As things transpired Bestie announced his retirement in a letter to the board. At the time he was the highest paid player at the club but was out of sorts with what he wanted out of life. At 26 it was crazy that he wanted to call it a day but the George Best story at United was not quite over!

Regarding a new manager, United had already set things in motion because in the crowd at Selhurst Park was my former boss at Chelsea, Tommy Docherty. And within a few days 'The Doc' was appointed the third Manchester United manager in as many years. Tommy had been in the frame when McGuinness got the nod and Matt had sounded him out on a number of occasions but they just hadn't been able to make it happen. Docherty had finally landed his dream post but it was a difficult time, as the dressing room was not united. New additions were either not good enough or in Buchan's case, had vast potential but had struggled to settle into new surroundings. But we had hope that Tommy could pull things around quickly.

I'd been managed by a variety of managers but none more outspoken than The Doc. Controversial and a real personality, hacks loved Tommy because they knew a story would not be far away. In fact, during my era as a professional footballer only Cloughie courted more publicity. Tommy had managed a host of clubs with varying degrees of success but Chelsea, Rotherham, QPR, Aston Villa and Oporto did not have the history of United. Docherty was a strong character and United needed that but when the board appointed him I had mixed feelings, after all he'd sold me to United but he'd also gone on to manage Scotland so knew Morgan and Buchan. The Scots boys reassured me that Tommy was a great motivator, tactically astute and backed his players to the hilt.

The Doc had vast experience, had handled high profile players, liked to play attractive football and was a disciplinarian. The club needed shaking up and Tommy would do that. He appointed Paddy Crerand as his assistant and Tommy Cavanagh, a tough disciplinarian, as coach. The Doc's management style was very much 'in your face'. He wanted his team to play football but if they were not capable then he was not afraid to adopt a more physical approach. Tommy had built an exciting young team at Chelsea in the mid-sixties that blew winning the league and lost an FA Cup final so hoped to go one better at United but that was for the future. For the meantime, a chaotic period ensued with players coming and going.

The lads met Tommy at Mottram Hall where pleasantries were exchanged. Within five days of Docherty arriving at Old Trafford the Scottish invasion started with the transfer of experienced Arsenal midfielder George Graham for £120,000 followed by promising Partick Thistle full-back Alex Forsyth at 100,000 and another young Scot, Jim Holton at £80,000 from Shrewsbury Town. The Doc's purchases for the season were completed with Celtic striker Lou Macari for £200,000. The arrival of Lou, who turned down joining Liverpool in favour of United, took the number of Scottish internationals at the club to six. The added experience was welcome but I also knew that if Scotland turned over England in the Home Internationals I'd want to keep my distance from Buchan, Forsyth, Graham, Holton, Morgan, Macari and Law for a while!

The defence now included Buchan, Forsyth and Holton alongside Tony Young, who had broken into the side. James had dropped down the pecking order at centre-half and Sadler, like other European Cup winners, was out of favour as Graham moved into midfield. In attack Davies and

MacDougall were axed after 13 starts together. MacDougall joined West Ham for a cut-price £170,000. Kidd would return but his days at United were numbered.

In our first victory under Docherty, Charlton scored twice against our FA Cup conquerors, Wolves, but the revamped team was struggling to knit. Just 13 games remained and United had a point advantage over Crystal Palace, Birmingham City and West Brom but all three had games in hand. The Wolves win though had given us a boost and after a defeat at Ipswich, Macari grabbed the winner against West Brom and though Birmingham defeated us, the result preceded an eight-match run that took us to safety. Holton was on target as we defeated Newcastle and Southampton while Kidd and Morgan earned a massive win over Palace. Willie secured a 2–2 draw at Stoke and a 1–0 victory at Leeds ensured safety. The goal came from Trevor Anderson, a youngster purchased by O'Farrell from Portadown for a nominal fee. His goal was welcome and one of only two in his short stay at United. There was a mighty relieved visitors' dressing room at Elland Road. The imports had made an impact but incredibly Charlton was top scorer with just six goals!

United finished 18th, seven points clear of relegated Palace and West Brom. In the end, our football was unspectacular, indeed we did not score more than two goals in any game but most importantly morale was back up and Docherty has to be credited for achieving that but he was only papering over the cracks, as a massive rebuilding job was needed. However, with Docherty you knew where you stood. Tommy listened and explained exactly what was expected. It was clear that he relished the challenge to make United great again.

The end of the season brought the curtain down on

United's greatest player of his generation, Bobby Charlton. When he scored the opening goal at Southampton in our 2–0 win during the run in it proved to be his last first class goal for the club. Bobby decided to call it a day on his own terms and went out at the top. It was an emotional day at Old Trafford for our final home match of the season when we faced Sheffield United. With both clubs safe, the game meant little in terms of the result. We lost 2–1 but Bobby received a standing ovation before the game when both teams lined up to salute him after almost 20 years at the club. Bobby signed off at Chelsea when again he got a rapturous send off but there was one more appearance when he scored twice against Verona in the Anglo-Italian tournament. I didn't play in the match and we failed to make the semi-final stages but earlier in the tournament, which comprised four group games at different stages in the season, Matt Busby organised an audience with Pope Paul when we faced Lazio in Rome. Visiting the Vatican was an unforgettable experience as was the view from the top of St Peter's from the highest point of the dome.

United wanted Bobby to stay one more season but he declined and as things transpired it was for the best as he'd have been heartbroken to go out in a season when the club was relegated. At the time, Bobby was United's record appearance holder and England's record goal scorer. Ryan Giggs has since taken the club mark and his England distinction could yet fall to the current United great, Wayne Rooney. From Munich to Wembley, Bobby had straddled a period of United's history that defined a generation and his legacy is there for all time. Bobby, for me, was the best striker of a ball from distance. I lost count of the goals he thumped home from 30 or 40 yards. When Bobby caught the ball right no keeper had a chance and he scored his fair share of headed goals too. Still a regular at Old Trafford, Bobby is United's ultimate ambassador. Of the European Cup 1968 team only Charlton, Foulkes, Dunne and Crerand had won league and FA Cup winners' medals. I still hoped to join this elite list.

During the close season changes were planned and by the start of the new campaign Denis Law had controversially returned to former club Manchester City on a free transfer. The manner of Law's departure was handled badly and it was not something he deserved. Idolised by United fans, the news hurt Denis deeply as United were his club. An equal part of United's iconic trio Charlton-Best-Law, where Charlton was the ultimate professional and Best the flamboyant magician, Denis was the undisputed 'King' of the Stretford End with his trademark arm raised saluting another goal. When you consider United had three 'European' Footballers of the Year in the same team it must be some record. Denis was a wonderful player in his heyday, and around the 18-yard box there was nobody more clinical. If Law was a foot from the keeper you knew the ball was in the back of the net and his heading ability was tremendous. Denis's instincts and reactions were incredible. When a half chance occurred he could turn on a sixpence and put the ball away. Law was the most natural goal scorer and complete striker I played with during my career. A predator in the box, at the height of his powers, nobody could touch The King. There was also controversy when Tony Dunne was allowed to join Bolton Wanderers. Tony had plenty to offer and went on to serve his new club for a number of years. Another player to move on was my old goalkeeping rival Jimmy Rimmer who moved to Arsenal where he'd get more first team opportunities.

A pre-season tour in Spain saw us defeat Penerol of

Uruguay during the group games on penalties. I saved one and scored the winner, much to the amusement of my teammates, but it impressed Docherty enough to make a mental note for future consideration. We went on to play Murcia in the final. Looking ahead to the league campaign, pundits' had us down as relegation candidates. United were far more physical than in recent seasons because we did not have the playmakers of days gone by but I felt we had enough quality to survive.

When the season kicked off in earnest United had a fine start, winning two of our opening three games when centre-backs James and Holton scored in home wins over Stoke City and Queens Park Rangers. Defeats at Leicester and Ipswich knocked us back but I still fancied our chances for the return midweek fixture with Leicester at Old Trafford. The pre-match chat was normal but as we prepared to run out, Docherty announced I'd be taking penalties if they were awarded. There was stunned silence but Tommy meant it and asked if I was okay with the responsibility. Like all keepers I fancied myself as a goal poacher in five-a-side games but this was different to a kick-about. I'd rather a £200,000 striker line up a spot kick but it was not for me to argue with the boss and I did not have to think twice. If the opportunity arose, I'd give it my best shot. And incredibly, before I knew it a penalty was awarded at the Scoreboard End. Looking around, I jogged to the other end of the pitch. You could hear a gasp from home supporters and the look of shock on the Leicester players' faces was a picture as I picked up the ball and placed it on the spot. Peter Shilton's face was puzzled but when I sent him the wrong way he was not happy. The cheer from the Stretford End as I jogged back to the goal was unforgettable. Unfortunately we lost 2–1. A few days later, Kidd (2) and Storey-Moore struck in a 3–1 win over West Ham, which was a relief despite it being so early in the season. But sadly for Storey-Moore it would be his last first team game in football as an ankle injury in the gym ended his career prematurely. To date we'd won or lost games so 0–0 draws at Leeds, who had won the opening six games, and at home to Liverpool, represented a turnaround in fortunes as they were the leading sides at the time. But there was no disguising our biggest issue and that was in attack where Macari and Anderson failed to click.

And our struggles continued as any League Cup ambitions ended at the first hurdle when Middlesbrough, managed by Jack Charlton, claimed a top-flight scalp. Disappointing performances followed against Wolves and Derby before a 'Stepney special' defeated Birmingham City. I'd missed a spot kick at Wolves but felt confident as I ran up to take the penalty against Birmingham. My goal would be the only time I'd score a winning goal in a match but I still failed to take the main headlines because returning to the side after quitting the previous season was Bestie who though a shade heavier and lacking some of his spark added 5,000 to the previous gate! George coming back to Old Trafford was a risk but one that The Doc felt was worthwhile because we needed a spark and Bestie's arrival could potentially have had that effect. A capacity crowd was assured for a trip to Turf Moor but the only thing notable about our 0–0 draw at Burnley was the fact that it marked the last game of another European Cup winner in Sadler who soon after accepted an offer of regular first team football at Preston North End for a small fee. Only Kidd, Best and myself remained from that victorious team. Neither of the other two players would be around by the end of the season. George, during his 12-game spell, was no longer the influence on a game that he used to be. He opened his nightclub, Slack Alice, when he arrived with the best of intentions but during his final fling at United we claimed just one further win over Ipswich. And by his departure a few days after a 3–0 defeat at home by QPR on New Year's Day, we were in the bottom three ahead of West Ham and Norwich City.

More words have been written about George Best than any other player in British football and no doubt this discussion will continue whenever the 'beautiful game' from the swinging sixties is discussed. George was a one-off and his demise from top-flight football when in the prime of his career was terrible because everybody wanted things to work out for the maestro. His problems off the field dealing with the spotlight and his fame have been analysed many times but it must be remembered that Bestie was the first football superstar of what was a golden era of football. It's all very well pundits criticising that he was not managed better but United had a stringent code of practice for players and he was not able to adhere to it. Also, no one knew how to handle a top star in that era. George's passing at just 57 was tragic. He lived life to the full on and off the pitch and would be the first to say he wouldn't change a thing because after all the bad headlines have faded his footballing skills are still remembered.

George was a great trainer, a lovely lad and so unassuming, but his beloved Manchester United had no Busby around to put an arm around him any longer. Only Matt got the best from Bestie and although he played on for a few clubs including Fulham, Bestie was never the same player again although he enjoyed a brief spell in the States where the atmosphere was more laid back. It's been well documented that George never fully reached his potential and he should have had another four years at least at the top but on his day, Bestie was the best player in Europe by a distance and only Pele matched him globally. I have so many memories of George as a player when he was truly magical on the ball. Television had started to cover highlights of games on a regular basis when Bestie was making his name but in reality there is not much coverage of George in his prime. There are clips of him in action but it's always the same footage. For example how he rode Chopper Harris's tackle in a League Cup tie before rounding Bonetti to score, his goal in the European Cup final against Benfica, and whilst playing for Northern Ireland robbing the unsuspecting Banks as he was about to the clear the ball only to have the goal chalked off. And off the field there is George at his state-of-the-art home in Manchester and relaxing at a nightclub with the champagne fountain of glasses. Away from off the field distractions there are the glorious football moments and one goal that is still in the memory bank, thanks to *Match of the Day* cameras, was in a home clash versus Sheffield United in October 1971. Both sides were heading the league at the time with newly promoted Sheffield a point ahead. Old Trafford was bursting with 51,000 inside and a further 15,000 locked out listening on transistor radios when four minutes from time Bestie struck one of the best goals you'll ever see. Picking the ball up on the left wing, *Match of the Day* (BBC Books) describes it perfectly:

> . . . Best picked up a Brian Kidd flick half way inside the Sheffield half. With the ball apparently glued to the outside of his right foot, he cut an unwavering diagonal line from left to right, accelerating across the path of four United defenders. As goalkeeper John Hope advanced, Best was still running away from goal towards the corner flag. How he cut the ball back inside the far post with his right foot

has never been satisfactorily explained—rather like what happened to the rest of his life . . .

The crowd went crazy. United went on to win 2–0 when Gowling added a second but Bestie had done the damage. We were top of the league and Bestie dominated the Sunday headlines. And that was George at his best, playing off the cuff but in full control because he lived for doing something special. Bestie wanted the plaudits on the back of every Sunday paper every week and he practised and practised to do something different week in week out. But as everyone knows, George had his disciplinary problems. I always recall the build up to an FA Cup clash with Northampton Town in 1970 when he hadn't practised for weeks following a ban but typical Bestie, he went out and banged in six goals during an 8–2 win. But that was George, sticking two fingers up to the FA—or was it six fingers? Bestie loved nothing more than waltzing past an opponent before firing home a goal or setting up a chance.

George was a true legend of the game and I was honoured to play alongside him in his heyday but as Bestie departed, United faced a relegation battle. Despite our predicament, Tommy was not afraid to throw in youngsters at the deep end. Making an impression were teenagers Sammy McIlroy and Brian Greenhoff who played with spirit and determination. And during a terrible run when we failed to register a single win throughout January and February the Doc continued to look to the future when he blooded Gerry Daly into the midfield. No side was thumping us but I didn't help matters when I missed what would be my last penalty for United in a 0–0 draw against Wolves. My spot kick escapades were over but my overriding memory was the bizarre situation that I found myself in as joint top scorer until Boxing Day for United. My two strikes are still a club record for a keeper in top-flight English football so I'm eternally grateful to Docherty for enabling me to hold the accolade. It's a record I've held for 36 years and long may it continue as I'm still dining out on it. Macari was the player to oust me from top spot and he was on target again to earn us a first win of the New Year when we edged past Sheffield United at Bramall Lane at the beginning of March. Twelve games remained and six points (two for a win) separated us from fourth bottom Chelsea. How times have changed!

As Leeds and Liverpool battled it out for the title, relegation looked a stark reality but in a desperate bid to avert the drop Docherty reacted by raiding the transfer kitty one final time backed up by some astute wheeler dealing. Kidd joined Arsenal and together with funds generated from the sale of Ray O'Brien, two more Scots in Stewart Houston for £50,000 and Jim McCalliog at £60,000 arrived from Brentford and Wolves respectively. Tommy liked to surround himself with players he had worked with before and Jim, a cultured playmaker, had started out with Docherty at Chelsea. McCalliog replaced Graham, who had skippered the team briefly in midfield, and was seen as the old hand to show the likes of Daly, McIlroy and Greenhoff the way. Kiddo's departure meant I was the sole survivor from the 1968 European Cup side.

The new arrivals sparked a mini-revival starting with a morale boosting 3–1 win over Chelsea but the odds were against a miraculous escape. Credit to Tommy though, despite all the pressure he continued trying to motivate us and unlike immediate predecessors there was no avoiding key issues with players and no hiding from the media. The Doc was fully aware that if United failed to stay up, history would show he was at the helm when we went down but he never baulked the challenge. Digging deep following our win at Stamford Bridge we drew 3–3 against Burnley prior to consecutive victories at Norwich and at home against Newcastle United and Everton. McCalliog in particular was having an impact and scored in the latter two games before notching another as we earned a draw at relegation rivals Southampton. Below Saints, apart from ourselves, were Birmingham and already doomed Norwich. Wins against Everton, Manchester City and Stoke City would be enough to see us safe but our position became precarious following a 1–0 defeat at Goodison Park.

Going into the penultimate game against City the writing was on the wall. Defeat would send us down and guess who was in the starting line up for City? The Lawman! During the season, as we struggled for goals, there were plenty of commentators noting how Denis could have helped our cause. Law had scored two goals on his City debut and 11 in 25 games coming into the key match with ourselves. Our top league scorer McIlroy was on six so pundits had a point but Docherty had made his decision and stuck by it. City turned out to be the beneficiaries when he teamed up with Lee, Bell and Summerbee. And not surprisingly he made his mark, helping them to a League Cup final where they lost to Wolves. This was the only time I faced Denis as an opponent.

The City game was a day to forget. In a game of few chances we went closest to breaking the deadlock only to be foiled by goal line clearances by Donachie and Barrett before the moment fans of both clubs always remember when Law scored a few minutes from time. As the ball came in across the six-yard box there appeared no immediate danger when my former teammate had his back to goal but in a flash Law stuck a boot out and wrong footed me. I looked up at Denis after the ball had passed me and I've never seen him look so

Thwarting Leeds United striker Allan Clarke in an FA Cup semi-final win, 1977

Finally claiming my 'treble' medal in the 1977 FA Cup final against Liverpool at Wembley

Taking a cross under pressure from Ray Kennedy (Liverpool) in the 1977 FA Cup final at Wembley

With Stuart Pearson and Paddy Roche meeting snookers stars Ray Reardon and Alex 'Hurricane' Higgins at the World Championships

Fun times with comic Bernard Manning at a Player of the Year ceremony

Meeting Pope Paul at the Vatican

My last season with Manchester United, taken August 1978   © Howard Talbot Photography

In action for Dallas Tornado in the NASL

Lining up at a seven-a-side tournament in Singapore. Others stars pictured are Liam Brady, Alan Ball, Tommy Docherty, Alan Kennedy, Gordon Strachan and Osvaldo Ardiles

With my sons John and Paul at a 40th anniversary European Cup dinner

At a gala dinner with Sheila

Visiting a street named after me in Tooting and Mitcham

With mates Paddy Crerand and Brian Kidd

At a celebration dinner with Sir Bobby

Stars of United's '68 European Cup winning team with Benfica star striker Eusebio

down after scoring a goal. Denis knew what his cheeky back heel meant. Credit to Denis, he just turned and walked away. There was no celebration and in fairness to the City lads any joy was kept to a minimum, as they knew the significance of the goal. The aftermath of the goal was a pitch invasion and referee David Smith had no alternative but to abandon the match. Due to results elsewhere relegation was confirmed and the score stood. The pitch invasion resulted in fans being fenced in at Old Trafford as the worst of hooliganism began to infiltrate the game. The match proved to be Denis' last game as a professional and bizarrely meant that my Division 1 career at the time started and ended with a United v City derby when Law scored!

Defeat at Stoke in the final game was academic as we dropped into Division 2 with Southampton and Norwich City. For United, relegation ended 37 years of top-flight football. No team has a divine right to stay in the top division and down the years many other teams followed us. Since 1973–74 all bar four teams (Liverpool, Arsenal, Everton and Tottenham Hotspur) have tasted relegation and the list makes interesting reading. Burnley, Birmingham City, Chelsea, Coventry City, Derby County, Ipswich Town, Leeds United, Leicester City, Manchester City, Newcastle United, Norwich City, QPR, Southampton, Stoke City, Sheffield United, West Ham and Wolves. And of this list only 12 were in the Premier League last season demonstrating how times change.

After eight seasons of top-flight football, I'd be playing in Division 2 for the first and hopefully the only time. Relegation was a sickening feeling and meant that I'd now play in all four Divisions of English professional football. I'd experienced relegation twice at Millwall and there was no worse feeling but looking ahead I could not help but feel positive about the new campaign because United had the basis of a promising team as youngsters such as McIlroy, Greenhoff, Holton, Macari, Daly and Forsyth had gained experience. We had a chance to resurrect the club's fortunes and The Doc made it clear the moment we got relegated that we'd bounce back at the first time of asking and in style.

Martin Buchan
Manchester United, 1971–72 to 1982–83

*When I made my debut for Manchester United in March
1972, Alex had already been at Old Trafford for five and a
half years and he was a reassuring presence between the
sticks. I've always said that when you line up for the kick
off before a game and can glance back over your shoulder
to see someone of Alex's stature filling the goal, it certainly
gives you a boost. I can only imagine what went through
Eusebio's mind when Alex advanced and made that famous
save from him at a crucial time in the 1968 European Cup
Final. His save prevented Benfica from taking a 2–1 lead in
the second half before United won in extra time.*

*Alex was a good reader of the game, which I attribute
to the fact that he was no mean outfield player in our five-
a-side games at training, whereas many other goalkeepers
are not happy with the ball at their feet and are no more
than shot stoppers. He would be extremely comfortable in
today's game where keepers cannot pick up a back pass
from a colleague, in fact he would probably dribble his way
out of trouble. And Alex put us all to shame in season 1973–
74 when he volunteered to take the penalties and scored
twice during a disastrous campaign when confidence was
at a low ebb and we were eventually relegated from the
top-flight.*

*I am somewhat surprised that he earned only one full
cap for England as I believe that he was at least the equal
of any of the goalkeepers around between the time when
Gordon Banks was number one and in the Shilton-
Clemence era. As a senior pro, Alex was a good influence in
the dressing room and extremely convivial company off the
field. He has an excellent sense of humour and was partial*

to the odd 'wind-up'. I'm only sorry that I've just found out his middle name is Cyril, as I could have used it in retaliation when I was on the receiving end of one of his pranks.

10

RED DEVILS' REVIVAL

Tommy Docherty was quick to dust himself down when the reality of relegation had set in and there was plenty of time for soul searching during the summer of 1974 as the World Cup in Germany took place. Whatever distractions had gone on off the pitch at Old Trafford, in the end it was down to the players and we had simply not been good enough. Over the previous season we'd suffered 20 defeats of which only four were by more than a goal. It did not take a genius to work out that a few extra goals would have made all the difference to survival. The bottom line was that United did not have the firepower to compete. Records showed that the defence shipped 48 goals in 42 league games. Only twice in two decades had United conceded fewer goals and on both occasions, 1964–65 and 1966–67, they'd won the league! On the attacking front records noted that in 1972–73 United set a 'low' record of 44 league goals and in the relegation season we found the net just 38 times. Goals win games and any team that finishes a league campaign when the top three goal scorers manage just 15 goals will struggle to survive. McIlroy led the way on six and four of those came when the teenager was a sub, Macari notched five and McCalliog four in 11 games. It was clear United needed a striker that could bag 20 goals a season.

Assessing his options, Docherty quickly entered the transfer market where he beat off Division 1 opposition to purchase Stuart Pearson from Hull City for £200,000. We needed a prolific striker and 'Pancho' Pearson had proved to be a top sharpshooter in the lower leagues. Pearson also had a reputation for leading the line with spirit. Only Mick Channon (Southampton) and Duncan McKenzie (Nottingham Forest) had scored more goals during the 1973–74 campaign in Division 2 so Pearson was a player with a growing reputation. It was a coup to get him, and at the same time Docherty decided to move Macari back into midfield. The decision would prove to be a masterstroke for Lou and United. As for myself, at no stage did I contemplate leaving United because having been at Old Trafford since 1966 I knew from talking to former players that once you left there was only one way to go and that was down. Division 1 or 2, United was still United. I was staying put. At my age though there was always going to be speculation that I'd be replaced and the main name being touted was Peter Shilton of Stoke City. But the gossip stayed just that . . . gossip. Shilton was a class keeper and eventually joined Cloughie at Forest where he'd win the league, European Cup and star for England in two World Cups.

Looking ahead to the 1974–75 campaign, I knew United would be the big game for every club in Division 2 just as they had been in Division 1 and nothing has changed all these years later. We'd play to packed houses on our travels but we'd have to be prepared because we could guarantee opponents home and away would be 'up for it'. Defeating United would be the highlight of the season for our opposition. There are very few positives to take from relegation but the one benefit it did give us was the chance to rebuild away from the spotlight. No matter what we did and how big a club we were, United would not occupy the back pages 'nationally' in Division 2, so Tommy had a chance to stamp his mark on the club.

When a team gets relegated the manager usually pays the price but the United board had made it clear they were going to let Tommy have a crack. Instantly achieving Matt Busby's success was an impossible task for all sorts of reasons so they recognised they would have to have patience. During preseason, Docherty emphasised how important it was to get off to a strong start. It was essential to impose ourselves on the league. We kicked off the season at Leyton Orient. I'd not heard of any Orient players but they were certainly fired up. United's starting XI of Stepney, Forsyth, Houston, Greenhoff, Holton, Buchan, Morgan, Macari, Pearson, McCalliog, Daly and substitute McIlroy all featured throughout the season with mainly James, Sidebottom, Coppell and Nicholl covering for injuries.

We made a flying start with a 2–0 win at Orient when our most experienced outfield player Morgan settled any nerves and it heralded an unbeaten nine-match run. I was delighted to see one of our youngest players, Daly, notch a hat-trick in the opening home fixture against my old club Millwall in a 4–0 win. Daly was on target again in further wins over Portsmouth and Cardiff City as we quickly led the way. Of all the fixtures I was looking forward to playing away the most was Millwall and the game soon appeared following draws versus Nottingham Forest and West Brom. It was the first time I'd returned to the club that gave me my big break and although not at all apprehensive because I was now a seasoned pro, I hoped to get a good reception. Speaking to former Millwall players the feedback was that so long as you had been a grafter at the club, no matter where you moved on to the fans gave you a good reception which was fair enough. Naturally, I understand resentment when players move on but past deeds should not be forgotten.

Sitting in the 'away' dressing room was strange as I'd only changed in the home one before. It was a surreal feeling but I had my match head on. Running out towards the Millwall supporters, I appreciated the applause but United had a match to win. To cap a great day a Daly penalty sealed a 1–0 victory. Our winning ways continued at home to Bristol Rovers and Bolton before Norwich City turned us over at Carrow Road.

Our confidence was sky high after the opening 10 matches. The only downside was that Pearson and Macari had picked up knocks but soon returned and started to bang in the goals. 'Pancho' Pearson found his scoring touch with a brace in a 2–1 win over Fulham, the winner against Southampton and a hat-trick as we thumped Oxford United 4–0, a match where Macari also scored. Macari's influence from midfield was beginning to take effect. The Doc's decision was proving inspirational as Lou had the freedom, guile and know-how to make an impact. And with the duo back on song it had the added effect of boosting the confidence of young striker, Sammy McIlroy. I was delighted to see McIlroy settle and look the part. Sammy had been in the side for a couple of seasons but like any young player he had his confidence knocked when we were relegated. Our good form brought the spark back into his game and McIlroy was demonstrating his potential to make it in the game.

As anticipated, and despite being in Division 2, we were still attracting massive crowds. The revenue was a windfall for many sides in the league but we had one objective only and that was promotion. McIlroy and Pearson both struck in an important 3–2 win over Sunderland in front of over 60,000 fans. The clash also marked the return of Holton in defence, which was welcome after suffering away defeats at Bristol City and Hull City in his absence but an eight-goal thriller at

Sheffield Wednesday was marred as Holton was stretchered off with a broken leg. And the 4–4 score was skewed as we shipped three goals inside 10 minutes after Holton departed. Losing Holton for the season was a massive blow as he was popular with fans and players alike with his wholehearted performances. Brave, committed and superb in the air, Holton, in his short time at the club, made a massive impact but wouldn't play again for United due to the eventual form of Greenhoff after Sidebottom and James deputised. Wednesday would be the only side to score more than two goals against us all season.

I've always enjoyed the buzz around Christmas fixtures and United followers were in fine voice for the first time in years when we scraped a win at York City prior to Christmas and again when Daly struck home a penalty for a victory over West Brom on Boxing Day. Daly was slightly built but blessed with a great attitude, boundless energy and 'bottle' when it came to taking spot kicks, and none more so than when he got the only goal of a League Cup third round win over our neighbours Manchester City who were looking to return to Wembley after losing in the final a year earlier. Not having a 'derby' clash had been a blow for United players and supporters who always looked forward to taking on our local rivals. Having lost to City a few months earlier as we slipped out of the league, the League Cup win gave us some much-needed bragging rights even if only for a night. It was also strange to be classed as 'giant killers' as we were from the lower league and this would be the only occasion I'd experience such a thrill. Our dressing room lapped up the moment even though the trophy was not our top priority.

As we approached the New Year there was a feel-good factor at the club and not only because of our league form. Following the win over City we'd progressed to the League

Cup semi-finals where we faced Norwich after taking Division 1 scalps in Burnley and Middlesbrough. In fact, the competition that season had three Division 2 sides and one from Division 3 in the last four as Aston Villa took on Chester. Naturally we fancied our chances of lifting the trophy for the first time in the club's history and it would be a first domestic cup trophy for me. But January was all about cup heartache as Walsall defeated us in the FA Cup and Norwich reached Wembley. Villa defeated Norwich in the final.

Around the time of the cup clashes we got the better of Sunderland but there was a brief backlash to our cup disappointments because we lost consecutive league games for the only time in the season, including our sole home defeat, when Bristol City became the only side to do the 'double' over us. Although still top we were no longer racing ahead of our rivals, including Villa. Playing with confidence they defeated us at Villa Park. Docherty told us a few home truths after the loss but it would be our last reverse of the season as we ended the campaign as confidently as we started it with an unbeaten 11-match run. A team always adapts during a season and a new arrival for the run in was yet another teenager, Steve Coppell, from Tranmere. Docherty was always looking to the future and in Coppell, blessed with pace, a good football brain and determination on the right flank, he'd found a real gem. Coppell made an immediate impact as a replacement for Morgan on the wing and to balance the books McCalliog departed to Southampton. McCalliog would come back to haunt us a year down the line! At the time though it was clear Docherty had made a shrewd long-term investment to supersede Morgan who joined Burnley at the end of the season.

Our best form had been saved for the end as we finished the season with eight victories and three draws to go up in style. Pearson and Macari were both on target in the first of those wins against Cardiff City and promotion was sealed with three games to spare when Macari scored the only goal at Southampton. The duo ended the season on a high with strikes in a 4–0 triumph against Blackpool. Ultimately, we finished three points ahead of runners up Aston Villa and eight clear of Norwich.

Manchester United's Division 2 title winning squad was Stepney 40, Forsyth 39, Houston 40, Greenhoff 39 (2), Holton 14, Buchan 41, Morgan 32 (2), Macari 36 (2), Pearson 30 (1), McCalliog 20, Daly 36 (1), McIlroy 41 (1), James 13, Sidebottom 12, Young 7 (8), Coppell 9 (1), Martin 7 (1), Davies (8), Albiston 2, Baldwin 2, Roche 2, McCreery (2), Graham (1), Nicholl (1). United's main scorers were Pearson 17, Macari 11 and McIlroy 11.

The most encouraging aspect of United's promotion season was that apart from a few old pros like myself, United had a young team so we knew we could only improve. We'd also been promoted playing open, attacking football in the best traditions of the club, which pleased all our supporters. Everyone connected with United could not wait to get back to playing the likes of Division 1 champions Derby County, Liverpool, Arsenal, Ipswich Town, Manchester City and all the other big guns. The United side had gelled mentally and physically, and looking ahead, I felt we could cope with the demands of top-flight football. Our young players in the squad instead of struggling away at the bottom of Division 1, which would have happened had we survived 12 months earlier, had been allowed to develop and express themselves away from the spotlight, which proved beneficial. Possessing the exuberance of youth sprinkled with experience, United were in far better shape than in the relegation season.

We'd skated away with the title and it was an enjoyable

season but worryingly in the game there was growing crowd trouble. It was a problem and United were not immune, especially on our travels. During the early part of the campaign smaller clubs could not cope with the sheer volume of United fans turning up to games so before Christmas the Football Association and Football League ruled that our away fixtures should be all-ticket. Playing in front of tight grounds with full houses was a learning experience for the younger lads but there were plenty of old pros to guide them.

I was delighted with my form throughout the campaign. While we dominated teams the key was concentration. I played 40 games and had a solid 'goals against' record. Forsyth and Houston had settled in at full-back while Buchan was consistent at the heart of our defence, especially after Holton broke a leg. And it was great to see our link up play develop through Daly, Greenhoff and McIlroy. While Pearson top scored with 17 league goals Macari struck the same figure in all games. It was fantastic to see Macari finally overcome a section of 'boo boys' that had given him stick following his big money transfer from Celtic. Joining a struggling club is not easy and it took Lou time to settle but the 'Mighty Mouse', as the press dubbed him, had found a role where he had regained his scoring prowess. Of course, the big challenge was to come but we could enjoy the close season with optimism. The Division 1 big guns were waiting but none would be too concerned about United. At Old Trafford there was a squad ready to stir things up at the top of English football.

After a decade at United, I'd achieved most of my ambitions apart from one, winning an FA Cup winners medal. As senior player on the books I realised my time was coming towards an end at Old Trafford so it was fantastic to be looking ahead to a new Division 1 campaign. The only downside were my occasional spats with the boss. After a decade in management at a number of clubs, The Doc took the United job determined to achieve success and changed the atmosphere for the better. Tough, opinionated and controversial in equal measure, Tommy could be one of the lads or read the riot act. Noted for his wheeler dealing in the transfer market, his training regimes were arguably the toughest I experienced. In the aftermath of promotion Docherty praised me for being a 'fatherly figure' to our young defenders but we had our differences.

Tommy had an ego and with us going well, left everyone in no doubt who was in charge. Winning the Division 2 title meant his swagger became overbearing occasionally. Docherty wanted to stamp his authority on everything but it did rebound at times and it came to a head on the post-season tour to the Far East and Australasia over players' expenses. Things needed sorting out and by the time we arrived in Hong Kong, Matt had flown in. The issues over expenses were resolved but it left a tense atmosphere and sadly my respect for Tommy dipped.

Reporting back to pre-season training I felt slightly uneasy and was suddenly at a crossroad when Docherty told me Paddy Roche would be the first team keeper. I was astounded because my form had been solid the previous season. Mulling things over, I said my piece but decided not to get involved in another spat. I'd bide my time to see what developed. The day before United took on Wolves at Molineux in the opening game, I reported for training at the Cliff with the reserves while the first team completed their preparations at Old Trafford. Loosening up, assistant manager Frank Blunstone told me Roche was out as his father had died so I had to report back to Old Trafford. Paddy's misfortune had brought about my recall but that can be the harsh reality of professional football. I didn't expect a long run in the team, as Tommy had been so clear that Roche was his first choice but after we won 2–0 with Macari scoring both goals, The Doc came into the dressing rooms and announced he'd play the same team at Birmingham City midweek.

After all the spats, I was back in the frame and could understand Tommy's decision. Whatever differences individuals have, the first rule of football is, don't change a winning team. It was only one match, but we'd played really well. Docherty was determined we'd play attacking football, which was in contrast to most sides who opted for a more cautious approach. Playing with an out and out winger in Coppell and both full-backs looking to attack we also had no holding midfielder in front of the back four. Our policy was to attack from the flanks with players supporting the strikers with runs from midfield. They say that attack is the best form of defence and this was our approach. United had received plenty of good reviews and they continued when we picked up another 2–0 win at St Andrews. This time McIlroy grabbed the goals to keep our perfect start going but Greenhoff gained more headlines as he ended the game in goal after I fractured my jaw following a collision with Birmingham striker Bob Hatton. There was no malice; it was just a hazard of the trade. There was little protection for keepers in my era, we knew the score and learnt how to protect ourselves when jumping. I was out cold briefly but soon came around after the 'magic sponge' from the trainer. There was no thought of coming off so I soldiered on till half time. In the dressing room, I felt okay even though my jaw started to swell up. Nowadays I'd have gone straight to hospital, as there would be a keeper on the bench, but in the mid-seventies a swelling meant you carried on. But early in the second half after picking up a ball from a back pass, I shouted to Buchan I was going to throw him the ball when I felt an enormous crack in my jaw. This time there were no heroics. I was on my way to Birmingham General Hospital to be wired up. Greenhoff went in goal and kept Wolves at bay. Brian dined out on that incident for months!

It may sound astonishing now, but I was back in goal on the Saturday when we thumped Sheffield United 5–1. Pearson opened his top-flight account with two goals in a thrilling display and our great run continued with a draw at Coventry before further victories over Stoke City and Tottenham Hotspur. We'd made an impressive start and led the league before a couple of setbacks but we soon bounced back with further wins over Leeds United and Arsenal when McIlroy and Coppell struck twice respectively. Pundits were talking up our chances in the league but Docherty was quick to point out that he'd reserve judgment at the end of the season. Publicly at least mid-table was the target.

Next up was a trip to FA Cup holders West Ham, who always looked to play football and they defeated us 2–1. I was responsible for one of the goals and held my hands up afterwards. Even so, I didn't expect to be dropped but that is exactly what happened. Docherty explained he'd not been fair to Roche. I thought, 'You're having a laugh, I've let in 12 goals in 14 league and cup games, the best record in the country,' but The Doc was adamant. I was livid and told him so but he soon reversed his decision when we lost at Liverpool and Arsenal in the next four league games. To make matters worse during the mini-slump we also lost a League Cup fourth round tie when City thumped us 4–0. Our neighbours went on to win the trophy—their last major honour as United fans keep reminding them!

When we went down 3–1 at Highbury, United's fans in the away end were shouting for my return. Docherty was under pressure and called me into his office on the Monday to inform me I was back in the side. Midweek I played in Paddy Crerand's testimonial match when the 1968 European Cup side took on the latest United XI. I kept a clean sheet in a win over Newcastle United and kept my place for the remainder of the season. Our spark was back in an 11-match unbeaten run that brought six victories as we stayed in touch at the top. For the first time in years, United had a team that was confident playing the ball out from defence. Instead of booting the ball to a front man, we had players to launch attacks from deep but hacks wondered whether our attacking approach would last the winter months when pitches became boggy or frozen. We quickly proved doubters wrong and had another player firing from the flanks in left winger Gordon Hill. Dubbed 'Merlin' by fans of his former club Millwall, Hill was a tricky winger with terrific pace who packed a powerful shot. Hill was seen as the final piece of The Doc's team and made an immediate impact scoring in wins over Sheffield United, Wolves and Queens Park Rangers. The win over Rangers was particularly important as they too were riding high.

Stan Bowles was Rangers mercurial talisman. Blessed with terrific skill, Bowles was one of a number of entertainers in the mid-seventies alongside the likes of Tony Currie, Charlie George, Duncan McKenzie and Frank Worthington. Dubbed 'mavericks' because of their ability to do the unexpected, all followed in the best traditions set out by my former teammate George Best. There is nothing like a crowd pleaser and when Bowles, Currie, George, McKenzie and Worthington played they displayed skills in abundance although they were all accused of not being 'team players'. But speak to fans from the era and all will remember these wonderfully gifted footballers.

Aston Villa were to end our unbeaten run but by now we had more than the league on our minds as our FA Cup campaign was gaining momentum. And our run to Wembley had a few anxious moments. Taking on Oxford United at Old Trafford should have been comfortable based on our respective league positions but 'The Cup' has a habit of levelling matters and Oxford gave us an almighty fright. In the end we were indebted to Daly who kept his cool to slot away two penalties. In round four, former United skipper Noel Cantwell was delighted when his Peterborough side drew a plumb tie at his former club. Describing the match as 'Posh's Wembley' we never looked in danger as Forsyth, McIlroy and Hill scored in a 3–1 win.

Every team needs some luck to win the trophy and we had our fair share against Leicester City at Filbert Street in a fifth round clash. My rift with Tommy was common knowledge at the time but we both had a professional outlook on the matter and I enjoyed one of those games when everything stuck. Macari and Daly put us in control but then we were under the cosh after Leicester got a goal back through Bob Lee. Worthington, Keith Weller and Jon Sammels threw everything at me but I was on song. They say fortune favours the brave and it was true in the closing stages. It is during games like this when you think to yourself, 'Our name is on The Cup'. Tommy and me were photographed in the dressing room but it all seemed a bit false as we posed. The main thing was that we were through to the next round. There were lots of notable performances on the night and getting praise is always appreciated. David Meek, recalling the game in *Manchester United Football Book No. 11* noted: 'The real saviour was Stepney. His timing, with runs off the line, was spot-on, and his reflexes against several well hit shots were as sharp as ever to see United through to a sixth round home tie against Wolves.' My hopes for a long awaited cup winner's medal were increasing.

We warmed up for a sixth round clash against Wolves by avenging a defeat to West Ham earlier in the season with a 4–0 thumping at home. Wolves were League Cup holders so knew what it took to win a trophy but we had enthusiasm and heart. And in front of a packed Old Trafford house you could sense FA Cup fever had gripped supporters. In a cagey affair, John Richards opened the scoring before Daly earned us a replay. Wolves had a good cup side in the mid-seventies and they swept into an early 2–0 lead. Credit to The Doc, he's never been afraid to make bold decisions and quickly substituted Macari, who was carrying a knock. Jimmy Nicholl moved into defence allowing Greenhoff to play in midfield. It's at times of adversity you discover what character a team has and we reacted in the right way by taking the game to Wolves. Pearson got us back in the game before half-time and Greenhoff took us into extra time. Looking at Wolves during the pep talk from Tommy, they were shell-shocked. McIlroy duly fired home the winner for a fantastic victory. A winning dressing room is always a great place and after our fightback the atmosphere was superb. The feeling among the lads was that this was our season—why not after that performance?

Confidence was sky high and further goal feasts followed against Leeds, Newcastle and Middlesbrough. Prior to playing Newcastle I chalked up my 500th league game in a draw at Norwich City but statistics were for retirement as massive games awaited United. We were viewed as entertainers as crowds flocked to see us. Entertainment was guaranteed but I was concerned at the number of goals being shipped. We needed to tighten up at the back no matter how many rave reviews we received as a semi-final with Derby County approached. I was only 90 minutes from a first FA Cup final appearance and Dave Mackay's Derby stood in our way but we were not going to be denied at Hillsborough. We prepared at Mottram Hall where partygoers disturbed one or two of the lads but we were focused. And with the exuberance of youth, our victory in the quarterfinals gave us all the confidence we needed against an experienced side that boasted great players in Bruce Rioch, Leighton James, Colin Todd, Archie Gemmell, Roy McFarland, Francis Lee and David Nish. Derby went into the game favourites but we had other ideas. Pearson led the line superbly, Hill was on fire and Buchan marshalled the defence superbly. Tearing into every tackle and attacking at will; from the moment Hill scored early on there was only one winner. Derby got frustrated at times, which resulted in some ugly moments but we deservedly booked our place at Wembley. In the other semi, Southampton defeated Crystal Palace in an all-Division 2 clash. Malcolm Allison was managing Palace by now and had enjoyed plenty of publicity, especially after knocking out Leeds but Saints ended his Wembley dreams.

Following our semi-final win the odds on us doing the double dipped but that was just paper talk. Yes, we were flying high but a 3–0 defeat at Norwich City brought us back to earth. And to make matters worse, Coppell picked up an injury. Pearson soon joined Steve on the treatment table with Wembley drawing ever closer so our focus was beginning to shift. A win at Burnley kept the pressure on Liverpool and Queens Park Rangers but a first league defeat at Old Trafford in 15 months against Stoke City ended our fading league title hopes. It was now a question of getting everyone fit for Wembley. And Docherty was taking no chances as Coppell, Pearson and McIlroy missed another loss, this time at Leicester. The league title had gone but European qualification had been achieved, which was terrific. However, facing Saints at Wembley was the only conversation in town.

United were favourites and I felt our young team could

handle the pressure and at last I'd win an FA Cup winners medal. Playing in an FA Cup final meant everything to me at this stage of my career and it was not long before we were being measured for our cup final suits. During the build up to Wembley there were many distractions with interviews and media commitments. In fact, in the seven years since I'd played at the Twin Towers, the media frenzy had increased massively. Everyone wanted a piece of United but the media knocked us when we asked for an improved fee for photographs and interviews. It was amazing because the amount generated by a players' Cup final pool was a pittance in reality.

Of more concern to me was the fact that I sensed a number of the lads were underestimating Southampton. It was as if we just had to turn up and win as we had finished third in Division 1 and Saints were a division below us. Based at Sopwell House, St Albans, it was a relief to make final preparations but some players were too relaxed. I had my match day head on and knew we'd be in a scrap as a number of the Saints players were nearing the end of high profile careers and it would be a last chance for them to win the FA Cup. I felt uneasy boarding the coach, especially as we made our way down Wembley Way and looked at Saints pen pictures—Channon, Osgood, McCalliog, Rodrigues, Stokes and Holmes. In Coppell, Hill, Pearson, Daly and Greenhoff we had youthful experience but we had to be on our 'A' game or we'd be turned over. Climbing off the coach we went for a walk around the pitch where I looked at the Saints lads and then ours. The contrast was stark. While the old hands at Southampton appeared serious, on the outside the United kids looked cocky. I thought to myself, 'This is a final and a one off game so if we don't play well Southampton could turn us over'. I genuinely felt this was my last chance to win an FA Cup winners medal. It was what I'd dreamed about as a kid. I knew we must not underestimate Saints and told the United lads so but I was not sure if my comments registered with all the hullaballoo going on around us.

FA Cup final, Wembley Stadium
(1 May 1976)

Manchester United: Stepney, Forsyth, Houston, Daly, Greenhoff, Buchan (c), Coppell, McIlroy, Pearson, Macari, Hill. Sub: McCreery (for Hill). *Southampton*: Turner, Rodrigues (c), Blyth, Steele, Peach, Holmes, Gilchrist, McCalliog, Channon, Osgood, Stokes. Sub: Fisher.

The Doc said all the right things in the dressing room. He wanted a tight defence, the offside game, battles around Saints' 18-yard box and shots at goal. Tommy told the lads to attack as we'd done all season and reminded us for one last time how Sunderland had overcome the odds against Leeds United three years earlier. Lining up in the Wembley tunnel, even with all my experience, there were plenty of nerves but as we walked out the noise was terrific. After meeting the dignitaries it was game on.

We needed a solid start but we couldn't find our form against the 5–1 underdogs. Hill looked dangerous on occasion but Rodrigues soon got his measure down the left flank and with Peach using his experience to stifle the threat of Coppell we struggled to dominate as we'd done in so many games during the season. Our instinctive play wasn't there. We weren't snapping into tackles or dictating play. The occasion had got to some of our players who froze. At times you would not have realised we were the top-flight side because despite having pace all over the park we couldn't penetrate. We did go close but Saints enjoyed that stroke of luck needed in a cup final when a McIlroy header hit the bar from a Pearson flick. It would be the nearest we'd go to scoring. Hill in particular had a poor game and missed a clear opening when Turner made a smart save. McCreery replaced Hill just after the hour. Macari also struggled to make an impact but we discovered he'd played for an hour with a broken toe! Southampton grew in confidence, as we became frustrated. Defensively, Buchan and Greenhoff marshalled Osgood and Channon with comfort but I had to make a save from Channon when he found space. In midfield the experience of McCalliog eventually told seven minutes from time when he put a ball through for Stokes to score with a shot that zipped off the pitch. On the replay Stokes looked offside but that was immaterial. What annoyed me most was that we'd been caught flat in defence in a split second. When Bobby, God bless him, struck the ball, I knew it was going to my left, but because the shot was slightly miss-hit I went early and the ball bounced past me. If Stokes had hit the ball true I'd have saved it. We pushed forward but there was no way back as Saints fought to hold on to the lead.

Lawrie McMenemy's team had caused a major cup final upset, which is what the FA Cup is all about. But at the final whistle my first thought was that my last chance of getting my 'treble' medal of Division 1, European Cup and FA Cup had gone. Seeing the joy on the Saints old pros faces I yearned to have that moment of winning the FA Cup. Of course, everybody was courteous when I offered my congratulations, as they knew how low I felt. I'd suffered losing semi-finals and relegation but this was the biggest disappointment of my career. I wanted so much to follow the heroes of my childhood like Matthews, Milburn, Trautmann and Lofthouse up those Wembley steps. After receiving my runners up medal from The Queen, walking off the pitch and down the tunnel, I was inconsolable and back in the dressing room the lads were also distraught. Tommy called on us to bounce back and win the trophy next year but his plea fell on deaf ears as we changed in silence. We attended a planned post-match dinner at the Hotel Russell but it was not the raucous celebratory occasion it should have been. It was certainly not an evening to remember. Twenty-four hours later 20,000 fans greeted us at St Peter's Square for a civic reception. The scenes got to a number of the players but the loudest cheer was when The Doc told United fans we'd come back stronger and win next season.

A few days later we won our final game of the season against City. Hill and McIlroy got the goals but it was no consolation. If only we'd displayed the same zip a few days earlier. We finished third; the highest United had finished since 1967–68. In a season that had so many positives, bizarrely our points total of 56 would have won the title the previous season when Derby were crowned champions with just 53 points! Overall, it had been a successful season and even the manager commended my performances in his end of season appraisal in the *Manchester United Football Book No.11*:

> Alex's experience after 10 years at Old Trafford and playing over 500 games in the course of his league career was invaluable to us. What impressed us most was the way he knuckled down and fought his way back into the team after I had dropped him earlier in the season. He showed great character. There was no malice on either side and he settled down to play as well as ever. He is a good professional and a great influence on the young players, always encouraging and helping to create a good team spirit.

By the end of the campaign I'd played more games for United than any other post-war keeper, I also created a bizarre record of having played against every one of the 92 football league clubs in 1975–6 bar five. Blackburn Rovers, Bury, Cambridge United, Carlisle and Manchester United! Records aside, looking back on the campaign during what was a sweltering summer, if anyone had told me pre-season United would qualify for Europe and reach the FA Cup final, I'd have thought they were being a tad optimistic as United's young side had to prove themselves at the top level. We'd overachieved yet there was such a sense of anti-climax. For the young lads there would be more opportunities of big match football but at 33 years of age my top class career was winding down and FA Cup glory seemed a distant dream. Little did I know what lay ahead 12 months down the line.

11

CUP MAGIC

Following our FA Cup final defeat to Southampton I was in reflective mood during the close season. Being at the veteran stage of my career and knowing Docherty was building a young team, the position of keeper would be on his agenda so I had no idea if I'd be first choice again. However, with my testimonial year coming up I knew I'd be busy organising events and it was a comfort that those closest to me believed my career was far from finished. By the time I reported back for training I was ready to go and it was clear that the heartbreak we suffered against Saints had hardened the players' resolve to kick on. Even Tommy seemed to have mellowed and with high hopes domestically together with European football to look forward to again after an eight year gap, the atmosphere was great. The down side of having a young squad is that they can be unprepared for big occasions, however much the backroom team prepare them, but the plus side is that they quickly get over disappointments. From adversity there are two ways to react at a football club, players either up their game or wallow in self-pity. The signs looked good for the coming season.

The Doc informed me that I was in the team from the start, which gave me a real boost, although our opening game at home ended disappointingly as we drew 2–2 with Birmingham

City. But we suffered just one defeat in the opening eight games, versus Tottenham 3–2 after letting slip a 2–0 lead. Three consecutive wins included a 3–1 'derby' triumph at City to keep us in the early mix. Our form was solid but it dipped when the heart of our defence was disrupted after skipper Martin Buchan was injured playing for Scotland. Buchan missed two months of the campaign when we failed to win a league game. And our UEFA Cup adventure ended after we defeated Ajax in the opening round. Buchan had played in both legs but was sidelined when we bowed out to Juventus. We edged the home leg against the Italians with a Hill goal but went down 3–0 in Turin. Buchan's absence was not the sole reason for losing but against the likes of Causio and Boninsegna we needed our first choice defence. And chasing the game with Zoff in goal was tough. Boninsegna scored twice before Bennetti grabbed a third to seal the tie. Going out of Europe was disappointing as there is nothing like the electric atmosphere of a European tie. Players loved the extra buzz they generated, as the games were a special experience, unlike today with the Champions League when so many European sides qualify for the group stage.

During this period Macari also missed some vital games and the only solace was our form in the League Cup where we reached the fifth round. Our run had seen us defeat Tranmere Rovers, Sunderland after two replays and Newcastle United when we achieved a club record 7–2 win in the competition. It was also the biggest victory over any side since we thumped Northampton Town and West Brom during the 1969–70 season. On a night when finally the team clicked, Hill notched a hat-trick. The result though failed to spark us into life as we went out in the next round to Everton at home and continued to struggle in the league. Tommy decided to enter the transfer market and produced one of his best signings for United when he overcame competition from Everton and West Ham to purchase Stoke City striker Jimmy Greenhoff for £120,000. Elder brother of Brian, Jimmy was one of the unlucky players never to win an England cap. United had lost some of its spark from the previous season and Jimmy arrived at just the right time. It took a few games for the Greenhoff-Pearson partnership to gel but the strike force brought about a move back into midfield for McIlroy, which in turn saw Daly depart to Derby County for £180,000. Daly's departure was somewhat surprising as he'd more than played his part in the clubs' renaissance but the changes had a massive impact on the spine of the team especially with Buchan back alongside Greenhoff in defence. United looked solid.

McIlroy was the last player from the academy team set up by Matt Busby to make the grade and his move to midfield was a masterstroke. As a striker, McIlroy was not prolific but moving to the middle of the park made him a superb player. Because of his roots in Belfast, McIlroy was dubbed the 'next' Georgie Best but that was never going to be the case. Credit to Sammy though, he came in as a teenager alongside Best and remained part of the first team set up through to the Docherty era. The Pearson-Greenhoff partnership was not typical of most clubs who had a big centre-forward with a smaller player picking up the scraps. Both were target men but also mobile. Docherty knew Greenhoff would take pressure off Pearson as he had the ability to shield a ball and slow the game down bringing our wingers into play but Jimmy was far more than just a goal scorer and The Doc knew it.

The subtle changes in personnel changed our fortunes around as the turn of the year brought a 4–0 rout against Everton and a comfortable win over Aston Villa before we embarked on another FA Cup run. The defeat to Saints still rankled and we were desperate to return to Wembley. Despite our patchy form we were among the favourites and determined to go one better than the previous season. The draw was kind to us as we faced Walsall at home in the third round but after Hill opened the scoring we just did enough to make it through without too many scares. We had another home tie in the fourth round, this time against Queens Park Rangers. Runners up in the league the previous season, Rangers were not going as well this time around but we all knew it would be a tough affair. And there was some doubt whether the tie would take place because the pitch was in such a poor state. Soft on one flank and rock hard on the other, Hill and Coppell lined up in different studs. We came out flying to create a number of chances and got our reward when Macari was quickest to react to head home a McIlroy shot that Parkes could only parry. In the second half Rangers hit the cross bar twice as lady luck shone on us but we were also indebted to a superb display by Buchan marshalling the defence.

The draw for each round took place on a Monday after the games and players gathered around to listen to the radio. It was all very ad hoc and there was certainly none of the razzmatazz as with modern day televised draws. As our name was drawn out of the hat, there was plenty of fist pumping when the fifth round offered us a chance of revenge against Southampton. The general feeling was 'bring it on'. Travelling to The Dell would be a severe test but coming into the tie we'd hit a rich vein of form. Unbeaten in seven games, we'd won six matches, including away wins at Birmingham City and Tottenham. Greenhoff had also notched a hat-trick against Newcastle in the match preceding the tie so the lads were in fine spirits during the trip to the South Coast.

The Dell was a tight ground and always generated a cracking atmosphere. Macari and Hill gave us the lead twice only for Peach and Holmes to equalise. With Saints pushing us back towards the end I enjoyed one of those games when everything stuck. There was a sense of disappointment that we had not held onto the lead but we knew that we could finish the job at home. But before the replay there was the small matter of another 'derby' at home to City and we warmed up for Saints by defeating City 3–1. Coppell, Hill and Pearson scored.

Over 60,000 fans packed Old Trafford for the 'derby' win and another massive crowd returned three days later for our cup quest. A big cup night at Old Trafford was, and still is, a special occasion and the majority of a packed house was convinced we were on the road to Wembley again. Greenhoff gave us an early lead before Southampton got back into the game courtesy of a controversial penalty award by ref Clive Thomas. Peach equalised but we were not to be denied and Greenhoff struck his second of the night to send us through. Jimmy grabbed the headlines but Thomas was also the centre of attention when he sent off Saints defender Steele after hacking Greenhoff down twice in quick succession. The decision was correct but Thomas would court controversy further along in the competition. We knew our fate before kick off and sitting in the dressing room the lads chatted about our quarterfinal tie, again at home, versus Aston Villa. Coming into the match Villa had taken on Everton in the League Cup final at Wembley and in a midweek replay when they conceded a last gasp equaliser. A second reply was on the horizon and having been through the emotional upheaval a cup final brings, there was a feeling in the press that Villa may feel jaded. But any possibility of tiredness was unfounded when Little rifled in a 30-yard strike. However Houston thumped home a free kick before Macari provided the match winner. Villa were crestfallen but had the consolation of lifting the League Cup.

The build up to the semi-finals where we'd face Leeds United saw us win just two out of seven games. But our focus was on winning the FA Cup and we dusted ourselves down at

Mottram Hall Hotel before arriving at Hillsborough fired up. The match was predicted to be a close game but we got off to a flyer with two goals in the opening 14 minutes from Greenhoff and Coppell. We never looked in danger despite Clarke scoring a penalty 20 minutes from time. Our dressing room was buzzing at the final whistle and I had another chance to get my hands on a cup winner's medal. But we did not know whom we'd face in the final as Liverpool and Everton had drawn 2–2 in the other semi-final. Everton felt particularly aggrieved not to be in the final because they had a late goal chalked off by referee Thomas. And viewing the replay on *Match of the Day* that night, Everton had cause to bemoan the decision. Liverpool outplayed Everton in the replay to book a place at Wembley with a comfortable 3–0 win.

While Liverpool wrapped up the league title our form was woeful as we picked up just two wins in the run in. United finished sixth but it could have been a whole lot better. Liverpool would be going for a unique treble as they faced Borrusia Monchenglabach in Rome four days after the final in the European Cup. Bob Paisley's team was a formidable outfit full of household names. The dominant side in the country, with Ray Clemence, Kevin Keegan, Jimmy Case, Terry McDermott and Ray Kennedy not to forget Emlyn Hughes, Tommy Smith and Phil Neal lining up against us, we'd be in for a massive challenge. One player missing though was striker John Toshack, which was a blow for them as his partnership with Keegan was a key feature of their attack. Craig Johnson, somewhat surprisingly, was preferred to 'supersub' David Fairclough to partner Keegan, who would be playing his last domestic match for Liverpool before a big money move to Hamburg.

Docherty secured an early morale victory when he changed hotels to Selsdon Park where both Southampton and Sunderland had stayed prior to FA Cup final triumphs. Both teams caused big cup upsets but if we won it would not be classed in the same manner although we were underdogs in the eyes of bookmakers. Staying at Selsdon Park generated predictable headlines but we knew there was no such thing as a 'lucky' hotel or dressing room. It was a question of having the right approach and we had the experience of the previous final. We knew the desolation of a losing dressing room, now we wanted to experience that winning feeling. In contrast to the team's attitude before playing Southampton, everyone was mentally focused. Credit to Tommy, his preparation for the game was spot on. And my relationship was far better with him than at any time since he took charge at Old Trafford. Pre-season he'd promised to help with my testimonial year and had been as good as his word. My testimonial match against Benfica attracted an attendance of 38,000 for what was a memorable night.

On the injury front Houston was out of the Wembley showdown after dislocating an ankle at Bristol City a week earlier and Buchan was facing a fight for fitness after picking up an injury in the final game at West Ham. By midweek his chances of making the 'Jubilee' Cup final were slim and physio Laurie Brown had his work cut out in giving our skipper every opportunity to play. Buchan's availability was massive for us, as the defence was suddenly looking shaky especially if two of the regular first teamers were out. Docherty was not one to shirk problems though and made it clear he'd play teenager Arthur Albiston at left back and would leave it late before deciding on Buchan. In the end, Martin declared himself fit, much to everyone's relief in the United camp. The team was relaxed and ready.

There was great rivalry between both clubs and its supporters in my day but this rivalry has intensified since then for Liverpool fans in particular during the Ferguson era, as

United have eaten away at the Anfield clubs' record 18 league titles. Liverpool, as they are reminded every season by the media and United followers, have not won the league since 1990 and each year that goes by those feelings of frustration intensify for diehard Liverpool fans, not that I find it upsetting! But the situation for United supporters was similar when it took until 1993 to win the Premier League all those seasons after 1967. With Liverpool on part two of the treble there was no danger of underestimating the opposition but I genuinely believed we had a team that could compete against any side in a one off cup tie.

FA Cup final, Wembley Stadium
(21 May 1977)

Manchester United: Stepney, Nicholl, Albiston, McIlroy, Greenhoff, Buchan (c), Coppell, Greenhoff, Pearson, Macari, Hill. Sub: McCreery (for Hill). *Liverpool*: Clemence, Neal, Jones, Smith, Kennedy, Hughes (c), Keegan, Case, Heighway, Johnson, McDermott. Sub: Callaghan (for Johnson).

United had a team full of pace and in front of me our side was packed with youngsters confident in their ability to produce the goods. Full-backs Jimmy Nicholl and Arthur Albiston were at the start of terrific careers. Nicholl made a massive impact when he replaced Forsyth. Although not the swiftest of our defenders Nicholl had terrific ball control and passing ability, which he used to great effect both defensively and on overlapping runs. Albiston was at home in the United defence from his first game. An injury gave him his opportunity and he went on to play in three FA Cup winning teams for the club. Two-footed, Albiston rarely attracted the headlines but was such a consistent player whether distributing the ball, digging us out of trouble with last ditch tackles or supporting the attack. Neither Brian Greenhoff nor Martin Buchan could be classed

the archetypal 'stopper' centre-back. Both were under six foot, which was short for a centre-half but could motor back when opponents got down the flanks. Whilst Greenhoff was not the most naturally gifted footballer he made up for it with his whole-hearted approach. Committed, brave and industrious in either midfield or defence, Brian's efforts were always noteworthy. Buchan was confident in his own ability, read the game superbly, tackled clinically and controlled the back line. Calmness personified, skipper Martin led by example and spoke his mind if teammates were not pulling their weight. Buchan was the first name on the team sheet after the Busby era.

Sammy McIlroy harassed opponents into mistakes in midfield. With his boundless energy, McIlroy was arguably the fittest player in our side. A converted striker, Sammy was not known as a tackler in the Stiles mould, but from the left side of midfield buzzed about all over the park. McIlroy was in opponents' faces all the time using his pace and football brain to great effect. In the heart of midfield was Lou Macari. A playmaker and inspiring figure in the dressing room, United's young lads looked up to Lou as he'd seen and done it all at Celtic. A box-to-box player, one moment Macari would be supporting the defence and the next he'd be on hand to get his share of goals. Energetic, brave and a hard worker, Macari took plenty of knocks but never let on to opponents. A terrific header of a ball, as a former striker, Lou knew his way around the box. Macari was also the joker in the dressing room, constantly taking the mickey. Nobody was safe when Lou was in the mood to have some fun.

On the flanks United had Steve Coppell and Gordon Hill. Off the field, Hill was a real extrovert and kept the lads entertained. He'd wear my cap for impressions of comic Norman Wisdom and was also a dab hand at impersonating singer Max Bygraves. On the park, Coppell and Hill had raw

pace and were great outlets when needed to break from defence. Both struck their share of goals but Coppell put more into every game so I was not surprised his England career lasted longer. Whereas Steve was always looking to get involved and demanding the ball, Hill would drift in and out of a match before producing a flash of brilliance. During his early years at the club, Coppell was a flying winger, taking on opponents before firing in pinpoint crosses but after Docherty left, Steve played a more measured game on the right of midfield but was still influential as a playmaker. When on song Hill lived up to his nickname of 'Merlin' but though blessed with wonderful skill he could also frustratingly drift from a game. Possessing lightning pace and a powerful strike, Hill brought the crowd to its feet on many occasions.

Stuart Pearson and Jimmy Greenhoff took knocks that came with being a striker and proved a terrific combination. Pearson's clenched fist goal salute was his trademark but he offered much more. 'Pancho' was the focal point of attack and adept at taking the ball in a flash before laying it off with a deft flick or touch for either his strike partner, wingers or supporting midfield players. Strong in the air and packing a powerful shot, Pearson was a great leader of the line. Unselfish, classy and skilful, Greenhoff was the final piece of the 1977 cup final team and made it possible for United to deliver the sharp one and two touch football that Docherty liked us to play. Jimmy was also just as capable as his strike partner to link play with consummate ease. Neither players were prolific strikers but helped make us tick. Substitute David McCreery was a bubbly character. Like Fairclough at Liverpool, McCreery was something of a 'supersub' as he always seemed to make an impact. Whether replacing a midfielder or striker, McCreery worked tirelessly for the team and his efforts were always important.

At the pre-match players meeting there was a determination

to win I'd not seen before in the team. The atmosphere was buzzing during the coach journey to Wembley, the walk around the pitch and preparations in our dressing room. As the lads changed, I could not help but spare a thought for Houston who had been in the side a year earlier. The Doc made sure he was part of the occasion. Tommy went through his last minute reminders about set plays and individual responsibilities then in no time we were lining up again in the tunnel. Glancing across at the Liverpool lads I knew we'd be in for a battle but they had all the pressure as the bookies favourites. Looking at our lads they'd grown mentally from the year before and were ready for the challenge ahead. I knew deep down this was my last chance of FA Cup glory and walking out of the tunnel there was an even bigger roar than 12 months earlier. Inside Wembley there was an incredible sense of anticipation and after the formalities of meeting dignitaries for the occasion it was game on.

Kicking off, my main concern was whether Albiston could handle the pressure in his first cup-tie but from the early skirmishes it was clear that I did not need to worry. And any doubt over Buchan also disappeared when he contested and came out unscathed from a 50–50 ball with Liverpool 'hard man' Smith. Pre-match punditry predictions that our best chance was to go flying at Liverpool were way out. In sunny conditions there was no way we would be going 'gung ho' at Liverpool as we'd soon burn out so instead adopted a more measured passing game. During the half, Liverpool enjoyed far more possession with Keegan prominent and they did create the better opportunities. When Kennedy arrived late to a Case cross I had to be sharp to stop his effort and I watched a Jones effort whistle over the bar. We also got lucky when Kennedy headed against a post but it's moments like that when you think maybe your name is on the Cup. Macari went closest for us when he hit the side netting and Hill forced Clemence into a

sharp tip over the crossbar but apart from Coppell giving Jones a few scares down the wing in reality we rarely threatened the Liverpool goal. Leaving the field at half time with the score 0–0 was fine and sitting down in the dressing room several of the lads said how they noticed a number of Liverpool players looking shattered. The weather had been warm but the game had not been helter-skelter like many league games so we had a positive dressing room. During the interval, Tommy told us to be patient and if we stuck to our guns chances would come.

The Doc could not have dreamed of a better start to the second half as we opened the scoring on 50 minutes. Greenhoff flicked a long ball from McIlroy to Pearson, who had not scored in the cup run. 'Pancho' said he'd deliver in the final, and true to his word, steadied himself before beating Clemence. It was a great strike but knowing Ray, he'd have been disappointed to be beaten at his near post. It's always a dangerous time for a side when they have just scored, as they tend to relax rather than stay on their mettle. And so it proved when just two minutes after taking the lead Liverpool hit back when Case chested down a Jones cross with his back to goal, turned and volleyed into the top left hand corner. I got a hand to the ball but couldn't save it. Our disappointment did not last long. Whether Liverpool, in turn, relaxed was hard to tell but I could sense the lads urging each other on at the kick off. Greenhoff again was involved in the build up as he won a battle with Smith, the ball ran loose and Macari was on the spot with a strike that ricocheted off Greenhoff before spinning into the goal past Clemence and Neal to put us 2–1 ahead. United's fans again erupted and this time there was no way I was going to be beaten. Liverpool brought on Callaghan for the ineffective Johnson and pushed Case into attack. Case was on song and did go close with a strike, as did Kennedy when he struck a stanchion, but that was the closest Liverpool came to finding a

second equaliser. With McCreery coming on for Hill we were able to shut up shop effectively. There was late pressure but I mainly had to deal with bread and butter crosses. At the final whistle, I fell to my knees to offer a silent prayer. I could not believe it. After years of trying, I had my 'treble'. We'd won the FA Cup.

The main feeling was one of relief to have come through the toughest test but that was soon replaced by pure joy as we congratulated each other. I made a point of going over to all the Liverpool lads because I knew how they felt, especially the ones not in the 1974 cup-winning team. Going up to the Royal Box, at last I was able to receive my winner's medal from The Duchess of Kent and watching Buchan lift the FA Cup was a magical moment. Following the official group shot it was time for the lap of honour, which was fortunately not as chaotic as the last time I'd jogged around Wembley with a trophy. Back in the dressing room we toasted our success with a swig of champagne from the trophy. I even found time to sit back and take in the atmosphere knowing it would most likely be my last chance to savour a cup winning moment at the Twin Towers.

United's victory was a tremendous achievement especially after the disappointment of 1976. The lads showed tremendous character to win. But that is what happens in football. United's defence gained tremendous acclaim. Albiston performed superbly and deservedly picked up the man of the match award. Lining up against Case and Keegan at the top of their games was no easy task but young players either buckle under pressure or revel in the adrenaline rush a cup final brings. Against Southampton, United's younger lads froze but a year on knew what to expect. Albiston took it all in his stride to help secure the first major trophy at the club since United's unforgettable European Cup triumph. I had been concerned about the back four but the quartet delivered in spades. Nicholl performed

heroically, Buchan had been an injury doubt but was rock solid alongside Greenhoff who never put a foot wrong.

Pam and our two sons, John (10) and Paul (7), were in the stadium and at the celebration party that took place at the Café Royal prior to further celebrations at the Royal Garden Hotel, Kensington where the team stayed that night. And the following day it was time to return home. The Doc made my boys' day by placing the FA Cup on our table for the train journey back to Manchester. For the first time in my career I returned to Manchester with a trophy for a victory parade and a civic reception at the Town Hall—it was incredible.

United received plenty of plaudits but it was not long before the club were fielding questions of a different nature when news broke that Tommy was to set up home with the wife of United physio Laurie Brown. I knew instantly The Doc's position was untenable and he was sacked after an emergency board meeting. All these years later I don't think he should have departed for what was a private matter but I understood the politics behind the scenes. Fortunately, what happens on a football pitch is far more lasting for supporters.

Docherty had a tough task when he joined United but he led the club to promotion, cup finals and brought the first piece of silverware back to Old Trafford after Matt Busby. Tommy had begun a huge rebuilding programme and his team produced exciting football. The Doc signed Pearson, Houston, Macari, Hill, Coppell, Forsyth and Holton; all played international football. Brian Greenhoff also played for England and Albiston went on to represent Scotland. You can't keep a good man down and Tommy resurfaced at Derby before serving other clubs prior to retiring. I come across The Doc from time to time on the after dinner circuit and he is still cracking jokes as a sought after speaker.

During the close season I joined a whistle stop trip organised by Bobby Charlton as part of an all-star football team. My teammates included, Ian Callaghan, Jack Charlton, Ralph Coates and Alan Ball. Mixing business and pleasure, the trip was an interesting experience where the quality of football was not top of the agenda. It gave me an insight into how the football world was beginning to change as the corporate and sporting world integrated. The schedule took in Denmark, Norway, Iceland, Hong Kong, Indonesia, Australia and the United States. During the summer, I also had a surprise when my voluntary work for the blind was marked with an invitation to board the royal yacht Britannia during the Queen's northern tour. Like most footballers, helping to raise funds for a charity was encouraged and over many years I had marvelled at the work done at Henshaw's School for the Blind. The invite was a terrific honour and I was privileged to meet the Queen. My thoughts though soon turned to the new season when a new manager would be at the helm but nothing could eclipse my joy at finally winning an FA Cup winners medal. I'd at last joined Charlton, Dunne, Crerand and Foulkes as the only United players to win league, FA and European Cup titles. Of course that list has been added to by a host of players since the Fergie revolution but without diminishing their achievements in any way, during our era you had to be champions to get a crack at the European Cup. My childhood dreams had been realised and the memories will live with me forever.

Arthur Albiston
Manchester United and Scotland

Playing at the back you need a lot of communication between the defenders but primarily you have it with the 'keeper and Alex was not shy in coming forward. Being a London lad, and a Cockney, Alex was vocal and let us know what he wanted. Alex was great to play with because you knew as soon as he got the ball what was happening. We played from the back to get the ball out to the full-backs and Alex would say, 'You'll be fed up of me throwing the ball to you because you'll be getting it all the time'. I'd think, 'That's great, as long as I know it's coming then that's fine'. Alex was not one to bamboozle you with tactics.

It can be difficult when you are young trying to break into a side, let alone Manchester United, but the experienced players made it easier for young lads like Jimmy Nicholl and myself. Alex was great company off the field and made all the young lads feel welcome. It could have been difficult for us to mix as there was 10, 12 or 14 years age difference but Alex was terrific company. He loved his golf and made everything easy when I got in the side. Alex was one of the big wind-up merchants at the club. Alongside Lou Macari they were a real double act and you had to be on your toes all the time.

During that first FA Cup final for me against Liverpool in 1977, I felt a bit of an imposter and would not have been playing if Stewart Houston had been fit. In a roundabout way I didn't feel any pressure, I just felt sorry for Stewart. Alex didn't say a lot before the game but he did make me feel at ease. He just said that the manager had picked me because he thought I was good enough so I should play my normal game. I did, and it was an unforgettable occasion.

As a 'keeper, Alex was very agile, a good shot stopper, great on crosses and kicking. In fact, he was good at everything. Alex would also tell you that he was a good outfield player as well!

I'd probably disagree having seen him play on a Friday morning five-a-side but he was top goal scorer in 1973–74 when the team was having a rough time. Credit to Alex, he showed plenty of bottle to go up and take the penalties when the strikers and midfield players should have been doing it. You need bags of confidence as a 'keeper and need to be vocal to let everyone know what is going on. His forte was probably with crosses. When they came over you simply knew that he'd be coming for them to clear the danger. Alex was terrific at giving the back four confidence, especially when the heat was on in a tight match.

12

ALTRINCHAM VIA MANCHESTER AND DALLAS

Following the shock departure of Tommy Docherty, speculation mounted regarding his successor. Candidates emerged including Bobby Robson (Ipswich Town), Brian Clough (Nottingham Forest) and Johnny Giles (West Brom). News also broke that Queens Park Rangers manager Dave Sexton was departing to assist Terry Neill at Arsenal. Courteous and a man of integrity it soon transpired that Sexton, who had also managed Chelsea, was no longer going to Arsenal but had accepted the post at Manchester United. I'd met him a number of times over the years and found Sexton easy to get on with. He was a deep thinker and an innovative coach who would be a totally different proposition to Docherty for hacks looking for a scoop. And it was not long before our new boss was dubbed 'Whispering Dave'.

Embarking on pre-season training, Rangers 'keeper Phil Parkes warned me how hard goalkeeping sessions had been under Sexton. And Phil was right because my ageing bones certainly ached! Sexton was meticulous in his preparation as he put Paddy Roche and myself through our paces. Balls were

fired at us from opposite sides of the goal and when it came to my turn I was determined to keep going. The sessions benefited me enormously as I was fighting fit despite nearing my 35th birthday. United warmed up with games in Norway and I was delighted to face Liverpool in the Charity Shield at Wembley, who had been strengthened by new signing from Celtic, Kenny Dalglish. Playing at the Twin Towers is always special although the season curtain raiser was an unspectacular 0–0 draw.

We began the league campaign well, winning three of our opening four games. Macari was on fire, scoring a hat-trick at Birmingham before notching the only goal at Derby. But with injuries sidelining Pearson, both Greenhoffs and Macari, our league form dipped. We also exited both the League Cup and European Cup Winners Cup early. The European departure, in particular, rankled because we'd begun promisingly by knocking out St Etienne when a 2–0 'home' win in the second leg at Home Park, Plymouth proved decisive. Crowd trouble had marred the first leg in France as our hosts provided no segregation so the return leg was played 200 miles from Manchester. But we played at Old Trafford in round two against FC Porto. However, we gave ourselves a mountain to climb in the second leg after we lost 4–0 in Portugal. Unfortunately our preparations for the first leg clash were hampered by a friendly game in the Middle East. Governmental pressure had meant United playing a game to support a trade fair and, following their travel inoculations, a number of the lads were washed out for the opening Porto tie and we were still off it when we lost 4–0 to West Brom a few days later. Following the whistle stop friendly we almost pulled off a remarkable comeback at Old Trafford when we thumped Porto 5–2 but fell short on aggregate. The feeling of anti-climax in the dressing room was an understatement but there

was no time for moping about, as the next game is never far away. We needed a boost but it was not forthcoming at home to Arsenal and a third consecutive league defeat signalled a change in goalkeeper.

Although we'd been struggling, Sexton's decision to drop me was a tad surprising as my form was solid, however I heard on the grapevine that he was going to make an offer for his former 'keeper. Parkes had a growing reputation and it would not have surprised me but Sexton took me aback when he pulled me aside to explain it was time to give Roche a run as it might change the club's luck! Of all the reasons to drop me, I could not believe it. As things transpired, Parkes never signed and Roche kept goal until the middle of March 1978 when an injury brought about my first team return against of all clubs . . . City! Honours were shared in a terrific 2–2 draw.

Playing in the reserves had been soul destroying even though Jack Crompton made me captain. The acknowledgement was well intended and made my appearances more noteworthy but I was only marking time. Playing in a deserted ground was not for me even though against Liverpool six players had appeared in the cup final a few months earlier. Liverpool edged the game but it was competitive, which was more than could be said for the next clash at Sheffield Wednesday. I'd played at Hillsborough in front of packed houses many times but looking around at the vacant terraces I thought, 'What I am doing here?' I was determined not to end my career in reserve team football so when Newport County wanted to sign me on loan I was happy to go. Sexton refused, citing I was cover for Roche. I was not happy and let Sexton know my feelings in no uncertain terms but I duly got back into the side for what would be my final 'derby'.

With United out of the FA Cup there was only pride to play

for until the end of the season. We ended on a high with four consecutive wins prior to a 2–1 defeat at Wolves, which would prove to be my last first team game for the club. United finished a disappointing tenth. Pearson had been in and out of the side all season but came back to plunder goals in victories over Queens Park Rangers, West Ham and Bristol City. Our other victory was against Norwich and among the goal scorers in a 3–1 win was Joe Jordan who had joined from Leeds United for £350,000 just before the festive period. The arrival of Jordan gave us arguably the best front-runner in British football. A brave leader of the line, powerful, unselfish and wholehearted, Jordan's arrival signalled the end for Pearson who would join West Ham. A £500,000 British record saw Jordan's Leeds teammate Gordon McQueen arrive at Old Trafford shortly afterwards. Tough, uncompromising, competitive and powerful in the air, McQueen was the long term successor to Jim Holton and immediately looked the part. Both Scottish internationals, they quickly became crowd favourites. Putting his stamp on United, Sexton had raided our old rivals for its two star players, which caused a stir at Elland Road, not that we were complaining!

On the field, the freedom United displayed under The Doc when the youngsters came into the side had gone. The cavalier days were over and drew criticism from supporters who expected success in style. Changes were afoot as United moved from an attacking 4–4–2 formation to a more conservative 4–3–3 line up in a bid for consistency. Coppell, Greenhoff and McIlroy altered their roles in the team while top scorer Hill joined Docherty at the Baseball Ground. Hill left for £275,000 as Sexton sacrificed flashes of individual brilliance for teamwork. And looking to the future, United signed a young South African 'keeper, Gary Bailey, son of former Ipswich Town player Roy Bailey.

My days at United were numbered and I was out of the competition for the number one spot when I broke a finger in a pre-season game against Sheffield United. Roche started the season in goal but after United lost 5–1 at Birmingham City, news came that Sexton was to sign Coventry 'keeper Jim Blyth. At the time I was due to test out my injury in a reserve fixture when Blyth failed a medical. The on-off saga over Blyth resulted in Sexton recalling me for first team duty against Ipswich, as Roche was not in the right frame of mind. I was delighted at the recall but also amazed, as I'd not tested my injury in actual game play. I told Sexton it was a huge risk and felt it more sensible to play in the reserves first. Sexton and I agreed to disagree. The spat resulted in Bailey getting his big break and credit to Gary, he went on to become a fine 'keeper but I'd lost total respect for Sexton.

My final appearance in a United XI was against Real Madrid at Old Trafford when I played as a second half substitute to mark the clubs' centenary. Supporters were allowed to attend for free and many former players were invited for what was a memorable occasion. For the record we won the challenge match 4–0 with McIlroy and Jimmy Greenhoff scoring two goals apiece. It was nice to bow out by saving a penalty from Jose Pirri but there was nothing at stake although fans lapped up the nostalgia. The match marked 20 years since Munich and the club continues to commemorate the tragedy annually when the anniversary comes around. Every player that has represented United since is well aware of the blackest day in the club's history. Those who perished will never be forgotten.

As I pondered my next step, out of the blue I received a telephone call enquiring if I'd play in the North American Soccer League (NASL). I knew little about the league but was aware that English players were enjoying a final swansong so

I joined the American dream to try to establish professional 'soccer'. I signed for Dallas Tornado in February 1979. While I settled in Dallas, United finished ninth and agonizingly lost a memorable FA Cup final against Arsenal in the last minute.

I'd had a fantastic career at the greatest club in the world even though I'd experienced a few ups and downs over the years. During my years at the club, the record books show I played 549 games, kept 175 clean sheets and played, at the time, a record 92 consecutive games. My two penalties make me the club's all time top goalkeeper goal scorer. When I was at school, if anyone had told me that I'd be the final player Matt Busby would sign as he rebuilt his Manchester United team, I'd have given them a quizzical look. I was, and will always feel, fortunate to have been in the right place at the right time. Playing for Matt was an honour, as was lining up alongside the likes of Charlton, Law, Best, Stiles, Foulkes and Crerand. And I was delighted always to have a great rapport with the supporters. For years the Stretford End would sing 'Stepney . . . Stepney' when a penalty was awarded and it made me smile. There was always humour on United's terraces but in 1979 it was time to move on.

Joining the NASL was a great opportunity to experience football, or should I say 'soccer' as the Yanks call it, on another continent. An agent was looking to recruit English players for Dallas Tornado. Discussing the move, we agreed a two-year contract. Noel Cantwell and Freddie Goodwin were already out in the US and spoke positively about being in America where the standard of living was fantastic. The prospect to continue playing was paramount for me but I was also asked to help coach youngsters. I knew what I'd tell them. As Matt Busby always said before a game, 'Play your football and enjoy yourselves'.

The dream of professional soccer in the United States and Canada started in 1966. Administrators aimed to find a niche alongside American football, baseball, basketball and ice hockey. The 'big four' sports dominated TV networks but by 1975 crowds of 70,000 packed the Giants Stadium to watch New York Cosmos when Pele joined. Eusebio had preceded Pele joining American Soccer League team Rhode Island Oceaneers and then NASL team Boston Minutemen while hot on his heels from England were George Best at Los Angeles Aztecs and Rodney Marsh at Tampa Bay Rowdies. Georgio Chinaglia, Carlos Alberto and Franz Beckenbauer all joined Pele at New York, and the season I joined, acquisitions included Johan Cruyff (Los Angeles Aztecs), Johann Neeskens (New York Cosmos), Gerd Muller and Teofilo Cubillas (both Ford Lauderdale Strikers). In terms of British players, Bestie and Marsh were established heroes. Other Brits involved with the NASL in 1979 included Alan Ball, Colin Boulton, Charlie Cooke, Kevin Hector, Alan Hudson, Peter Lorimer, David Nish, Bob McNab, Willie Morgan, Harry Redknapp, Bobby Stokes, Keith Weller and Alan Woodward. Among the players to follow were crowd favourites Duncan McKenzie and Frank Worthington.

The powers that be in the US knew that for the game to grow they had to develop local stars. Pele retired in 1977 and his departure started an eight-year dip. The league eventually folded but resurged after the US hosted the 1994 World Cup and soccer is now on the map. David Beckham is the new Pele when it comes to top billing but there are plenty of home grown players. The national team is respected in football and they have reached the quarterfinals of a World Cup. US players have made their mark on the world stage and currently the Premiership boasts its fair share. I'm pleased I was involved in the formative years, if only for a short period.

Al Miller was the Dallas coach and the team played at the Ownby Stadium. On the roster, I knew Tony Simoes, as we'd faced each other in the European Cup final, and my old United teammate Jimmy Ryan. It was good to catch up with Jimmy in particular as we'd shared digs at United. Jimmy explained the set up and standard of football. It sounded a terrific finale to my career. Our 24-man squad comprised players from USA (5), Brazil (4), England (4), West Germany (4), Argentina (2), Denmark, Mexico, Portugal, Scotland and Yugoslavia. Our squad were not household names in the US but Pedro Gano, Steve Pecher, Zequinha, Willie Lippens and Tony Bellinger were first team regulars. The standard of football was decent and possession football was key, especially in the summer temperatures. Stat recognition is commonplace now in the English game but was part of the ethos in the US. Coaches adapted the system from its traditional sports. Every pass, tackle, assist, header and save was recorded so it was not just about goal scorers. Every player was recognised for the effort they gave in a game.

During my two seasons in the NASL there were 24 teams and the season ran April to August. Administrators tinkered with rules. The major differences revolved around offside with the 35-yard line, also no draws were allowed so after 90 minutes 'sudden death' 15-minute overtime periods and shoot-outs decided games. In my first campaign our 30-match season was a complicated format. Dallas Tornado were placed in the National Conference 'Central Division' alongside Minnesota Kicks, Tulsa Roughnecks and Atlanta Chiefs, playing them 'home and away'. Dallas also took on our American Conference 'Central Division' counterparts Houston Hurricane, Chicago Sting, Detroit Express and Memphis Rogues 'home and away'. Our schedule was completed with 16 games against National and American

Conference sides but we didn't play all teams 'home and away'. The schedule meant I faced New York Cosmos, Toronto Blizzard, Washington Diplomats, Rochester Lancers, Vancouver Whitecaps, Portland Timbers, Los Angeles Aztecs, Seattle Sounders, Tampa Bay Rowdies, New England Tea Men, California Surf and Edmonton Drillers. Travelling the length and breadth of America was illuminating to say the least.

Six points were awarded for a win plus an additional point for each goal up to a maximum of three per team. I missed two games of the 1979 season as we finished second behind Minnesota Kicks in our division, winning 17 of our 30 games to make the play offs. Among encounters that would have been a draw back home was an overtime win against Chicago and three shoot-out victories versus Vancouver, Atlanta and Seattle. In the Conference quarterfinals we lost to Vancouver in both play off legs. Vancouver then stunned favourites New York Cosmos in the semi-finals and defeated Tampa Bay Rowdies in the Soccer Bowl. Fabbiani (Tampa Bay), Chinaglia (New York) and Muller (Ford Lauderdale) were leading scorers. Chinaglia is the most prolific goal scorer in NASL history.

During the close season the NASL, like all American sports, utilised a draft system so struggling teams got first pick to strengthen their squads. If a club chose to trade you in the draft system, as in American Football, baseball or basketball, you had to move otherwise you didn't get paid. I was immune from the draft as I had a straight contract so returned home and played part time for Altrincham until February 1980. Altrincham played in the Alliance Premier League (now known as The Conference), which was in its debut season. The league comprised 13 teams from the Southern League and seven from the Northern Premier League. Administrators hoped it would become the most notable semi-professional league in England and Wales. I thoroughly enjoyed my spell at The Robins in a season when they clinched the league ahead of Weymouth by two points but there was no automatic promotion in those days. In the end of season re-election system league members voted against Altrincham joining the Football League.

Altrincham were also renowned FA Cup giant killers so it was terrific to help them overcome Crewe Alexandra and Rotherham United in the first and second rounds. Reaching the third round meant I'd won a game in every round of the competition. Leyton Orient knocked us out in a replay 2–1 after we'd drawn 1–1 at home. It was certainly exciting going into the 'hat' before the replay one more time. I'd loved to have drawn United but the lads were more than happy to draw eventual cup winners West Ham but we missed out on a fourth round clash. For me there is nothing like the FA Cup. Playing for Altrincham kept me in shape before I departed for my second season in the NASL.

Dallas Tornado switched to the Texas Stadium where Dallas Cowboys used to play. The stadium was vast, seating 60,000, not that we ever came close to filling it. We played on Astroturf and it took time to get used to the bounce. Records show the most we attracted was 13,475 spectators for the visit of New York Cosmos. I made 26 appearances in our 32-game schedule, which again was not straight logic in terms of 'home and away' games. Dallas played in the National Conference 'Central Division' alongside Minnesota Kicks, Tulsa Roughnecks and Atlanta Chiefs facing them 'home and away'. Dallas also took on American Conference 'Central Division' counterparts Houston Hurricane, Chicago Sting, Detroit Express and Memphis Rogues 'home and away'. Our schedule was completed with 18 games against all bar two of the

National and American Conference sides, and again not all 'home and away'. The schedule meant I didn't face New England Tea Men or Edmonton Drillers.

During the season I picked up some niggling injuries but we topped our division, winning 18 games to make the play offs. Again, I revelled in the 'sudden death' element of the games. Both fixtures versus Portland went to shoot-outs and we won a game each, whilst we prevailed in overtime against Atlanta during the run in to the divisional title. In the Conference first round play offs we defeated Minnesota Kicks in both legs but tied the semi-finals with the mighty New York Yankees. In fact, after losing our home leg 3–2 we thumped New York in their back yard 3–0. But in the play-off series unlike in European competitions if games were tied at one leg each the 'away' goal rule was irrelevant. A mini-game took place following the second game and we lost 3–0. New York went on to lift the Soccer Bowl by defeating Fort Lauderdale. For Dallas it was a case of so near yet so far. Chinaglia again topped the goal scoring charts. I was asked to stay on at the end of my contract but my injuries were becoming more frequent so I declined. Looking back, I loved living in America and travelling around the country playing at all the big stadia. I returned to Altrincham again briefly and helped them land the 1980–81 Alliance title again. They also defeated Scunthorpe United in the FA Cup but I didn't face Liverpool when they drew them in the third round. For me, it was time to hang up my gloves.

13

LIFE ON CIVVY STREET

Pondering the future after retiring as a player I took my coaching badges through the Professional Footballers Association. I did the usual things ex-footballers do so ran a pub and had a go at management with Droylsden before working in the transport industry. You never know what is around the corner but nobody was more surprised than me when a chance came to get back into football in the early nineties. I'd experienced a number of challenges in the intervening years. Pam and I had divorced in 1986 and sadly she succumbed to breast cancer seven years later. During this period, my new partner Sheila's eldest daughter, Samantha, was killed in a car crash a couple of years before Sheila and I married in 1991. We honeymooned in the United States and nowadays we're based on the Fylde coast, which is a nice part of Britain to live. Sheila's younger daughter, Natalie, lives close by with her partner Lee and I have a great relationship with my sons. John and Jaqui live in Sale while Paul and Julie are in Altrincham. I also enjoy spoiling our three grandchildren Harry, Scarlet and Miles.

On the football front, my return to the game came about when I attended a Sportswriters dinner at the Savoy. At my table were a number of ex-players including Alan Ball who was managing Exeter at the time. Ballie and I happened to be sitting next to each other and the conversation turned to scouts. In his distinctive voice, Ballie quipped that he didn't have such luxuries so I said I'd do it for nothing. I finished work at lunchtime on Saturdays and was based near a number of local clubs in his division so it would be easy. Ballie looked at me quizzically but I assured him I was up for it, as it meant I'd get out and about instead of sitting at home watching the box. Ballie couldn't believe it and snapped my hand off so rain or shine I was back involved with football. Ballie would ring up, 'Alex, can you go watch so and so at Bury. Let me know what you think'. It was terrific and I loved the involvement.

Out of the blue, Ballie landed a job at Premier League Southampton and asked me to be his North West scout. Finishing work at lunchtimes I'd tootle off to a local match and it was similar for a night game. And it was not long before I accompanied Southampton into a tournament in Singapore. During the trip Ballie asked me to be his goalkeeping coach but pointed out that, football being football, if I moved to Southampton you never knew what was around the corner. Mulling things over, I decided it was not for me. And then blow me down; Ballie was given the Manchester City post and offered me the goalkeeping coach post. I could not believe my good fortune. City legend Francis Lee was chairman while Tony Book, Mike Summerbee and Colin Bell were also around. It was just like the old days and the easiest decision of my life. I jumped at the chance and during six years there from 1995 to 2001 I enjoyed every minute of working with the 'keepers. And City fans were terrific with me, despite my background! The banter, coaching and especially seeing young 'keepers develop was fantastic. The only disappointment during my time at City was that Nicky Weaver didn't reach his full potential.

When it came to spotting potential 'keepers, I needed to see them three games on the bounce. City reserves used to play at

Whitton Albion and a young kid at Mansfield Town impressed me in a match. Looking at him, he looked older than his age. I went home and got my Rothman's book out . . . Weaver, aged 17. I thought, I'll take another look at the kid. Looking at the fixture list, Mansfield had a game coming up against Stockport County and Weaver was playing. Mansfield lost but Weaver was impressive clearing the ball left foot, right foot, was a sound shot stopper and had a clear idea of his angles. I thought to myself, 'This kid's got a chance'. I watched Weaver in the next game and again he impressed. Frank Clark was by now City manager and I told him to snap Weaver up. City paid £100,000. I told Weaver to stay with me and if he followed my advice he'd be a first team 'keeper within three years. But things were not going well in the first team and City got relegated to the third tier of professional football, Division 2. Joe Royle was now at the helm and relegation meant big changes. I told Joe to give the kid a chance. Weaver had a blinding season and got City promoted with an amazing performance against Gillingham at Wembley in the play off final. City fans still talk about that incredible day for the club as they came back from the dead to win a penalty shoot out.

Weaver was a hero overnight and had an unbelievable debut season in Division 1. City won the last game at Blackburn Rovers to gain promotion to the Premier League. To cap a great campaign, Weaver broke into the England U21 side. The other keeper was Paul Robinson of Leeds United. Getting experience at international level was essential for his development and he impressed everyone. Pre-season, things looked terrific. I had my training routines all set out for the keepers. I handed out the programme with the aim to push on but Weaver said he couldn't do my routine, as he had to follow a different schedule mapped out by the England coaches. I was shocked and told him that it was up to him, he could stay with me or do his own thing. Weaver decided to do his own thing. Shortly afterwards City appointed Kevin Keegan who brought in a goalkeeping coach. I bumped into Nicky at a corporate event some years after his career had gone downhill and fair play to him, he acknowledged his errors. But it's a crying shame because Nicky Weaver should have been playing at the top level today and could have been in the England set up.

In recent years I've entertained on the after-dinner circuit, hosted *The Legends Football Phone In* on Century Radio and worked in corporate hospitality at Old Trafford. Wherever I am conversation always revolves around football and I'm often asked to compare the United team I played in when we won the European Cup and subsequent European Cup winning United teams. The game has changed enormously. Physically, modern day United teams are faster, fitter, bigger and stronger but training methods, nutrition and medical facilities are on a different scale. You can only judge on your era and we had a team blessed with world class players that could rip any side apart. In our prime, we were a match for any team and proved it. I'm also quizzed on my views about Sir Matt Busby and Sir Alex Ferguson. With Matt there was so much admiration for the history he created, especially after Munich, that the next person in the hot seat was on a hiding to nothing. Matt built three teams and each had a place in United supporters' hearts. And moving on to Alex, who has won more honours than Matt, both are rightly held at a similar level. There will always be a special place for the Busby Babes and 1968 European Cup winners but Alex has also produced teams that are deservedly acclaimed. You cannot compare different generations but without taking anything away from Alex's achievements, Matt had a much smaller squad. These days, football is a global sport and Manchester United is a well-known brand. An area both managers had to contend with was massive expectations from supporters and they achieved it brilliantly.

No conversation ever seems to goes by without someone asking what it was like to play alongside Charlton, Law and Best and it's a subject I never tire of discussing. The trio seemed to sum up an era when football really was the beautiful game and I was lucky to play with them many times. Charlton was indispensable to the team. Packing an almighty shot, Bobby was as destructive from distance as anyone in the game during his heyday. Blessed with incredible drive he demonstrated sportsmanship in every game. The quietest of the trio, his serious nature was mistaken because Bobby was a prankster and loved a laugh. On away trips he was organiser of the crib tournaments that passed away the hours but once on the park, in full flight Charlton was wonderful to watch before he unleashed a venomous drive.

Law was a showman and it was no surprise he was dubbed the 'King' of the Stretford End with his sleeves pulled down and trademark fist salute after scoring a goal. A handful for any defence, razor sharp and inventive in the penalty box, no defender was safe in his company. Denis also brought his wit to the game. On more than one occasion he'd look along the line for offside and as the linesman's flag was going up, Denis would wag a finger at him to admonish his early delivery. The linesman would laugh along with the crowd during a time when the game was played in a better spirit. Brave as a lion, Law had many a battle with the hatchet men of the era. Whether it was Hunter, Harris or Smith these battle-hardened defenders rarely floored Denis. And there was never any animosity. At full time there would be handshakes after a rip-roaring battle.

In his heyday Bestie was unstoppable. The most naturally gifted footballer to come from these shores, George had everything . . . balance, shooting ability, a deft touch, strength, stamina and an unnerving ability to ride flying tackles. George was also no slouch when it came to heading and won the ball back with ease. Of course his dribbling ability set him apart and there was no one better when in full flight.

A youth policy has served United magnificently down the years. I've documented Matt's successes already but in recent times Alex has had the Neville brothers, Nicky Butt, Paul Scholes, Ryan Giggs and David Beckham to name just a few of the elite players. Gary Neville and Scholes have served the club superbly while Phil Neville and Butt were also hits. Beckham is an unbelievable player and for me his best game was in the European Cup final against Bayern Munich in 1999. When things were not going right he worked his socks off. David is a workhorse and has been exceptional down the years for England. It's a tragedy he missed out on the 2010 World Cup finals. As for Giggs, he is as excited about winning honours two decades on from when he first broke into the side. Alex has looked after Giggs like Matt looked after Bestie in his heyday. Giggs is United's record appearance holder, most decorated player and a role model for modern footballers. Alex has also not been averse to buying players. Cantona was a maestro and the missing link at a crucial time. He turned around the fortunes of the club and was the best business Alex did. Just as importantly, Alex has never been afraid to drop or sell a player in his prime such as Ince, Beckham, Cole, Stam, van Nistelrooy, Tevez and Ronaldo. Moving players on has arguably been his greatest strength. Nobody is bigger than United. Alex knows what he wants, continually builds and is ahead of anyone else as the ultimate manager.

When Ronaldo broke onto the scene at Sporting Lisbon, Alex bought the kid and never regretted his decision. Ronaldo improved constantly, rewriting the record books at United. On the ball, Ronaldo is so tricky, a defender does not know whether he'll go on the outside or cut infield. He also has a cracking strike. Real Madrid paid £80 million, which is crazy money but in the modern game every player has a price. And then there is Wayne Rooney who broke onto the scene as a kid at Everton. Rooney is a fiery guy and it was clear he could make it straight away. Everton had financial restraints; Alex saw the opportunity and went for it. Rooney is a street fighter but Alex will curb his temperament. You have to remember Wayne is still a young player and will only get better, which is a frightening prospect because he's already world class. In 2009/10 Rooney was phenomenal. Strong as an ox and blessed with an astonishing first touch there is nothing Wayne cannot achieve. If he stays injury free Rooney will become an all time great of world football. He should also reset the record books for England in terms of caps and goals because he has a decade at the top ahead of him. Players like Rooney win trophies, they may self-destruct on occasion but they have some amazing talent.

Competition is always a big debating point and weak outfits cannot live with top teams over a season. In the Premier League there are the big four, then 10 clubs doing enough to stay mid-table and a bottom six scrapping to avoid relegation. The days when a club can get promotion and win the league are long gone. Further down the road I'd like to see Celtic and Rangers join the Premiership. Too many games are predictable and it would be a terrific boost. Supporters would love the rivalry. Football is about big business and entertaining supporters. Having Celtic and Rangers in the Premiership would be a huge bonus. Of course it would decimate the Scottish League but Celtic and Rangers cannot hope to compete in Europe unless they get a share of the Premiership pot. It's not an idea that is popular with everyone but the benefits are obvious and would help the Scottish national team as its home grown players would be competing at a higher level every week. The media has debated this topic for a long time and whenever I meet supporters of the two Scottish giants there is increasing support. However much Scottish administrators procrastinate I think it could happen sooner rather than later. As for the domestic trophies, both the FA and League Cups are sadly devalued due to the Champions League. When Sunderland won the Cup in '73, Southampton in '76 and West Ham in '80 it was fantastic for the game and gave any club hope of enjoying a glory day out at Wembley. Everyone likes an underdog but that seems impossible now.

Football finances have spiralled out of control but clubs have to decide what they can afford as a business model and act accordingly. It's obvious that the football landscape has changed forever. Ground sharing, wage capping and European Super Leagues will continue to be debated for years to come. What clubs pay players does not interest me, that is between the club and the player, and of course star players earn even more because of endorsements. But I do get frustrated when I see highly paid players just going through the motions and understand why supporters vent their anger at them during games and on phone-in shows. It's all very well taking the big bucks but you need to give everything on the park. When it comes to stadia that supporters flocked to in massive numbers in the fifties and sixties, they have improved beyond recognition because in my heyday they had, in the main, terrible facilities and appalling pitches. Ground improvements were rare but nowadays there has been a lot of investment up and down the country. And many of these new all-seater stadia are fantastic to watch a game of football at, although they don't quite have the same atmosphere. The days are long gone when footballers played on pitches like Derby County's Baseball Ground caked in mud or on a rock hard surface or a pitch with one half frozen and one half soft so no one knew which studs to wear. Time has moved on and traditionalists have to get over the fact that the game has changed.

Looking back on my football career, I was so fortunate. I gave my all for every club I represented and at different times the breaks I needed came my way. I wasn't flashy, it was all about angles, being in the right place at the right time, concentration and working hard. People always go on about the money side of football but I've never looked at it that way. I had a great career and enjoyed every minute whether playing in the Isthmian and Alliance Leagues right through to being a professional at all levels of the Football League and NASL. I played with, and against, many of the greatest players to kick a football. I would not change a thing. Dream teams are something that is always fun to select and years ago I featured in two Manchester United XIs selected by Bill Foulkes and Jack Crompton in book seven of the annual *Manchester United Football Books* (1966–80). Foulkes XI ran out as Stepney, Dunne, Byrne, Colman, Jones, Edwards, Berry, Whelan, Taylor, Law and Best. The Crompton XI was Stepney, Dunne, Aston, Crerand, Carey, Edwards, Delaney, Law. Taylor, Whelan and Rowley. I'd loved to have played in either fictional XI. There are plenty of legendary United players missing but the name Stepney appears in both. That will do for me.

Appendix, Alex Stepney's Playing Career

Season	Team	League	FA Cup	League Cup	European Cup	European Cup Winners Cup	UEFA Cup	World Club Championship	FA Charity Shield	Watney Cup	Anglo-Italian Tournament	Totals
1963/64	Millwall	46	2	5								53
1964/65	Millwall	46	5	2								53
1965/66	Millwall	45	2	4								51
1966/67	Chelsea	1										1
1966/67	Manchester United	35	2									37
1967/68	Manchester United	41	2		9				1			53
1968/69	Manchester United	38	5		6			2				51
1969/70	Manchester United	37	9	8								54
1970/71	Manchester United	22								3		25
1971/72	Manchester United	39	7	6						1		53
1972/73	Manchester United	38	1	4							2	45
1973/74	Manchester United	42*	2	1								45*
1974/75	Manchester United	40	2	7								49
1975/76	Manchester United	38	7	2								47
1976/77	Manchester United	40	7	6			4					57
1977/78	Manchester United	23	4	1		4			1			33

Total **707***

Other Appearances: Tooting & Mitcham (1961/62 and 1962/63, Isthmian League) 61**, Dallas Tornado (1979 and 1980, North American Soccer League) 61*** and Altrincham (1979/80, Allaince Premier League) 17****

England U23s versus France U23, Yugoslavia U23 and Turkey U23 in 1965/66. Young England versus England XI in 1965/66. Stepney gained 1 full international cap for England versus Sweden in 1967/68.

* = scored two goals, ** = league and cup games, *** = includes play-off games and **** = on loan